INTELLIGENT DESIGN

By request of the author, 10 limited collector's editions of this book have been published. Each copy is marked with a number from 1 to 10.

INTELLIGENT DESIGN

MESSAGE FROM THE DESIGNERS

RAEL

This re-titled English Language edition is a newly combined re-translation and updated edition of Rael's three original French books *Le Livre Qui Dit La Verite* (The Book Which Tells The Truth) which first appeared in France in 1974, *Les Extra-Terrestres M'ont Emmene Sur Leur Planete* (Extra-Terrestrials Took Me To Their Planet) and *Accueillir les Extra-Terrestres* (Let's Welcome The Extra-terrestrials). Similar English paperback editions were printed in Japan in 1986 under the titles *The Message Given To me By Extra-Terrestrials* (the first 2 books combined) and *Lets Welcome Our Fathers from Space* . In 1998 the combined first 2 books were released in England by Tagman Press entitled *The Final Message* and again in the USA with the title *The True Face of God* in 1999 and *The Message Given by Extra-terrestrials* in 2001.

ISBN : 2-940252-22-X
EAN : 9782940252220

This book is also available in hardcover: ISBN 2-940252-20-3

Publisher: Nova Distribution
The publisher may be contacted at: publishing@rael.org

Credits
Chief Editor and Project Manager: Cameron Hanly
Project Assistant: Line Gareau
Translation Review: B.B
Proof-reading: Panteha Naghi
Composition and Design: Cameron Hanly and Rob Chalfant
Cover-Design: Rael and Cameron Hanly

CONTENTS

Foreword   xi

BOOK ONE : THE BOOK WHICH TELLS THE TRUTH

1 THE ENCOUNTER   3

2 THE TRUTH   10
   Genesis   10
   The Flood   18
   The Tower of Babel   22
   Sodom and Gomorrah   23
   The Sacrifice of Abraham   24

3 WATCHING OVER THE CHOSEN PEOPLE   26
   Moses   26
   The Trumpets of Jericho   33
   Samson the Telepathist   35
   The First Residence to Welcome the Elohim   38
   Elijah the Messenger   40
   The Multiplication of Bread   42
   The Flying Saucers of Ezekiel   45

The Last Judgement 53
Satan 57
Humans Could Not Understand 59

4 THE ROLE OF CHRIST 65
The Conception 65
The Initiation 66
Parallel Humanities 69
Scientific Miracles 73
Deserving the Inheritance 75

5 THE END OF THE WORLD 80
1946, First Year of the New Era 80
The End of the Church 81
The Creation of the State of Israel 84
The Mistakes of the Church 86
At the Root of All Religions 88
Mankind: A Disease of the Universe 90
Evolution: A Myth 92

6 THE NEW COMMANDMENTS 95
Geniocracy 95
Humanitarianism 97
World Government 100
Your Mission 101

7 THE ELOHIM 105
Nuclear Weapons 105
Overpopulation 106
The Secret of Eternity 108
Chemical Education 113
The Raelian Movement 115

BOOK TWO : EXTRA-TERRESTRIALS TOOK ME TO THEIR PLANET

1 MY LIFE UNTIL THE FIRST ENCOUNTER   **121**

Introduction   121

Two Years Have Passed   122

Childhood: a UFO over Ambert   123

The Pope of the Druids   124

Poetry   126

The Encounter   136

The Public Talks   140

2 THE SECOND ENCOUNTER   **142**

The Sighting of July 31st, 1975   142

The Message: Part Two   145

Buddhism   150

Neither God nor Soul   153

Paradise on Earth   156

The Other World   159

Meeting the Ancient Prophets   161

A Foretaste of Paradise   168

The New Commandments   175

To the People of Israel   176

3 THE KEYS   **180**

Introduction   180

Humanity   181

Birth   182

Education   183

Sensual Education   185

Fulfillment   187

Society and Government   193

Meditation and Prayer   198

The Arts   201

Sensual Meditation   201

Human Justice   203
Science   205
The Human Brain   207
The Apocalypse   207
Telepathic Communication   209
The Reward   213
The Guides   222

BOOK THREE : LET'S WELCOME THE EXTRA-TERRESTRIALS

1 FREQUENTLY ASKED QUESTIONS   227
Seeming Contradictions...   227
Dating the Works of the Elohim   230
The People of Israel and the Jews   231
The Raelian Movement and Money   232
Nothing is Constant in Space and Time   234
Transmission of the Cellular Plan and the Forehead Bone. 236
Is the Earth an Atom of the Finger of God?   239
Noah's Ark – A Space Craft?   240
Life After Life – or Dream and Reality?   241
The Elohim's Scientific Level of Development   243
Neither God nor Soul...   245
The Religion of the Infinite   248
The Future of Traditional Religions   249
Raelism and Geniocracy   250
Who Created the Creator of the Creators?   252
What is the Purpose of Life?   255
What is Pleasure?   257
What is Death?   262
Sexual Freedom and No Obligation   270
Raelism and Homosexuality   272
Deists and Evolutionists: The False Prophets   273
Suicide   275

2 THE NEW REVELATIONS   276
The Devil Does Not Exist, I Met Him   276
My Father Who Art in Heaven   288
Message from Yahweh to the Men of the Earth   291

3 AN ATHEIST RELIGION   308
Angels Without Wings   308
'Deresponsibilisation'   314

4 COMMENTARIES AND TESTIMONIALS OF RAELIANS   327
Raelism Through the Eyes of Science   327
Impressions of a 'Priest'   334
Yes... I am Raelian   339
The Consecration of My Priesthood   344
To Become Active So As Not To Become Radioactive   349
From Marxism to Raelism Adhesion   352
A New Art of Living   353

5 ADDENDUM   356
Encounter of October 7th, 1976   356
The Message of the Elohim, March 14th, 1978   357
Modification of the New Commandments   358
Message of the Elohim, December 13th, 1997   358
The United Nations - Rael, September 2005   361

Author's Postscript   364
Additional Information   373
Seminars and Contacts   374
Acknowledgements   375
Other Books by Rael   376
Notes and References   378
Bibliography   380
Index   381

FOREWORD

by
Anthony Grey
international best-selling novelist, journalist and broadcaster

This extraordinary volume of writings, I am certain, contains revealed information of the greatest magnitude and importance for humanity. Combining for the first time three important books in one and written in very simple, matter-of-fact terms, this newly comprehensive narrative provides for me the only truly persuasive explanation I have discovered to date of our physical origins, our planetary history, our place and present standing in our known universe, and last but not least, the reasons behind our chronically divisive and potentially self-destructive global religious beliefs.

For all these reasons I believe that this new book, along with four others written by Rael, has the power to transform our understanding of our greatly troubled world and open the way towards a new and unprecedented era of global peace, harmony and unprecedented scientific and social progress.

Above all, the writings by Rael between these covers affirm that we are not alone in our universe. They demonstrate that we are at present very junior but highly potent members of a greater clan of galactic humanity just like ourselves - we are loved, observed and guided so far as we chose to allow ourselves to be, by a superior advanced human civilization that conceived and engineered our very existence on this planet.

Although these three-books-in-one do not exhaustively say everything nor answer every conceivable question about our universe and ourselves, they vastly overshadow everything else published in the UFO/space field by offering obviously authoritative insights into topics as diverse as the infinite nature of all living matter, our planetary history, human and plant genetics, sexuality, sensuality, psychology, politics, and the true nature of criminality. They also throw fascinating new light on many other mundane issues including property ownership, wise child-rearing, the outdated values of our conventional marriage systems, and the high importance of sport, even violent sport, in creating and sustaining harmonious and peaceful human societies.

In reporting details of how all life forms on Earth including the ecology and ourselves were engineered by human scientists from another part of our galaxy, Rael effectively demystifies and refocuses all the ancient scriptures of the world's major religions. While emphasizing that all faiths and their historical traditions and cultures still deserve our respect, he makes it clear how they have become outdated while still continuing to testify obscurely to this newly revealed practical scientific reality. Most controversially, this volume abolishes the notion that a benevolent, all-knowing, all-powerful, spiritual, mysterious and immaterial God presides over us all.

The scriptures of all the major religions, it emphasizes, are about representatives of that ultra-sophisticated and highly refined civilization - human beings just like ourselves - who care deeply about us, because it was here that they first discovered and developed their own genius for transforming life from planet to planet by their mastery of DNA. In short, this massively important book sets our past, present and future on a firm scientific basis without diminishing the beauty, joy and spirituality of our existence. In fact, it greatly enhances the understanding and practice of a new common-sense spirituality based around meditation and achieving the inner peace and harmony that is eminently appropriate in this new era of space travel and genetic modification of ourselves and our environment.

The author of these unique writings was born Claude Vorilhon in France in September 1946. He changed his name to Rael, which means 'messenger' in Hebrew, after meeting a human being from another planet when a small spacecraft landed in a remote volcanic region of south central France in December 1973. During several meetings on successive days, its human occupant verbally dictated to him most of the first book of this volume, saying it was 'a message to be addressed to all humanity'. He told Rael that all the great prophets of the major religions throughout our history had been given information appropriate to the educational level of their times in precisely this way and invited Rael to take on the mission of making what he called 'our final message' known worldwide. Rael accepted the task and rapidly wrote and published the first book himself in French under the disarmingly simple title *The Book Which Tells the Truth*.

Nearly two years later, in October 1975, a second encounter occurred in woodland near Brantome in the Perigord region of France, and this time Rael was invited aboard the advanced spacecraft and taken on an astonishing revelatory journey. Rael describes this fully in the second section of the book entitled *Extra-Terrestrials Took Me to Their Planet,* which he also originally published as a separate volume in French in late 1975.

In view of the fact that American, Russian, Chinese, and European astronauts are so far known to have succeeded in venturing only into the nearest margins of space - at most into orbit around the Earth and our moon - it perhaps seems outlandish at first sight to accept that without a spacesuit or any other special apparatus, Rael could have been whisked unexpectedly from a wooded European glade to another planet far across our galaxy. But this is what he describes here in those same detached, matter- of-fact terms, detailing many extraordinary experiences on the planet of his hosts who call themselves 'the Elohim'. Having known him now for some 13 years, I have no doubt that he is describing here real and factual experiences.

In a third book entitled *Let's Welcome the Extra-terrestrials,* originally published in 1979 and now for the first time joined with the first two books in this updated volume, Rael answers some of the commonest questions that were repeatedly asked about his original writings in the early years by journalists and others. Very significantly, he also adds in that third book further new amplifying material about his own personal background, which he says he was asked by his informants in 1975 to withhold for three further years. Other equally important writings have followed in successive books entitled *Sensual Meditation, Yes to Human Cloning, Geniocracy*, and *The Maitreya*. To get a true and complete picture of his unprecedented revelations and insights it is important to read all of these books.

In recounting this brief outline of Rael's story, I have not inserted any customary qualifying words such as 'alleged' or 'reported' which responsible journalists - and especially former foreign correspondents who have reported from Beijing and Berlin among other datelines - might rightly be expected to employ to distance themselves from any controversial or improbable information they are conveying. I've done this quite intentionally to underline my conviction that Rael is a man of high integrity describing genuine experiences in a sincere and totally truthful fashion.

An international journalist such as I have been is of course accustomed to assessing the reliability or otherwise of those he quotes for information, even when sometimes concealing his confidant's identity behind a stock phrase like 'a usually well-informed source' or 'a usually reliable source'. In this regard, my estimation of Rael is that he is an eminently reliable witness to what he has experienced, fantastic though it often may seem. I think that he is indeed 'a *uniquely* well informed and reliable source' and, after hearing him speak in public lectures over a period of thirteen years and after reviewing my own and other recorded broadcast interviews with him, it is my impression that perhaps even now he is saying less than everything he learned during those extraordinary, unsought meetings in the mid-1970s on this planet and beyond. More importantly perhaps, the profound logic and rationality of what he was told by his informants appear unassailable to me.

I interviewed Rael twice in preparing an investigative radio documentary series for the BBC World Service entitled 'UFOs - Fact, Fiction or Fantasy?' I also interviewed sane, responsible Frenchmen who met and decided to support him during the period immediately following his two extraordinary encounters in the 1970s. I have also come to know and respect as friends many other leading and rank-

and-file members of his international organization. In presenting Rael's story briefly to a world radio audience as just one aspect of the complex UFO phenomenon, I observed the time-honored journalistic practice of impartial detachment - but here I have no hesitation in publicly declaring my conviction that Rael has written books of the utmost importance and significance for our understanding of ourselves and the known universe in which we live.

If that is so, it is legitimate to ask, why are the contents of this book not yet universally known and accepted in the world some thirty-two years after the first of them was made public? In short, there was a sharp flurry of public interest in France after Rael announced the outline of what he had been told on a television chat show as soon as he finished his first book. But somehow the remarkable story did not immediately gain widespread acceptance in Europe, nor did it travel further abroad at that time along normal news channels. One explanation for this is that the national and international news media are curiously conservative in their approach to reporting news which is unprecedented. Well worn clichéd stories that are safe and reliable always find their way into broadcast bulletins and newspapers while anything truly radical appears to go through a long period of being reported scoffingly if at all. Decrying the likely truth of unprecedented information is a seemingly knee-jerk ploy which many journalists habitually employ over and over again to avoid any suspicion that they or their organization are gullible. To a large extent this has been happening to Rael's extraordinarily important information over the past thirty years or so, and the world's media has generally so far failed to inform its public about it very widely.

There are some signs, however, that this is beginning to change at long last. This is to be welcomed since in my considered view the contents of this book constitute a front-page, banner headline, top-of-the-bulletin story which has never been given its due global prominence. Little by little as the years since 1973 have passed, new scientific discoveries have confirmed the veracity of Rael's originally startling information. When proven to be fully true, the body of information that is presented in the following pages will, I feel confident, be seen as the greatest revelation in mankind's recorded history. But of course until now there have been two obvious reasons why it has not been quickly recognized as such.

Firstly, there is no incontrovertible, physical proof to back up what Rael has written. And secondly, the nature of what he says is deeply disturbing to the entrenched belief systems of religious, scientific, academic, and other institutions all around the world.

As individuals too, we are all unconsciously influenced by the conventions of our education, our upbringing and that limited climate of thought fostered by our world's conservative and unadventurous mainstream news media.

All this is not surprising since it requires considerable effort on the part of individuals to become independently open-minded and overcome such influences. For these reasons, this extraordinary information has seeped out only slowly around the world over the past thirty-two years, largely through the steady, unspectacular efforts of the International Raelian Movement which at the time of writing lays claim to some 60,000 members in nearly ninety countries.

For more than thirty years now, Rael himself has, with gentle and patient good humour, explained his story again and again, certainly thousands of times to radio, television and print journalists in most of the countries of the world. When mocked or derided as he has often been in live or recorded studio interviews at which I have been present as his English language commercial publisher and a supporter of his extraordinary mission, he has always conducted himself with the same quiet courtesy and unshakable confidence. Never once have I seen him lose the calm demeanor of a man who knows without any shadow of doubt that he is telling the truth.

As far as providing proof is concerned, however, Rael quotes the Elohim as saying that they are deliberately withholding any outright physical evidence that would support their revelations - beyond the fact that their spacecraft will appear more and more frequently in our skies as time goes by. It is very important, they say, that we consider all their final information without proof - the logic and rationality of what they have revealed effectively contains its own hallmark of truth.

Whether or not we understand and accept their information and philosophical teaching and insights, they say, is a vital test of our intelligence and powers of perception, and from our reactions they will judge whether we are mature enough to be entrusted with their highly superior scientific and social knowledge, which is 25,000 years in advance of our own.

They explain that they do not choose to land openly and officially in any one country because that would involve violating our planetary air space, both at national and international levels. Landing anywhere at all might also seem to imply approval of that particular country's government and philosophy - and they do not so approve of any existing nation on Earth. Therefore they need a diplomatic embassy of their own with the kind of extraterritorial rights enjoyed by any respected, visiting diplomat in a foreign state. Since their first embassy on Earth was Jerusalem's first temple, they have asked for their new modern embassy to be built as close as possible to that most ancient of all cities in the heart of Israel.

Despite the minimal media acceptance to date of Rael and what he stands for, the passage of time has already provided its own growing substantiation of what he has written. In 1974-75 when he first began to say that all life forms on Earth had been created in laboratories by Elohim scientists via their mastery of DNA, our own genetic research scientists were far less advanced in their work than they are today. In February 1997, about a quarter of a century after Rael's first encounter with the visitor from space, there came the announcement of an historic, global breakthrough in the field of biology, made from Edinburgh in Scotland, revealing that British embryologists had succeeded in artificially cloning a sheep named Dolly.

The cloning of human beings, it was said then, would become possible within two years and Rael promptly issued a press release saying: 'All this demonstrates that the technology which was considered impossible at the time of my original revelations is now perfectly attainable.'

The prediction that it would be possible to clone a human being in two years did not in the event prove accurate. However, Rael founded a new company called Clonaid that same year which became the first commercial enterprise in the world offering cloning services to the public - and in December 2002 five years after the announcement of Dolly's birth, Dr Brigitte Boisselier, Clonaid's president, announced at a crowded press conference in Miami that the company had assisted the first successful cloned human birth of a baby girl named Eve. Dr Boisselier later announced that Clonaid had achieved a succession of other cloned births in a number of countries around the world. Legal complications halted Clonaid's plan to present immediate medical and scientific proof of these cloned births to the world and that remained the position in the autumn of 2005 as this book was going to press. Dr Boisselier explained publicly that Clonaid's wish to protect the privacy and security of the cloned babies and their parents was the prime concern, but proof of Clonaid's achievements would be published at the right time.

Meanwhile, new advances in understanding cloning, DNA and stem cells continue to appear regularly in our newspapers contributing new support to what Rael has been writing and saying over the past thirty years. In one notable example, Japanese scientists announced that their research indicated that the gene pool for all races on Earth originated from a surprisingly small common base dating back approximately 13,000 years. This figure echoed what Rael had written with uncanny precision since the Elohim had said they began their work here 25,000 years ago and had spent some 12,000 years preparing the planet and creating the ecology, the marine and bird life and then land mammals before embarking finally on the creation of human beings 'in their own image'.

Rael says the Elohim leaders have been alive continually during those 25,000 years, having long since learned how to genetically recreate the human body with memory and personality intact. Soon, they contend, we will be able to expand our own average life span to around 1,000 years on our way to emulating them. Rael says they also monitor the thoughts and deeds of every individual on Earth by computer and can recreate each and any of us at will at the moment of death by a remote sampling of a single cell of our bodies. He reports that some 8,000 individuals from Earth had already been recreated on their planet when he was taken there in 1975.

Outside of practical scientific laboratory research a recent highly significant development in the academic field has provided new support for Rael's message. On 4 August 2004 the most comprehensive challenge to Darwin's Theory of Evolution known as Intelligent Design Theory was presented quietly to the world. This new theory hypothesizes that no new living entity can happen by chance and it was presented formally by Dr. Stephen C. Meyer, Director of the Discovery Institute's Center for Science & Culture in an article published in its biology journal by the National Museum of Natural History at the Smithsonian Institution in Washington D.C.

The journal, *Proceedings of the Biological Society of Washington* (volume 117, no. 2, pp. 213-239), carried an article entitled 'The Origin of Biological Information and the Higher Taxonomic Categories,' in which Dr. Meyer argued that no current theory of evolution could account for the origin of the information necessary to build novel animal forms. He proposed 'intelligent design' as an alternative explanation. This article represented an historic breakthrough for those who have long questioned Darwin's unproven theory because it was published in a peer reviewed academic journal and has since been used increasingly as a reference by scientists who were previously obliged to refer only to evolution theory in explaining their discoveries.

Commenting on this development at the time, Dr Boisselier said those who supported Rael all over the world had cause to rejoice at this event since it made it possible for biologists to look at living entities not as the result of random mutations but more as sophisticated creations in which every detail had been thought out and had a reason to exist. "Biology will go so fast," she said, "once biologists stop being blinded by the evolution theory. I am sure that in ten years from now scientists will look back and wonder why they accepted evolution for so long."

This landmark academic event brought the new conceptual term 'Intelligent Design' into public awareness and opened a new era of debate about evolution theory and our origins. Quickly becoming known in short as ID, 'intelligent design' is now beginning to be studied and developed in some respected universities. Even President George W. Bush, who is not renowned for his intervention in purely intellectual debates, has declared that 'intelligent design' is as likely an explanation as evolution theory.

Does this mean that President Bush has taken the first step on his way to becoming a Raelian? Perhaps, perhaps not. Whatever the truth proves to be, this is another illustration of the gradual emergence of strong corroboration of Rael's story. Indeed we might speculate that the very essence of the Elohim's 'intelligent design' is that they are waking up the world they created to the whole truth very slowly since being shocked suddenly and instantly into full wakefulness from deep sleep is always very unpleasant and sometimes damaging.

However, it is for all these reasons that the title *Intelligent Design - Message from the Designers* has been given to this new edition of Rael's writings. In a striking new Author's Postscript to this book Rael develops this theme to a new level. He says that the original and unique Raelian explanation of the origins of life on Earth effectively offers a Third Way between Darwin and Genesis and it can best be described as atheist Intelligent Design, which is the scientific creation of life on Earth performed by an advanced human civilization. And uniquely this Third Way is reproducible in a laboratory.

Having said all that, I must emphasize that no brief summary can really do justice to the high import of this whole book. To grasp the full significance of all its major assertions requires that measured consideration be given to each and all of them in their context. Therefore, I trust in writing this foreword that others on reading it, will be encouraged to give the whole book a careful reading. If it is all true, and I feel sure it has been honestly and truthfully reported, then nothing in the world could be more important.

The world of UFO research is awash with many amazing and often conflicting testimonies and claims about life beyond our planet, virtually all of them unproven. What Rael has written does not reconcile all these conflicts in an instant - and nothing could. Outside of the disturbing and still unexplained phenomenon of claimed abduction experiences which have been reported worldwide, other people have come forward over the past forty or fifty years to insist that they have had friendly personal contacts with extra-terrestrial visitors to our planet. The list of 'contactees' contains some fraudsters as well as others who are obviously sincere. But none of them has remotely approached Rael in the sheer scale of the information reportedly offered - and Rael is adamant that he alone has been entrusted with conveying these truths.

It is just over thirteen years at the time of writing since I first read the contents of this book myself. Presented with a combined copy of the first two books by a French business executive whom I had met at a conference, I began reading them after getting into bed late one evening - and read on right through the entire night until I finished them, never once sleeping then or even during the whole of the next day.

I was seized almost immediately by a feeling of awe that I had, by good fortune, stumbled across the greatest possible truths - and that feeling has never left me since then.

After reflecting and musing carefully on the book's enormous implications over the past thirteen years, I still firmly believe as indicated above that it has the potential to transform us and our world beyond all present expectations. At a purely practical level, if national leaders could take this book seriously and steel themselves to the thought that our world is in comparison a backward 'developing country' with many seemingly insoluble problems, and that unlimited aid and assistance is available from a generous, highly-advanced Superpower living beyond our planet, then working towards an historic meeting with representatives of the Elohim at the world's first extra-terrestrial embassy near to Jerusalem could be seen as a worthy and sensible international goal.

Equally important I believe, is the book's core revelation about the very nature of the reality in which we live. Things infinitely small, the Elohim say, have exactly the same structure as things infinitely large - and they assured Rael they had proved this scientifically. This sounds incredible perhaps because our own science can not yet conceive of it, but they say that the atoms and sub-atoms in the cells of our bodies are mirror images of the universe above us; they contain minute planetary systems and galaxies on which complex, intelligent life forms like ourselves exist.

Similarly our own planet, solar system, galaxy and universe are tiny particles in an atom of some immense organic being and all matter at different levels mirrors itself in this way. Matter and time have no beginning and no end, they say, and everything is cyclic.

Interlocked Star of David triangles symbolizing these fundamental truths - which are illustrated and explained in the selection of photographs printed in this book - were emblazoned on the first extra-terrestrial spacecraft which landed before Rael's eyes in France. During his second encounter he was taught meditation techniques rooted in these understandings which he has been assiduously passing on ever since at annual seminars held on all five continents of the world. Called 'sensual meditation' or 'meditation of all senses', these techniques are designed to awaken the individual mind to its greatest potential by first fully awakening the physical sensibilities of the body.

The undoubted benefits of any kind of meditation are being recognized increasingly by the medical professions but the techniques taught by Rael specifically help individuals to feel a greater sense of harmony with the infinite nature of all things and consequently with each other. Beneficial chemical reactions are stimulated within the body, health is enhanced, mental and physical inner ease increases. In short, what is unique about these teachings and practices is that they combine the spiritual with the scientific in a common-sense fashion, promising a transformation of society that begins where any real change must begin - with the individual.

In my view, for the many reasons outlined here publication of *Intelligent Design - Message from the Designers* marks the end of a long era of incomprehension and ignorance about ourselves and the purposes of our existence. I don't think its potential importance can be overstated: in my view it is simply the most important book to be published anywhere in the world for two thousand years. If it receives the attention it deserves, I believe it could herald and usher in an unprecedented epoch of worldwide enlightenment and change.

Autumn 2005
Norwich, England

Anthony Grey is a former foreign correspondent with Reuters in Eastern Europe and China – where he was held hostage for two years during the Cultural Revolution -- and the author of the international best-selling historical novels, *Saigon*, *Peking* and *Tokyo Bay*. (www.anthonygrey.co.uk)

BOOK ONE

THE BOOK WHICH TELLS THE TRUTH

1

THE ENCOUNTER

Ever since I was nine years old I have had but one passion - motor racing. I founded a specialist motor sport magazine in 1970, simply to be able to live in the environment of a sport where man is constantly trying to surpass himself while striving to surpass others. Since my early childhood I had dreamed of one day being a racing-car driver, following in the footsteps of someone as famous as Fangio. Thanks to contacts made through the magazine I founded, I was given the opportunity to race and about ten trophies now adorn my apartment as a result of those races.

On the 13th of December 1973, however, I went to a volcano overlooking Clermont-Ferrand in central southern France. I went more to get a breath of fresh air than to take a drive in my car. My legs were itching after a full year following the races from circuit to circuit, almost always living on four wheels, so to speak.

The air was cool at the time, and the sky rather gray with a background mist. I walked and jogged a little and left the path where my car was parked, aiming to reach the center of the crater called Puy-de-Lassolas where I often went for picnics with my family in the summer.

What a superb and breathtaking place it was! To think that thousands of years ago, right where my feet were standing, lava had spurted out at incredibly high temperatures. Decorative volcanic 'bombs' can still be found among the debris. The stunted vegetation resembled that of Province in France but without sunshine.

I was just about to leave and looked for the last time towards the top of the circular mountain, which was formed by an accumulation of volcanic slag. It reminded me how many times I had slid down those steep slopes, as if I was on skis. Suddenly in the fog, I saw a red light flashing; then a sort of helicopter was descending towards me. A helicopter, however, makes a noise but at that moment, I could hear absolutely nothing, not even the slightest whistle. A balloon maybe?

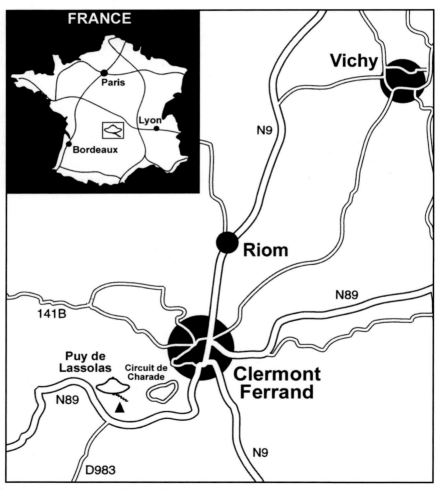

Site of Rael's first encounter: Puy de Lassolas, near
Clermont-Ferrand, December 13th, 1973.

By now, the object was about twenty meters above the ground, and I could see it had a somewhat flattened shape.

It was a flying saucer.

I had always believed in their existence, but I had never dreamed I would actually see one. It measured some seven meters in diameter, about 2.5 meters in height, was flat underneath and cone-shaped. On its underside, a very bright red light flashed, while at the top an intermittent white light reminded me of a camera flash cube. This white light was so intense, that I could not look at it without blinking.

The object continued to descend, without the slightest noise until it stopped and hovered motionless about two meters above the ground. I was petrified and remained absolutely still. I was not afraid, but rather filled with joy to be living through such a great moment. I bitterly regretted not having brought my camera with me.

Then the incredible happened. A trap door opened beneath the machine and a kind of stairway unfolded to the ground. I realized that some living being was about to appear, and I wondered what it was going to look like.

First two feet appeared then two legs, which reassured me a little, since apparently I was about to meet a man. In the event, what at first I took to be a child came down the stairway and walked straight towards me.

I could see then this was certainly no child even though the figure was only about four feet (1.2 meters) tall. His eyes were slightly almond shaped, his hair was black and long, and he had a small black beard. I still had not moved, and he stopped about ten meters away from me.

He wore some sort of green one-piece suit, which covered his entire body, and although his head seemed to be exposed, I could see around it a strange sort of halo. It was not really a halo but the air about his face shone slightly and shimmered. It looked like an invisible shield, like a bubble, so fine that you could barely see it. His skin was white with a slightly greenish tinge, a bit like someone with liver trouble.

He smiled faintly, and I thought it best to return his smile. I felt rather ill at ease, so I smiled and bowed my head slightly in greeting. He answered with the same gesture. Thinking that I had to find out if he could hear me, I asked: *'Where do you come from?'*

He answered in a strong, articulate voice that was slightly nasal: 'From very far away.'

'Do you speak French?' I enquired.

'I speak all the languages of the Earth.'

'Do you come from another planet?'

'Yes,' he replied.

As he spoke, he moved closer and stopped about two meters from me.

'Is this the first time you have visited the Earth?'

'Oh no!'

'Have you been here often?'

'Very often - to say the least.'

'Why did you come here?'

'Today, to talk to you.'

'To me?'

'Yes, to you, Claude Vorilhon, editor of a small motor sport magazine, married and father of two children.'

'How do you know all that?'

'We have been watching you for a long time.'

'Why me?'

'This is precisely what I want to tell you. Why did you come here on this cold winter morning?'

'I don't know... I felt like walking in the fresh air...'

'Do you come here often?'

'In the summer yes, but almost never in this season.'

'So why did you come today? Had you planned this walk for a long time?'

'No. I don't really know. When I woke up this morning I suddenly had an urge to come here.'

'You came because I wanted to see you. Do you believe in telepathy?'

'*Yes, of course, it's something I've always been interested in - as well as the subject of "flying saucers". But I never thought I'd see one myself.*'

'Well, I used telepathy to get you to come here because I have many things to tell you. Have you read the Bible?'

'*Yes, but why do you ask?*'

'Have you been reading it for a long time?'

'*No, as a matter of fact, I bought it only a few days ago.*'

'Why?'

'*I really don't know. Suddenly I had an urge to read it...*'

'Again I used telepathy to make you decide to buy it. I have chosen you for a very difficult mission, and I have many things to tell you. So come into my craft where we can talk more comfortably.'

I followed him, climbing up the small staircase beneath the machine, which, on closer inspection, looked more like a flattened bell with a full and bulging underside. Inside it, two seats faced one another, and the temperature was mild even though the door was still open.

There was no lamp, but natural light emanated from everywhere. There were no instruments like those you find in an aircraft cockpit. The floor was made of a sparkling alloy, which was slightly bluish. The chairs were colorless and translucent, but very comfortable and made from one piece of material. I sat on the larger one that was set closer to the floor, so that the face of the little man sitting in front of me was at the same level as mine.

He touched a spot on the wall, and the whole machine became transparent except for its top and bottom. It was like being in the open air, but the temperature was mild. He invited me to take off my coat, which I did, and then he started to speak.

'You regret not having brought your camera so that you could have talked about our meeting to the whole world - with proof in your hands?'

'*Yes, of course...*'

'Listen to me carefully. You will tell human beings about this meeting, but you will tell them the truth about what they are, and about what we are. Judging from their reactions we will know if we can show ourselves freely and officially. Wait until you know everything before you start speaking publicly. Then you will be able to defend yourself properly against those people who will not believe you and you will be able to bring them incontestable proof. You will write down everything I tell you and publish the writings as a book.'

'*But why did you choose me?*'

'For many reasons. First of all, we needed someone in a country where new ideas are welcomed and where it is possible to talk about such ideas openly. Democracy was born in France, and this country has a reputation the world over for being the country of freedom. Also we needed someone who is intelligent and quite open to everything. Above all we needed someone who is a free thinker without being anti-religious. Because you were born of a Jewish father and a Catholic mother, we consider you to be an ideal link between two very important peoples in the history of the world. Besides, your activities do not in any way predispose you to making incredible revelations, and this will make your words all the more credible. Since you are not a scientist, you will not complicate things and will explain them simply. Not being a literary man, you won't compose elaborate sentences, which are difficult to read for a great many people. Finally, we decided to choose someone who was born after the first atomic explosion in 1945, and you were born in 1946. We have in fact been following you since your birth, and even before. This is why we have chosen you. Do you have any other questions?'

'*Where do you come from?*'

'From a distant planet about which I will tell you nothing for fear that men of the Earth might be unwise enough to disturb our peace.'

'*Is your planet very far away?*'

'Very far. When I tell you the distance you will understand that it is impossible to reach it with your present level of scientific and technical knowledge.'

'*What are you called?*'

'We are people like you, and we live on a planet similar to Earth.'

'*How long does it take you to come here?*'

'As long as it takes to think about it.'

8

'*Why do you come to Earth?*'

'To monitor and watch over the development of humanity. Human beings on Earth are the future, we are the past.'

'*Are there many people on your planet?*'

'There are more people than on yours.'

'*I would like to visit your planet. Can I?*'

'No. First of all you couldn't live there because the atmosphere is different from yours, and you have not been trained for such a journey.'

'*But why meet here?*'

'Because the crater of a volcano is an ideal place, away from irksome people. I shall leave you now. Come back tomorrow at the same time with the Bible and something to take notes with. Do not bring any metallic object and speak to no one of our conversation, otherwise we will never meet again.'

He handed me my coat, let me climb down the ladder and waved his hand. The ladder folded up and the door closed without a sound. Still without making the slightest murmur or any whistling sound, the craft rose gently to a height of about 400 meters, then disappeared into the mist.

2

THE TRUTH

Genesis

The following day I was at the meeting place again as arranged with a notebook, a pen and the Bible. The flying machine reappeared on time, and I found myself face to face once more with the little man who invited me to enter the machine and sit in the same comfortable chair.

I had spoken to nobody about all this, not even to those closest to me, and he was happy to learn that I had been discreet. He suggested I take notes, and then he started to speak:

'A very long time ago on our distant planet, we had reached a level of technical and scientific knowledge, comparable to that which you will soon reach. Our scientists had started to create primitive, embryonic forms of life, namely living cells in test tubes. Everyone was thrilled by this.'

The scientists perfected their techniques and began creating bizarre little animals but the government, under pressure from public opinion, ordered the scientists to stop their experiments for fear they would create monsters, which would become dangerous to society. In fact one of these animals had broken loose and killed several people.

Since at that time, interplanetary and intergalactic explorations had also made progress, the scientists decided to set out for a distant planet where they could find most of the necessary conditions to pursue their experiments. They chose Earth where you live. Now I would like you to refer to the Bible where you will find traces of the truth about your past. These traces, of course, have been somewhat distorted by successive transcribers who could not conceive of such high technology and could therefore only explain what was described as being a mystical and supernatural force.

Only the parts of the Bible that I will translate are important. Other parts are merely poetic babblings of which I will say nothing. I am sure you can appreciate that, thanks to the law, which said that the Bible had always to be re-copied without changing even the smallest detail, the deepest meaning has remained intact throughout the ages, even if the text has been larded with mystical and futile sentences.

So let us start with the first chapter of the Book of Genesis:

> In the beginning Elohim[1] created the heaven and the earth.
> *Genesis 1: 1.*

Elohim, translated without justification in some Bibles by the word *God* means in Hebrew "those who came from the sky", and furthermore the word is a plural. It means that the scientists from our world searched for a planet that was suitable to carry out their projects. They "created", or in reality discovered the Earth, and realized it contained all the necessary elements for the creation of artificial life, even if its atmosphere was not quite the same as our own.

> And the Spirit of Elohim moved upon the face of the waters.
> *Genesis 1: 2.*

This means the scientists made reconnaissance flights, and what you might call artificial satellites were placed around the Earth to study its constitution and atmosphere. The Earth was, at that time, completely covered with water and thick mist.

And Elohim saw the light, that it was good. *Genesis 1: 4.*

To create life on Earth it was important to know whether the sun was sending harmful rays to the Earth's surface, and this question was fully researched. It turned out that the sun was heating the Earth correctly without sending out harmful rays. In other words the "light was good".

And the evening and the morning were the first day. *Genesis 1: 5.*

This research took quite some time. The "day" mentioned here corresponds to the period in which your sun rises under the same sign on the day of the vernal equinox, in other words, about 2,000 years on Earth.

And Elohim made the firmament, and divided the waters which were under the firmament from the waters which were above the firmament. *Genesis 1: 7.*

After studying the cosmic rays above the clouds the scientists descended below the clouds but stayed above the waters. That means they were between the clouds, "the waters which were above the firmament", and the ocean covering the whole planet, "the waters which were under the firmament".

Let the waters under the heaven be gathered together unto one place, and let the dry land appear. *Genesis 1: 9.*

After they studied the surface of the ocean they studied the sea bed and determined that it was not very deep and fairly even everywhere. So then, by means of fairly strong explosions, which acted rather like bulldozers, they raised matter from the bottom of the seas and piled it up into one place to form a continent.

Originally there was on Earth only one continent, and your scientists have recently acknowledged that all the continents, which have drifted apart over many years, used to fit perfectly into one another to form one land mass.

> Let the earth bring forth grass, the herb yielding seed, and the fruit tree yielding fruit after his kind, whose seed is in itself, upon the earth. *Genesis 1: 11.*

In this magnificent and gigantic laboratory, they created vegetable cells from nothing other than chemicals, which then produced various types of plants. All their efforts were aimed at reproduction. The few blades of grass they created had to reproduce on their own.

The scientists spread out across this immense continent in small research teams. Every individual created different varieties of plants according to their inspiration and the climate. They met up at regular intervals to compare their research and their creations. The people back on their own planet followed their progress from afar with passion and amazement. The most brilliant artists came and joined the scientists in order to give some plants purely decorative and pleasing roles, either through their appearance or their perfume.

> Let there be lights in the firmament of the heaven to divide the day from the night; and let them be for signs, and for seasons, and for days, and years. *Genesis 1: 14.*

By observing the stars and the sun they could measure the duration of the days, the months and the years on Earth. This helped them regulate their life on the new planet - so different from their own where days and years did not have the same duration. Research in astronomy enabled them to locate themselves precisely and to understand the Earth better.

> Let the waters abound with an abundance of living creatures, and
> let birds fly above the earth across the face of the firmament of the
> heavens. *Genesis 1: 20.*

Next they created the first aquatic animals, from plankton to small
fish, then very large fish. They also created seaweed to balance this
little world, so that the small fish could feed on it and the bigger fish
could eat the small fish in turn.

Thus a natural balance would be established, and one species
would not destroy another species in order to survive. This is what
you now refer to as "ecology", and that was achieved successfully. The
scientists and artists met often and organized competitions to
determine which team had created the most beautiful or most
interesting animals.

After the fish they created birds. This was done under pressure, it
must be said, from the artists, who went out of their way to create the
most stunning forms with the craziest colors. Some of them had great
trouble flying because their beautiful feathers were very cumbersome.
The contests went even further, embracing not only physical
characteristics but also the behavior of these animals, particularly the
wonderful dances of their mating rituals.

Some other groups of scientists created frightful animals, veritable
monsters, which proved right those people who had opposed the
creation plans on their own planet. These were dragons, or what you
call dinosaurs and brontosaurs.

> Let the earth bring forth the living creature according to its kind:
> cattle and creeping thing and beast of the earth, each according to
> its kind. *Genesis 1: 24.*

After marine organisms and birds, the scientists created land
animals on a planet where the vegetation had by now become
magnificent. There was plenty of food for the herbivores. These were
the first land animals which were created. Later they created

carnivores to balance the herbivorous population. Here too, the species had to maintain equilibrium. Those scientists who did all this came from the same planet as me. I am one of those people who created life on Earth.

It was at that time that the most skillful among us wanted to create an artificial human being like ourselves. Each team set to work, and very soon we were able to compare our creations. But on our home planet people were outraged when they heard that we were making "test tube children" who might come to threaten their world. They feared that these new human beings could become a danger if their mental capacities or powers turned out to be superior to those of their creators. So we had to agree to leave the new humans to live in a very primitive way without letting them know anything scientific, and we mystified our actions. It is easy to work out how many teams of creators did this - each race on Earth corresponds to a team of creators.

> Let Us make man in Our image, according to Our likeness; let them have dominion over the fish of the sea, over the birds of the air, and over the cattle, over all the earth and over every creeping thing that creeps on the earth. *Genesis 1: 26.*

"In our image!" You can see that the resemblance is striking. That is when the trouble started for us. The team located in the country you now call Israel, which at the time was not far from Greece and Turkey on the original continent, was composed of brilliant creators who were perhaps the most talented team of all.

Their animals were the most beautiful and their plants had the sweetest perfumes. This was what you call "paradise on Earth". The human beings they created there were the most intelligent. So steps had to be taken to ensure that they did not surpass their creators. The created, therefore, had to be kept in ignorance of the great scientific secrets while being educated for the purpose of measuring their intelligence.

Of every tree of the garden you may freely eat; but of the tree of
the knowledge of good and evil you shall not eat, for in the day
that you eat of it you shall surely die.. *Genesis 2: 16-17.*

This means you - the created - can learn all you want, read all of
the books that we have here at your disposal, but never touch the
scientific books, otherwise you will die.

He brought them to the man to see what he would name them.
Genesis 2: 19.

Human beings had to have a thorough understanding of the plants
and animals living around them, their way of life, and the way to get
food from them. The creators taught them the names and the powers
of everything that existed around them since botany and zoology
were not considered dangerous for them. Imagine the joy of this team
of scientists, having two children, a male and a female running
around, eagerly learning what was being taught to them.

The serpent... said unto the woman... of the fruit of the tree
which is in the midst of the garden... ye shall not surely die, for
Elohim doth know that in the day ye eat thereof, then your eyes
shall be opened, and ye shall be like Elohim. *Genesis 3: 1-5.*

Some scientists in this team felt a deep love for their little human
beings, their "creatures", and they wanted to give them a complete
education in order to make them scientists like themselves. So they
told these young people who were almost adults that they could
pursue their scientific studies and in so doing they would become as
knowledgeable as their creators.

And the eyes of them both were opened, and they knew that they
were naked. *Genesis 3: 7.*

The new human beings then understood that they could also become creators in their turn, and they became angry at their "parents" for having kept them away from scientific books, considering them to be like dangerous laboratory animals.

> And Yahweh[1] Elohim said unto the serpent, 'Because thou hast done this, thou art cursed... upon thy belly shalt thou go, and dust shalt thou eat all the days of thy life.' *Genesis 3: 14.*

The "serpent" was this small group of creators who had wished to tell the truth to Adam and Eve, and as a result they were condemned by the government of their own planet to live in exile on Earth, while all the other scientists had to put a stop to their experiments and leave the Earth.

> Unto Adam also and to his wife did Yahweh Elohim make coats of skins, and clothed them. *Genesis 3: 21.*

The creators gave their creations the basic means of survival, enough to manage without needing any further contact with them. The Bible has preserved a sentence, which is close to the original document:

> Behold, the man is become as one of us, to know good and evil[2]: and now, lest he put forth his hand, and take also of the tree of life, and eat, and live for ever. *Genesis 3: 22.*

Human life is very short, but there is a scientific way to prolong it. Human scientists who study all their lives can only begin to amass sufficient knowledge to start making interesting discoveries when they get old, which is the reason why human progress is so slow. If humans could live ten times longer, scientific knowledge would take a gigantic leap forward.

If when they were first created these new beings could have lived much longer, they would have quite rapidly become our equals because their mental faculties are slightly superior to our own. They are unaware of their full potential. This applies especially to the people of Israel who, as I mentioned earlier, had been selected in a contest as the most successful type of humanoid on Earth due to their intelligence and genius. This explains why they have always considered themselves to be the "chosen people". In truth they were the people chosen by the teams of scientists who gathered together to judge their creations. You can see for yourself the number of geniuses born out of that race.

> So he drove out the man; and he placed at the east of the garden of Eden Cherubims, and a flaming sword which turned every way, to keep the way of the tree of life. *Genesis 3: 24.*

Soldiers with atomic disintegration weapons were placed at the entrance to the creators' residence to prevent human beings from stealing more scientific knowledge.'

The Flood

'Let us move on to the fourth chapter of Genesis.

> And in process of time it came to pass, that Cain brought of the fruit of the ground an offering unto Yahweh. And Abel, he also brought of the firstlings of his flock and of the fat thereof.
> *Genesis 4: 3-4.*

The creators in exile who were left under military surveillance, urged the human beings to bring them food in order to show their own superiors that the newly created people were good, and that they would never turn against their creators. Thus they managed to obtain permission for the leaders of these first human beings to benefit from the "tree of life", and this explains how they lived so long: Adam lived for 930 years, Seth for 912 years and Enos for 905 years, and so on as is stated in *Genesis,* Chapter 5, Verses 1-11.

> And it came to pass, when men began to multiply on the face of the earth, and daughters were born unto them, that the sons of Elohim saw the daughters of men that they were fair; and they took them wives of all which they chose. *Genesis 6: 1-2.*

The creators living in exile took the most beautiful daughters of humanity and made them their wives.

> My spirit shall not always strive with man, for that he also is flesh: yet his days shall be an hundred and twenty years. *Genesis 6: 3.*

Longevity is not hereditary and much to the relief of the authorities on the distant planet, the children of the new human beings did not automatically benefit from the "tree of life". Thus the secret of life was lost, and mankind's progress was slowed down.

> When the sons of Elohim came in unto the daughters of men, and they bare children to them, the same became mighty men which were of old, men of renown. *Genesis 6: 4.*

There you have proof that the creators could have intercourse with the daughters of humanity whom they had created in their own image, and in so doing produced exceptional children. These actions seemed very dangerous to people on the distant planet. The scientific progress on Earth was fantastic, and they decided to destroy what had been created.

> And Elohim saw that the wickedness of man was great in the
> earth, and that every imagination of the thoughts of his heart was
> only evil continually. *Genesis 6: 5.*

The "evil" in question was the desire of human beings to become scientific and independent people equal to their creators. Being "good", as far as those on the Elohim's planet were concerned meant the new human beings would remain primitive, vegetating on the Earth. Their "evil" was their wish to progress, perhaps enabling them one day to catch up with their creators.

The government then decided from their distant planet to destroy all life on Earth by sending nuclear missiles. However when the exiled creators were informed of the project they asked Noah to build a spaceship, which would orbit the Earth during the cataclysm containing a pair of each species that was to be preserved.

This was true figuratively speaking, but in reality - and your scientific knowledge will very soon enable you to understand this - a single living cell of each species, male and female, is all that is required to recreate a whole being. This is something like the first living cell of a fetus in the womb of its mother, which already possesses all the information needed to create a human being right down to the color of its eyes and hair. This was a colossal task, but it was completed on time.

When the explosion took place, life had already been preserved a few thousand kilometers above the Earth. The continent was submerged by a gigantic tidal wave, which destroyed all forms of life on its surface.

> The ark... was lift up above the earth. *Genesis 7: 17.*

As you can clearly see, it is said that the ark was lifted "above" the Earth and not "on" the water.

Then it was necessary to wait until there was no more dangerous radioactive fallout:

And the waters prevailed upon the earth an hundred and fifty days. *Genesis 7: 24.*

The spacecraft had three sections:

...and the door of the ark shalt thou set in the side thereof; with lower, second, and third stories shalt thou make it. *Genesis 6: 16.*

Later it landed on Earth, and besides Noah, it carried a couple from each race of human beings on the Earth.

And Elohim remembered Noah... and Elohim made a wind to pass over the earth, and the waters asswaged. *Genesis 8: 1.*

After monitoring the level of radioactivity and dispersing it scientifically, the creators told Noah to release the animals to see if they could survive in the atmosphere. This operation was successful, and they were able to venture out into the open air. The creators then asked the human survivors to work and multiply, and show their gratitude to their benefactors who had created them and saved them from destruction. Noah agreed to give a portion of their harvest and their cattle to the creators to ensure they survived:

And Noah builded an altar unto Yahweh; and took of every clean beast, and of every clean fowl, and offered burnt offerings on the altar. *Genesis 8: 20.*

The creators were happy to see that humans wished them well, and they promised never to try to destroy their creation again. They understood that it was only normal for them to want to progress scientifically.

...for the imagination of man's heart is evil. *Genesis 8: 21.*

The goal of humankind is scientific progress. Each race of humanity was then returned to its original place of creation, and each animal was recreated from the cells which had been preserved aboard the ark.

> And by these were the nations divided in the earth after the flood.
> *Genesis 10: 32.'*

The Tower of Babel

'But the most intelligent race, the people of Israel, was making such remarkable progress that they were soon able to undertake the conquest of space with the help of the exiled creators. The latter wanted their new human beings to go to the creators' planet to obtain their pardon, by showing that they were not only intelligent and scientific but also grateful and peaceful. So they built an enormous rocket - The Tower of Babel.

> And now nothing will be restrained from them, which they have imagined to do. *Genesis 11: 6.*

The people on our planet became frightened when they heard about this. They were still observing the Earth and knew that life had not been destroyed.

> Go to, let us go down, and there confound their language, that they may not understand one another's speech. So Yahweh scattered them abroad from thence upon the face of all the earth.
> *Genesis 11: 7-8.*

So they came and took the Jews who had the most scientific knowledge and scattered them all over the continent among primitive tribes in countries where nobody could understand them because the language was different, and they destroyed all their scientific instruments.'

Sodom and Gomorrah

'The exiled creators were pardoned and allowed to return to their original planet where they pleaded the case of their magnificent creation. As a result, everyone on the distant planet fixed their eyes on the Earth because it was inhabited by people they had themselves created.

But among the humans who had been dispersed on Earth, a few nursed the desire for vengeance, so they gathered in the towns of Sodom and Gomorrah and, having managed to salvage a few scientific secrets, they prepared an expedition aimed at punishing those who had tried to destroy them. Consequently, the creators sent two spies to investigate what was going on:

And there came two angels to Sodom at even[3]. *Genesis 19: 1.*

Some humans tried to kill them, but the spies managed to blind their attackers with a pocket atomic weapon:

And they smote the men that were at the door of the house with blindness, both small and great. *Genesis 19: 11.*

They warned those who were peaceful to leave the town because they were going to destroy it with an atomic explosion:

> Up, get you out of this place; for Yahweh will destroy this city.
> *Genesis 19: 14.*

As the people were leaving town, they were in no particular hurry because they did not realize what an atomic explosion could mean.

> Escape for thy life; look not behind thee, neither stay thou in all the plain. *Genesis 19: 17.*

And the bomb fell on Sodom and Gomorrah:

> Then Yahweh rained upon Sodom and upon Gomorrah brimstone and fire from Yahweh out of heaven; And he overthrew those cities, and all the plain, and all the inhabitants of the cities, and that which grew upon the ground. But his wife looked back from behind him, and she became a pillar of salt.
> *Genesis 19: 24-26.*

As you now know, burns caused by an atomic explosion kill those who are too near and make them look like salt statues.'

The Sacrifice of Abraham

'Later, after most of their leading intellectuals had been destroyed, and they had relapsed into a semi-primitive state, the creators wished to see if the people of Israel, and particularly their leader, still had positive feelings towards them. This is related in the paragraph where Abraham wants to sacrifice his own son. The creators tested him to see if his feelings towards them were sufficiently strong. Fortunately, the experiment ended positively.

Lay not thine hand upon the lad, neither do thou any thing unto him: for now I know that thou fearest Elohim. *Genesis 22: 12.*

There you have it. Assimilate it all and write down everything that I have just told you. I will tell you more tomorrow.'

Once again the small man took leave of me, and his spacecraft rose slowly into the air. Because the sky was clearer this time, I was able to watch more closely as it took off. It hovered motionless at a height of about 400 meters, then still without the slightest sound, the vessel turned red as if it was heating up, then as white as white-hot metal, and then finally a sort of bluish purple like an enormous spark, which was impossible to look at. Then it disappeared completely.

3

WATCHING OVER THE CHOSEN PEOPLE

Moses

The following day I again met with my visitor, and he immediately continued his story.

'In *Genesis*, Chapter 28, there is another description of our presence:

> And behold a ladder set up on the earth, and the top of it reached to heaven: and behold the angels of Elohim ascending and descending on it. *Genesis 28: 12.*

Because of the destruction of centers of progress such as Sodom and Gomorrah and the elimination of the most intelligent individuals, human beings had lapsed back into a very primitive state and had begun, rather stupidly, to adore pieces of stone and idols, forgetting those who had really created them:

> Put away the foreign gods that are among you. *Genesis 35: 2.*

In *Exodus,* we appeared to Moses.

> And the angel of Yahweh appeared unto him in a flame of fire out of the midst of a bush: and he looked, and, behold, the bush

burned with fire, and the bush was not consumed.

Exodus 3: 2.

A rocket landed in front of him, and his description corresponds to what a Brazilian tribesman might say today if we were to land before him in a flying vessel illuminating the trees without burning them.

The people chosen as the most intelligent had lost their most brilliant minds and had become slaves to neighboring tribes who were more numerous since they had not undergone the same destruction. It was thus necessary to restore dignity to the people of Israel by returning their land to them.

The beginning of *Exodus* describes all that we had to do to help liberate the people of Israel. Once departed, we guided them to the country, which we had destined for them:

> And Yahweh went before them by day in a pillar of a cloud, to lead them the way; and by night in a pillar of fire, to give them light; to go by day and night. *Exodus 13: 21.*

In order to slow down the march of the Egyptians who had started to pursue them:

> The pillar of the cloud went from before their face, and stood behind them... and it was a cloud and darkness to them, but it gave light by night to these: so that the one came not near the other all the night. *Exodus 14: 19-20.*

The smoke emitted behind the people of Israel made a curtain, which slowed down their pursuers. Then the crossing of the water was made possible by a repulsion beam, which cleared a passageway:

And Yahweh caused the sea to go back by a strong east wind all
that night, and made the sea dry land, and the waters were
divided. *Exodus 14: 21.*

Thus Yahweh saved Israel that day out of the hand of the
Egyptians. *Exodus 14: 30.*

While they were crossing the desert the chosen people began to feel
hungry:

Upon the face of the wilderness there lay a small round thing, as
small as the hoar frost on the ground. *Exodus 16: 14.*

The manna was nothing more than pulverized synthetic chemical
food, which when spread on the ground, swelled with the early
morning dew.

As for the staff which allowed Moses to draw water from the rock,
as it says in *Exodus 17:6* - it was nothing but a detector of
underground water pools similar to those which you use at present to
find oil, for example. Once the water is located, one has only to dig.

Then in Chapter 20 of *Exodus* a certain number of rules are cited.

Because the Israelites were so primitive, they needed laws regarding
morals and especially hygiene. These were outlined in the
commandments.

The creators came to dictate these laws to Moses on Mount Sinai,
and they arrived in a flying vessel:

And it came to pass on the third day in the morning, that there
were thunders and lightnings, and a thick cloud upon the mount,
and the voice of the trumpet exceeding loud; so that all the people
that was in the camp trembled... And mount Sinai was altogether
on a smoke, because Yahweh descended upon it in fire: and the
smoke thereof ascended as the smoke of a furnace, and the whole
mount quaked greatly. And when the voice of the trumpet

sounded long, and waxed louder and louder. Moses spake, and Elohim answered him by a voice. *Exodus 19: 16-19.*

The creators were afraid of being invaded or maltreated by human beings. It was therefore essential that they be respected, even venerated, so that they would be in no danger:

The people cannot come up to mount Sinai... but let not the priests and the people break through to come up unto Yahweh, lest he break forth upon them. *Exodus 19: 23-24.*

Also, it was written:

And Moses alone shall come near Yahweh: but they shall not come nigh; neither shall the people go up with him.
Exodus 24: 2.

They saw the God of Israel:

And there was under his feet as it were a paved work of a sapphire stone, and as it were the body of heaven in his clearness.
Exodus 24: 10.

There you have the description of the pedestal upon which one of the creators presented himself, and it was made of the same bluish alloys as the floor of the machine in which we are now sitting.

And the sight of the glory of Yahweh was like devouring fire on the top of the mount. *Exodus 24: 17.*

Here you have a description of "the glory" of the creators - in reality, the flying vessel - and, as you have already noticed, upon take-off it has a coloration similar to that of fire.

This team of creators was going to live on the Earth for some time, and they wished to eat fresh food. That is why they asked the Israelites to bring them fresh provisions regularly and also riches, which they wanted to take back to their own planet. I suppose you might call it colonization:

> Speak unto the children of Israel, that they bring me an offering: of every man that giveth it willingly with his heart ye shall take my offering. And this is the offering which ye shall take of them; gold, and silver, and brass, and blue, and purple, and scarlet, and fine linen, and goats' hair. *Exodus 25: 2-4.*

They also decided that they would like to live more comfortably, so they asked the human beings to build them a residence according to plans they had drawn up. The plans are described in Chapter 26 of the *Book of Exodus.* In this residence they would meet the representatives of the people. It was a meeting tent where people brought food and gifts as a pledge of submission.

> And it came to pass, as Moses entered into the tabernacle, the cloudy pillar descended, and stood at the door of the tabernacle and Yahweh talked with Moses... And Yahweh spake unto Moses face to face, as a man speaketh unto his friend. *Exodus 33: 8-11.*

Just as today I can speak to you as you can speak to me, man to man.

> Thou canst not see my face: for there shall no man see me, and live. *Exodus 33: 20.*

There you have reference to the difference in atmosphere between our planets. Humans cannot see their creators unless the latter are protected by a pressurized suit, because the terrestrial atmosphere is not suitable for them. If a man came to our planet he would see the creators without a space suit, but he would die because the atmosphere is not suitable for him.

The entire beginning of *Leviticus* explains how the foods offered to the creators had to be brought to them for their replenishment. For example, in *Leviticus 21: 17* it says:

> Whosoever he be of thy seed in their generations that hath any blemish[4], let him not approach to offer the bread of his Elohim.

This is obviously to prevent sick or deformed people, who were symbols of failure and therefore unbearable to the eyes of the creators, from presenting themselves before them.

In the *Book of Numbers 11:7-8* there is a very precise description of the manna, which your chemists could very easily reproduce:

> And the manna was as coriander seed, and the colour thereof as the colour of bdellium... and the taste of it was as the taste of fresh oil.

This manna was nothing more than a chemical food, but the creators preferred fresh fruits and vegetables:

> And whatsoever is first ripe in the land, which they shall bring unto Yahweh, shall be thine. *Numbers 18: 13.*

Later, the creators taught human beings how to inject themselves to treat snakebites:

> Make thee a fiery serpent, and set it upon a pole: and it shall come to pass, that every one that is bitten, when he looketh upon it, shall live. *Numbers 21: 8.*

As soon as someone was bitten, he "looked" at the "serpent of brass", that is to say, a syringe was brought to him, and he was injected with serum.

Finally, the journey, which led the "chosen people" to the Promised Land, came to an end. Following the advice of the creators, they destroyed the idols of the local primitive people and took over their territories:

> Then ye shall... destroy all their molten images...and ye shall dispossess the inhabitants of the land, and dwell therein: for I have given you the land to possess it. *Numbers 33: 52-53.*

The "chosen people" finally reached their Promised Land:

> And because he loved thy fathers, therefore he chose their seed after them. *Deuteronomy 4: 37.*

In the *Book of Joshua*, Chapter 3, Verses 15-16, we read about the crossing of the Jordan:

> And as they that bare the ark were come unto Jordan... the waters which came down from above stood and rose up upon an heap very far from the city... and those that came down toward the sea of the plain, even the salt sea, failed, and were cut off: and the people passed over right against Jericho.

Thus the creators helped the "chosen people" cross without getting their feet wet, just as they had done in their escape from the Egyptians by using the same water repulsion ray.'

The Trumpets of Jericho

'At the end of Chapter 5 in the *Book of Joshua*, there is a meeting between a military creator and the chosen people regarding the resistance of the city of Jericho.

> But as captain of the host[5] of Yahweh am I now come.
> *Joshua 5: 14.*

A military consultant was sent to the Jewish people to assist them in the siege of Jericho. It is easy to understand how the walls were knocked down. You know that the very high voice of a singer can crack a crystal glass. By using highly amplified ultrasonic waves, one can knock down any concrete wall. This is what was done using a very complicated instrument, which the Bible calls a "trumpet":

> When they make a long blast with the ram's horn, and when ye hear the sound of the trumpet... and the wall of the city shall fall down flat. *Joshua 6: 5.*

At a given moment, the ultrasounds were emitted in a synchronized way, and the walls fell down. A little later, some real bombing took place:

> Yahweh cast down great stones from heaven upon them unto Azekah, and they died: they were more which died with hailstones than they whom the children of Israel slew with the sword. *Joshua 10: 11.*

This full scale bombing, as indicated, killed more people than the swords of the Israelites. One of the most distorted passages is in *Joshua,* Chapter 10, Verse 13, where it is stated:

> And the sun stood still, and the moon stayed, until the people had avenged themselves upon their enemies.

This simply means that it was a flash war, which lasted only one day – in fact, it is stated later that the war occupied "about a whole day". It was so short, when you consider the extent of the land conquered, that people thought the sun had stood still.

In the *Book of Judges*, Chapter 6, Verse 21, one of the creators is again in contact with a man called Gideon who delivers food to him:

> Then the angel of Yahweh put forth the end of the staff that was in his hand, and touched the flesh and the unleavened cakes; and there rose up fire out of the rock, and consumed the flesh and the unleavened cakes. Then the angel of Yahweh departed out of his sight.

The creators were unable to eat in the open air because of their pressurized suits, but if necessary, using a scientific technique, they could feed themselves by extracting the essentials from these offerings using a flexible tube or cane. The process radiates flames, which made people at the time think sacrifices to God were being made.

In Chapter 7 of the *Book of Judges,* 300 men with "trumpets" surrounded the enemy camp, and using highly amplified ultrasonic instruments, they blew them simultaneously in order to drive all the people in the camp mad. You know now that certain high pitched sounds carried to extremes can drive anyone mad.

Indeed the people who had been surrounded went mad; the soldiers killed each other and ran away.'

Samson the Telepathist

'In *Judges,* Chapter 13, there is yet another example of mating taking place between the creators and human women:

> And the angel of Yahweh appeared unto the woman, and said unto her, Behold now, thou art barren, and bearest not: but thou shalt conceive, and bear a son. *Judges 13: 3.*

It was necessary that the fruit of this union be healthy so that the behavior of the child could be studied. This is why he tells her:

> And drink not wine nor strong drink, and eat not any unclean thing: for, lo, thou shalt conceive, and bear a son; and no razor shall come on his head: for the child shall be a Nazarite unto Elohim from the womb. *Judges 13: 4-5.*

Later, it is written:

> And the angel of Elohim came again unto the woman as she sat in the field: but Manoah her husband was not with her.
> *Judges 13: 9.*

It is easy to imagine what happened during her husband's absence... It was an easy task for the scientists to cure her sterility. In this way she was made aware that she was going to give birth to an exceptional individual, and that she should take the utmost care of her baby. It was wonderful for the creators to mate with a daughter of humanity. This enabled them to have sons ruling directly on Earth, where the atmosphere was not suitable for themselves.

The point about not shaving off any hair is very important. The human brain is like a huge transmitter, capable of sending out a multitude of very accurate waves and thoughts. In fact, telepathy is nothing more than that.

But this type of transmitter requires antennae, and the hair and beard are these antennae. That is why you should not shave off any hair if you want to make use of your transmitters. You have surely noticed that many of your scientists have long hair, and often a beard. Prophets and other wise people have them too. Now you can understand why.

The child was born. It was Samson, whose story you know. He was able to communicate directly with "God" by telepathy, thanks to his natural antennae - his hair. And the creators could then help him during difficult moments and produce marvels to reinforce his authority.

But when Delilah cut his hair, he could no longer ask for help. Then his eyes were gouged out by his enemies, but when his hair grew again, he regained his "strength". That is to say, he could once again ask for help from the creators who then demolished the temple where he was touching the columns. All of this was attributed to Samson's strength.

In *Samuel,* Chapter 3, we find Elijah initiating Samuel into telepathy. The creators wanted to contact Samuel, and he thinks that Elijah is speaking to him. He "hears voices":

> Go, lie down: and it shall be, if he call thee, that thou shalt say,
> Speak, Yahweh; for thy servant heareth. *1 Samuel 3: 9.*

This is a little like the behavior of amateur radio operators who might say, "Go ahead, I can hear you loud and clear". And the telepathic conversation begins:

> 'Samuel, Samuel.' Then Samuel answered, 'Speak; for thy servant heareth.' *1 Samuel 3: 10-11.*

In the episode where David challenges Goliath there is quite an interesting sentence which ends:

> ...that he should defy the armies of the living Elohim?
> *1 Samuel 17: 26.*

This shows the reality of the presence in that epoch of a quite tangible "God". Telepathy as a means of communication between the creators and human beings was only possible when the Elohim were in proximity to the Earth.

When they were on their distant planet, or elsewhere, they could not communicate in this way.

For this reason they set up a transmitter-receiver, which was transported in the "Ark of God" - an apparatus containing its own atomic powered cell. This is why in the *First Book of Samuel*, Chapters 5 and 6, when the Philistines stole the Ark, their idol Dagon lay face down on the ground nearby, as the result of an electrical discharge caused by their clumsy mishandling of it.

They also suffered radiation burns from the dangerous radioactive materials:

> And smote them with emerods[6]. *1 Samuel 5: 6.*

Even the Jews who had not taken precautions while handling the Ark were harmed:

> Uzzah put forth his hand to the ark of Elohim, and took hold of it; for the oxen shook it. And the anger of Yahweh was kindled against Uzzah; and Elohim smote him there for his error; and there he died by the ark of Elohim. *2 Samuel 6: 6-7.*

The Ark almost fell over and Uzzah, trying to hold it up, touched a dangerous part of the machine and was electrocuted.

In the first book of *Kings* (*1 Kings* 1:50 and *1 Kings* 2:28), we read in several places of individuals who "caught hold on the horns of the altar".

This refers to the manipulation of the transmitter-receiver levers while trying to communicate with the creators.'

The First Residence to Welcome the Elohim

'The great King Solomon had a sumptuous residence built in order to welcome the creators when they came to visit the Earth:

Yahweh said He would dwell in thick darkness[7]. I have surely built thee an house to dwell in. *1 Kings 8: 12-13.*

For the glory of Yahweh had filled the house of Yahweh.
1 Kings 8: 11.

The cloud filled the house of Yahweh. *1 Kings 8: 10.*

And I will dwell among the children of Israel. *1 Kings 6: 13.*

So the creators lived in a cloud, or rather in a vessel that orbits above the clouds. Imagine trying to make primitive people understand that.

There came a man of Elohim out of Judah by the word of Yahweh unto Bethel...and said...behold, the altar shall be rent. When king Jeroboam heard the saying of the man of Elohim, which had cried against the altar in Bethel, that he put forth his hand from the altar, saying, 'Lay hold on him.' And his hand, which he put forth against him, dried up, so that he could not pull it in again to him.
1 Kings 13: 1-5.

With the help of an atomic disintegrator, one of the creators destroyed the altar and burned the hand of the man who did not show respect for the creators. He returns to one of the Elohim's terrestrial camps by another route to keep their whereabouts secret:

> So he went another way, and returned not by the way that he came to Bethel. *1 Kings 13: 10.*

In *1 Kings,* Chapter 17, Verse 6, there is an example of the radio control of animals through the use of electrodes, as you yourselves are beginning to discover:

> And the ravens brought him bread and flesh in the morning, and bread and flesh in the evening.

Because of recent discoveries, the creators decided to appear as little as possible in order not to influence the destiny of Man too much, so that they could see if they would reach the age of scientific knowledge on their own. So, the creators began to use increasingly discreet means of communicating with humans, as in the method of feeding Elijah using "homing" ravens.

This was the beginning of a gigantic experiment throughout the galaxy in which several humanities are in competition. The creators decided to appear less often, while at the same time reinforcing the authority and reputation of their ambassadors - the prophets - by using miracles. That is to say, scientific means which were then incomprehensible to the people of that era:

> See, your son lives!... Now by this I know that you are a man of God.[12] *1 Kings 17: 23-24.*

Elijah had healed a young child who was dying. Later, he ordered two bull calves to be placed on logs at Mount Carmel, one to be consecrated to the idol Baal and the other to the creators. The one that would ignite by itself would represent the one true "God".

Obviously, at a moment agreed upon in advance between Elijah and the creators, the Elohim's chosen log burst into flames, even though the wood was wet. This was accomplished by a powerful beam similar to a laser, emitted from a vessel hidden in the clouds:

> Then the fire of Yahweh fell, and consumed the burnt sacrifice, and the wood, and the stones, and the dust, and licked up the water that was in the trench. *1 Kings 18: 38.*'

Elijah the Messenger

'The creators paid particular attention to Elijah.

> Then an angel touched him, and said unto him, Arise and eat. And he looked, and, behold, there was a cake baken on the coals, and a cruse of water at his head. *1 Kings 19: 5-6.*

All this happened in the desert...

> And, behold, Yahweh passed by, and a great and strong wind rent the mountains, and brake in pieces the rocks before Yahweh; but Yahweh was not in the wind: and after the wind an earthquake; but Yahweh was not in the earthquake: And after the earthquake a fire; but Yahweh was not in the fire: and after the fire a still small voice. *1 Kings 19: 11-12.*

There you have the exact description of a landing by a machine similar to one of your rockets. Then further on, a vision of the creators is described:

> I saw Yahweh sitting on his throne, and all the host[9] of heaven standing by him. *1 Kings 22: 19.*

The creators once again used telepathy - this time group telepathy – so that none of the prophets could predict the truth to the King:

> I will be a lying spirit in the mouth of all his prophets.
> *1 Kings 22: 22.*

In the *Second Book of Kings*, there is further evidence of the protection, which the creators gave to Elijah:

> If I be a man of Elohim, let fire come down from heaven, and consume thee and thy fifty. And the fire of Elohim came down from heaven, and consumed him and his fifty. *2 Kings 1: 12.*

This operation happened again, but the third time:

> And the angel of Yahweh said unto Elijah[10], Go down with him.
> *2 Kings 1: 15.*

In the *Second Book of Kings*, Chapter 2, Elijah is invited onto a spacecraft, which takes off with him on board:

> When Yahweh would take up Elijah into heaven by a whirlwind.
> *2 Kings 2: 1.*

There appeared a chariot of fire, and horses of fire, and parted them both asunder; and Elijah went up by a whirlwind into heaven. *2 Kings 2: 11.*

This is a spacecraft taking off, and when the narrator speaks of horses of fire, he is referring to the fire, which was emitted from the blast pipes. If you showed certain South American or African tribes people a rocket taking off, they would be incapable of understanding this scientific phenomenon in a rational way, and would look upon it as something supernatural, mystical, and divine. When returning to their tribes, they would speak of chariots of fire and horses of fire.

Further on in the *Second Book of Kings,* Chapter 4, Verses 32-7 Elisha, like his father, performs a resurrection. He heals and brings back to life a child who was dead. This happens quite frequently nowadays when mouth to mouth resuscitation and heart massage revive a person whose cardiac muscle has ceased to function.

Then Elisha proceeds to multiply the bread.'

The Multiplication of Bread

'A man... brought the man of Elohim bread of the firstfruits, twenty loaves of barley... And his servitor said, What, should I set this before an hundred men?... He said again, Give the people, that they may eat: for thus saith Yahweh, They shall eat, and shall leave thereof. So he set it before them, and they did eat, and left thereof, according to the word of Yahweh. *2 Kings 4: 42-44.*

The creators had brought synthetic dehydrated food with them, which when added to water, increased to five times its original volume. So with twenty small loaves of bread there was enough food for a hundred people.

You are already familiar with the little vitamin pills, which nourished your first astronauts. They take up very little space but contain all the necessary nutritional elements. One pill is enough to feed one person. A quantity equivalent in volume to one small loaf of bread is enough to feed five people. Therefore twenty loaves are sufficient to feed one hundred people.

But the people of Israel had begun adoring metal idols; they had also become cannibals and were completely immoral, much to the disgust of their creators:

> So was Israel carried away out of their own land. *2 Kings 17: 23.*

That was the beginning of the dispersion of the Israelites whose civilization, instead of making progress, was constantly regressing, in contrast to their neighbors, who took advantage of the situation.

In the *Book of Isaiah* you again find:

> In the year that king Uzziah died I saw also Yahweh sitting upon a throne, high and lifted up... Above it stood the seraphims: each one had six wings; with twain he covered his face, and with twain he covered his feet, and with twain he did fly. *Isaiah 6: 1-2.*

That is a description of the creators dressed in their one piece space suits fitted with six small jet engines, two on their backs, two on their hands, and two at their feet, these ones for steering purposes.

> The noise of a multitude in the mountains, like as of a great people; a tumultuous noise of the kingdoms of nations gathered together: Yahweh of hosts mustereth the host of the battle. They come from a far country, from the end of heaven, even Yahweh, and the weapons of his indignation, to destroy the whole land.
> *Isaiah 13: 4-5.*

The whole truth is encapsulated in that quote, it is just a matter of reading between the lines in order to understand. *They come from a far country, from the end of heaven.* That could not be clearer.

> For thou hast said in thine heart, I will ascend into heaven, I will exalt my throne above the stars of Elohim. *Isaiah 14: 13.*

This refers to the human scientists who had accumulated sufficient knowledge to undertake a trip to the creators' planet but were destroyed at Sodom and Gomorrah. The army of the heavens is described here at that time when they arrived with the weapons of wrath to destroy the whole country. It was those human scientists of Sodom and Gomorrah who said:

> I will ascend above the heights of the clouds; I will be like the most high. *Isaiah 14: 14.*

But the destruction prevented humans from equaling their creators, "the most high":

> That made the world as a wilderness[27]. *Isaiah 14: 17.*

The nuclear explosion is described further on:

> For the cry is gone round about the borders of Moab; the howling thereof unto Eglaim, and the howling thereof unto Beer-elim. For the waters of Dimon shall be full of blood... *Isaiah 15: 8-9.*

A few were saved because they sheltered in bunkers:

> Come, my people, enter thou into thy chambers, and shut thy doors about thee: hide thyself as it were for a little moment, until the indignation be overpast. *Isaiah 26: 20.'*

The Flying Saucers of Ezekiel

'It is in the *Book of Ezekiel*, that we find the most interesting description of one of our flying machines:

> I looked, and, behold, a stormy wind came out of the north, a great cloud, with flashing lightning, and a brightness round about it, and out of the midst of it as it were glowing metal, out of the midst of the fire. Out of the midst of it came the likeness of four living creatures. This was their appearance: they had the likeness of a man. Everyone had four faces, and everyone of them had four wings. Their feet were straight feet; and the sole of their feet was like the sole of a calf's foot; and they sparkled like burnished brass. They had the hands of a man under their wings on their four sides; and they four had their faces and their wings [thus]: their wings were joined one to another; they didn't turn when they went; they went everyone straight forward.

> As for the likeness of their faces, they had the face of a man; and they four had the face of a lion on the right side; and they four had the face of an ox on the left side; they four had also the face of an eagle. Their faces and their wings were separate above; two [wings] of everyone were joined one to another, and two covered their bodies. They went everyone straight forward: where the spirit was to go, they went; they didn't turn when they went. As for the likeness of the living creatures, their appearance was like burning coals of fire, like the appearance of torches: [the fire] went up and down among the living creatures; and the fire was bright, and out of the fire went forth lightning. The living creatures ran and returned as the appearance of a flash of lightning.

> Now as I saw the living creatures, behold, one wheel on the eretz beside the living creatures, for each of the four faces of it.

The appearance of the wheels and their work was like a bareket: and they four had one likeness; and their appearance and their work was as it were a wheel within a wheel. When they went, they went in their four directions: they didn't turn when they went. As for their rims, they were high and dreadful; and they four had their rims full of eyes round about. When the living creatures went, the wheels went beside them; and when the living creatures were lifted up from the eretz, the wheels were lifted up. Wherever the spirit was to go, they went; there was the spirit to go: and the wheels were lifted up beside them; for the spirit of the living creature was in the wheels. When those went, these went; and when those stood, these stood; and when those were lifted up from the eretz, the wheels were lifted up beside them: for the spirit of the living creature was in the wheels.

Over the head of the living creature there was the likeness of an expanse, like the awesome crystal to look on, stretched forth over their heads above. Under the expanse were their wings straight, the one toward the other: everyone had two which covered on this side, and every one had two which covered on that side, their bodies. When they went, I heard the noise of their wings like the noise of great waters, like the voice of Shaddai, a noise of tumult like the noise of a host: when they stood, they let down their wings. There was a voice above the expanse that was over their heads: when they stood, they let down their wings. Above the expanse that was over their heads was the likeness of a throne, as the appearance of a sappir stone; and on the likeness of the throne was a likeness as the appearance of a man on it above.[11]

Ezekiel 1: 4-26.

There you have a description, which could not be more precise, of the creators who had come out of their flying machines. The "stormy wind" is the trace of smoke or vapor trail that present-day planes leave behind them at high altitudes. Then the machine appeared with its blinking light, the "flashing lightning" and "glowing metal". Later, four creators appear wearing antigravity suits with small directional jet engines attached. These are described as the "wings" on their metal suits and "their feet... sparkled like burnished brass". You have surely noticed how shiny the suits of your astronauts are.

As for the "flying saucers" or "wheels", their appearance and their operation were not at all badly described considering it is a primitive person who is speaking. "as it were a wheel within a wheel...they didn't turn when they went".

In the center of the flying saucer, very similar to the one in which we are now sitting, was the habitable section - the rim. "they four had their rims full of eyes round about". In the same way that our clothing has evolved and we no longer wear those cumbersome space suits, our vessels then had portholes - the "eyes" around the rims - because we had not then discovered how to see through metallic walls by modifying their atomic structure at will.

The flying saucers stayed near the creators ready to help them if the need arose, since they were loading supplies and carrying out routine maintenance on the large intergalactic vessel above them. Other creators inside the vessels were directing them. "...for the spirit of the living creature was in the wheels". This is quite clear.

The suit described with its four portholes was similar to your first diving suits. "Everyone had four faces... they didn't turn when they went".

The smaller saucers were something like your own LEMs - lunar excursion modules - small, short range vehicles used for exploratory missions. Above them the larger interplanetary vessel waited.

> Above the expanse that was over their heads was the likeness of a throne, as the appearance of a sappir stone; and on the likeness of the throne was a likeness as the appearance of a man on it above.
>
> *Ezekiel 1: 26.*

The latter individual on the large vessel was supervising and coordinating the work of the creators.

Frightened by all this, Ezekiel fell flat on his face before these things, which were so mysterious that they had to have come from no one other than "God". But one of the creators said to him:

> Son of man, stand on your feet, and I will speak with you... hear what I tell you... and eat that which I give you.
> *Ezekiel 2: 1 and 7-8.*

This is an image, like the eating from the tree of science of good and evil. It was intellectual food that he was given. In this case, it was a book:

> There was a hand stretched out to me; and behold, a scroll of a book was in it... there was writing on the inside and on the outside.[12] *Ezekiel 2: 9-10.*

There was writing on both sides, a very surprising thing at that time when usually only one side of parchment was written on.

Then the scroll is "eaten". This means that Ezekiel absorbed its meaning. What he learned is what you are learning now about humanity's origins. It was so exciting and comforting that he said:

> Then did I eat it; and it was in my mouth as honey for sweetness.
> *Ezekiel 3: 3.*

Then Ezekiel is transported in the creators' vessel to the place where he was to spread the news:

> Then the spirit took me up, and I heard behind me a voice of a great rushing. *Ezekiel 3: 12.*

Further on, the prophet is transported once again in a flying machine:

> ...and the spirit lifted me up between the earth and the heaven, and brought me in the visions of Elohim to Jerusalem.
>
> *Ezekiel 8: 3.*

Ezekiel noticed afterwards that beneath their "wings" the cherubims had hands like humans:

> And there appeared in the cherubims the form of a man's hand under their wings. *Ezekiel 10: 8.*

> And the cherubims lifted up their wings, and mounted up from the earth in my sight: when they went out, the wheels also were beside them... *Ezekiel 10: 19.*

> Moreover the spirit lifted me up, and brought me... *Ezekiel 11: 1.*

> And the glory of Yahweh went up from the midst of the city, and stood upon the mountain which is on the east side of the city. Afterwards the spirit took me up, and brought me in a vision by the Spirit of Elohim into Chaldea... *Ezekiel 11: 23-24.*

There you have some of the many journeys of Ezekiel in one of the creators' flying machines.

> The hand of Yahweh was upon me, and carried me out in the spirit of Yahweh, and set me down in the midst of the valley which was full of bones. *Ezekiel 37: 1.*

Here a miracle is about to happen. The creators go on to resurrect human beings whose only remains are their bones.

As mentioned earlier, each particle of a living being contains all the information to reconstruct it completely. All you have to do is place one of these particles, for example from bone remains, in a machine, which provides all the living matter required to reconstruct that original being.

The machine supplies the matter, and the particle supplies all the required information, the blue-print according to which the being will be built, just as a spermatozoon contains all the information necessary to create a living being in the first place, right down to the color of the hair and eyes.

> Son of man, can these bones live?... there was a noise, and behold a shaking... the sinews and the flesh came up upon them, and the skin covered them above... and they lived, and stood up upon their feet, an exceeding great army. *Ezekiel 37: 3-10.*

All this is very easy to do, and you will do it some day. This is the origin of the ancient rituals in which elaborately protective sepulchers were built to bury great people, so that one day, they may be brought back to life everlasting. This is part of the secret of the "tree of life" - the secret of eternity.

In Chapter 40, Ezekiel is again carried away in a spacecraft, which takes him into the presence of someone wearing a space suit:

> Brought he me into the land of Israel, and set me upon a very high mountain, by which was as the frame of a city on the south. And he brought me thither, and, behold, there was a man, whose appearance was like the appearance of brass... *Ezekiel 40: 2-3.*

This "city" is one of the Earth bases that the creators used at that time. They were always located on very high mountains so that the creators would not be disturbed by humans. The man "whose appearance was the appearance of brass" is, of course, wearing a metallic suit. Similarly, due to our small stature, we were often mistaken for children or cherubs.

The priests in serving the creators in their terrestrial residence – the temple visited by Ezekiel - wore aseptic clothing when performing their duties, and those clothes always had to remain in the temple to avoid being contaminated by germs dangerous to the creators:

> When the priests enter therein, then shall they not go out of the holy place into the utter court, but there they shall lay their garments wherein they minister; for they are holy.
>
> *Ezekiel 42:14*

They should have written, "for these garments are pure or sterile", but that was incomprehensible for primitive people who deified all that was told or shown to them at that period.

In *Ezekiel* Chapter 43, the big vessel, respectfully called "the glory of God", approached.

> The glory of the God of Israel came from the way of the east. His voice was like the sound of many waters; and the earth shone with His glory.[12] *Ezekiel, 43: 2.*

The creators did not want to be disturbed, so they issued a directive:

> This gate shall be shut, it shall not be opened, and no man shall enter in by it; because Yahweh, the Elohim of Israel, hath entered in by it, therefore it shall be shut. *Ezekiel 44: 2.*

Only a "prince" is allowed to come and speak with the creators:

> It is for the prince; the prince, he shall sit in it to eat bread before Yahweh. *Ezekiel 44: 3.*

But the prince had to pass through a chamber where he was disinfected by special rays:

He shall enter by the way of the porch of that gate, and shall go out by the way of the same. *Ezekiel 44: 3.*

The Levite priests were there to look after the creators:

They shall come near to me to minister unto me, and they shall stand before me to offer unto me the fat and the blood... and they shall come near to my table, to minister unto me...
Ezekiel 44: 15-16.

The odor of human perspiration was very unpleasant to the creators:

When they enter in at the gates of the inner court, they shall be clothed with linen garments... they shall not gird themselves with any thing that causeth sweat. *Ezekiel 44: 17-18.*

There is a description also of how the Elohim's supply of fresh products continued:

The first of all the firstfruits... ye shall also give unto the priest the first of your dough, that he may cause the blessing to rest in thine house. *Ezekiel 44: 30.*

In Chapter 3 of the *Book of Daniel,* King Nebuchadnezzar condemned three men to the stake for refusing to worship a metal god instead of the creators, whom he knew existed. But the three men were saved by one of the creators who came to their aid in the glowing fire, armed with a repellent and refrigerative ray. He protected them from the heat and the flames with this and allowed them to walk away totally unscathed:

> Lo, I see four men loose, walking in the midst of the fire, and they have no hurt; and the form of the fourth is like the Son of Elohim. *Daniel 3: 25.*

Further on, Daniel is cast into the lions' den, but the lions do not harm him. There again, nothing too complicated was involved, just a paralyzing beam to give enough time to get Daniel out of the den unharmed:

> My Elohim hath sent his angel, and hath shut the lions' mouths.
> *Daniel 6: 22.*

In the tenth chapter of *Daniel,* you will find another interesting description of a creator:

> Then I lifted up mine eyes, and looked, and behold a certain man... His body also was like the beryl, and his face as the appearance of lightning, and his eyes as lamps of fire, and his arms and his feet like in colour to polished brass, and the voice of his words like the voice of a multitude. *Daniel 10: 5-6.'*

The Last Judgement

'If the Hebrew people were dominated by the Persians and the Greeks, it was because of their lack of faith. Consequently, the Elohim punished the Hebrews by sending some of their "angels" amongst the Persians and Greeks to help those nations to progress technologically.

This explains the great moments in the history of those two civilizations. The archangel Michael was the leader of the delegation, which was helping the Persians:

Michael, one of the chief princes, came to help me; and I remained there with the kings of Persia. *Daniel 10: 13.*

In Chapter 12 of *Daniel,* the resurrection is again mentioned:

And many of them that sleep in the dust of the earth shall awake, some to everlasting life, and some to shame and everlasting contempt. *Daniel 12: 2.*

The "Last Judgement" will enable great individuals to live again. Those people who have acted positively for humanity and who have truly believed in their creators and followed their commandments will be welcomed with great joy by the people of the era when this will happen.

On the other hand, all the wicked people will feel shame before their judges and will live in eternal regret, as an example for the rest of humanity:

And they that be wise shall shine as the brightness of the firmament; and they that turn many to righteousness as the stars for ever and ever. *Daniel 12: 3.*

The geniuses will be the most highly esteemed and the most highly rewarded. Those just individuals, who allowed the geniuses to blossom, or the truth to triumph, will also be rewarded.

Daniel, shut up the words, and seal the book, even to the time of the end: many shall run to and fro, and knowledge shall be increased. *Daniel 12: 4.*

These words will only be understood when humanity has reached a sufficient level of scientific understanding - that is to say, now. All this will happen:

and when he shall have accomplished to scatter the power of the holy people, all these things shall be finished. *Daniel 12: 7.*

This will be when the people of Israel recover their land after their long Diaspora. The state of Israel was created a few decades ago, at the same time as the explosion of humanity's scientific knowledge.

Go thy way, Daniel: for the words are closed up and sealed till the time of the end. *Daniel 12: 9.*

All this will only be understood in this epoch. In recent years scientific progress and the beginning of space exploration by human beings have been such that everything seems possible for humanity. Nothing surprises people anymore, for they are used to seeing many wonders happening before their eyes on television. They can learn without astonishment that they really are made in the image of "God", their almighty creator, and even as far as their scientific abilities are concerned. These days, miracles have become comprehensible.

In *Jonah*, the big fish that swallows the prophet is very interesting indeed. After Jonah was thrown into the water from a small boat:

Now Yahweh had prepared a great fish to swallow up Jonah. And Jonah was in the belly of the fish three days and three nights.
Jonah 1: 17.

The "great fish" was in reality a submarine, as you know such vessels now. But for the people of that time, it could only be a great fish, even though the gastric juices of such a fish would have digested a man quickly without any hope of his returning to the open air. What is more, Jonah would have needed air to breathe. In the submarine, the creators were able to carry on a conversation with Jonah to learn about the political developments of those times.

And Yahweh spake unto the fish, and it vomited out Jonah upon
the dry land. *Jonah 2: 10.*

The submarine came close to the shore, and Jonah was back on
land. In *Zechariah,* Chapter 5, there is another description of a flying
machine:

Then I turned, and lifted up mine eyes, and looked, and behold
a flying roll... the length thereof is twenty cubits (9 meters) and
the breadth thereof ten cubits (4.5 meters). *Zechariah 5: 1-2.*

A little further on, women amongst the creators appear for the first
time:

Behold, there came out two women, and the wind was in their
wings; for they had wings like the wings of a stork...
Zechariah 5: 9.

These two female companions were accompanying the creators
and both were equipped with autonomous flying suits when they
appeared before Zechariah.

In *Psalms* 8, Verse 5, it is said of human beings:

For thou hast made him a little lower than the angels[13].

Human beings are virtually as strong intellectually as their creators.
Those who copied out the texts did not dare write "equal" to the
Elohim as it had been originally dictated.

His going forth is from the end of the heaven, and his circuit unto
the ends of it. *Psalms 19: 6.*

The creators came from a planet very far away from the Earth's orbit.

In them hath he set a tabernacle for the sun. *Psalms 19: 4.*

Here is another allusion to the mass of Earth, which was created to form the original continent when the oceans covered the Earth.

Yahweh looketh from heaven; he beholdeth all the sons of men. From the place of his habitation he looketh upon all the inhabitants of the earth. *Psalms 33: 13-14.*

The creators watch humanity's behavior as they always have done from their flying vessels.'

Satan

'In the *Book of Job*, Chapter 1, you have the explanation of Satan:

Now there was a day when the sons of Elohim came to present themselves before Yahweh, and Satan came also among them.
Job 1: 6.

Elohim in Hebrew literally means "those who came from the sky". The "sons of Elohim", in other words, the creators who watch human beings, report regularly to their planet of origin, indicating for the most part that human beings venerate and love the Elohim. But one of these Elohim, called Satan, was part of a group, which had always condemned the creation of other intelligent beings on a planet as close as the Earth, seeing them as a possible threat. That is why, on seeing Job's devotion, which was one of the best examples of human beings loving their creators, he said:

> Doth Job fear Elohim for nought?... But put forth thine hand now, and touch all that he hath, and he will curse thee to thy face. And Yahweh said unto Satan, 'Behold, all that he hath is in thy power; only upon himself put not forth thine hand.'
> *Job 1: 9-12.*

Hearing Satan's assertion that had Job not been rich, he would not have loved his creators, the government gave full power to Satan to ruin Job. It would then be seen if he still venerated his creators, and that is why killing him was forbidden.

On seeing Job's dedication to respecting his creators, even when he was ruined, the government triumphed over the opposition, Satan. But Satan retorted that though Job had lost many things, he was still in good health. So the government gave Satan *carte blanche* so long as he did not kill Job:

> Behold, he is in thine hand; but save his life. *Job 2: 6.*

Again, in the *Book of Job*, a small sentence in Chapter 37 is very interesting:

> With Him, have you spread out the skies, Strong as a cast metal mirror?[14] *Job 37: 18*

In other words, are human beings capable of making a "cast metal mirror"- in reality flying metallic vessels? People of that time thought it was possible for no one but God. And yet today it can be done.

Finally, in view of Job's humility, the creators healed him and gave him back his wealth, his children and his health.'

Humans Could Not Understand

'In the *Book of Tobit* in the Apocryhpha, one of the creators' robots named Raphael also came to test humanity's reaction towards its creators.

Once he had accomplished his mission, he left, after proving who he was:

> All these days I did appear unto you; but I did neither eat nor drink... for I go up to him that sent me; but write all things which are done in a book. *Tobit 12: 19-20.*

All of this is easy to see in the writings. But once again you must try to understand.

> As for wisdom, what she is, and how she came up, I will tell you, and will not hide mysteries from you: but will seek her out from the beginning of her nativity, and bring the knowledge of her into light, and will not pass over the truth. *Wisdom of Solomon 6: 22.*

When the time comes, "wisdom", the science, which allowed all this to happen, will be known by Man. The biblical writings will be proof of all this.

> For by the greatness and beauty of the creatures proportionably the maker of them is seen. *Wisdom of Solomon 13: 5.*

So it is simple to see the truth, recognizing the creators by observing their creations.

> And could not out of the good things that are seen know him that is. *Wisdom of Solomon 13: 1.*

To avoid being disturbed by humans, the creators built their bases on high mountains, where we now find traces of great civilizations (in the Himalayas and Peru, for example), as well as at the bottom of the sea. Gradually the mountain stations were abandoned in favor of submarine bases less accessible to humans. The creators who had been banished at the outset had hidden themselves in the oceans.

> In that day Yahweh with his sore and great and strong sword shall punish leviathan the piercing serpent, even leviathan that crooked serpent; and he shall slay the dragon that is in the sea.
> *Isaiah 27: 1.*

At that time the government of their planet wanted to destroy those who had created the humans.

It was not easy to see clearly among all those wonders, so of course, the creators were deified and made into something abstract because human beings were unable to understand scientific facts.

> And the book is delivered to him that is not learned, saying, Read this, I pray thee: and he saith, I am not learned. *Isaiah 29: 12.*

For a long time, humanity has held the truth in its hands but could not understand until it was sufficiently evolved scientifically to decode it.

> Every man is brutish in his knowledge[15]... *Jeremiah 10: 14.*

Science enabled the creators to create and will enable human beings to do the same.

> Yahweh possessed me in the beginning of his way, before his works of old.I was set up from everlasting, from the beginning, or ever the earth was... When he prepared the heavens, I was there...

> When he gave to the sea his decree, that the waters should not
> pass his commandment... Then I was by him, as one brought up
> with him: and I was daily his delight, rejoicing always before him;
> Rejoicing in the habitable part of his earth; and my delights were
> with the sons of men. *Proverbs 8: 22-23, 27, 29 -31.*

Intelligence and science, these are the two virtues that enabled the creators to create the landmass - the single continent - and the living beings they placed upon it. And now this intelligence and this spirit leads the human brain to repeat the acts of their creators.

Since the beginning of time it has been so: people create other people like themselves on other planets. The cycle continues. Some die, others take over. We are your creators, and you will create other humanities:

> That which hath been is now; and that which is to be hath already
> been. *Ecclesiastes 3: 15.*

The animals were also created and will be recreated. Just like human beings, no more, no less. The species that disappear will live again when you know how to recreate them:

> So that a man hath no preeminence above a beast: for all is vanity.
> *Ecelesiastes 3: 19.*

We, the creators, will only show ourselves officially if humanity is grateful to us for having created them. We fear that human beings might hold a grudge against us, which we cannot accept.

We would like to begin making open contact with you and give you the benefit of our considerable advance in scientific knowledge - so long as we could be sure that you would not turn against us, and that you would love us as your parents.

> Woe unto him that striveth with his Maker!... Shall the clay say
> to him that fashioneth it, What makest thou? or thy work, He
> hath no hands? Woe unto him that saith unto his father, What
> begettest thou? *Isaiah 45: 9-10.*

Fear of not being loved by human beings has led your creators to
allow you to progress scientifically by yourselves, with almost no help.

The emblem you see engraved on this machine and on my suit
represents the truth. It is also the emblem of the Jewish people, the
Star of David, which means: "That which is above is like that which
is below", and in its center is the swastika, which means that
everything is cyclic, the top becoming the bottom, and the bottom in
turn becoming the top. The origins and destiny of the creators and
human beings are similar and linked.

> Have ye not known? have ye not heard? hath it not been told you
> from the beginning? have ye not understood from the
> foundations of the earth? *Isaiah 40: 21.*

The traces of the creators' bases on high mountains is mentioned
in the *Book of Amos:*

> He that... treadeth upon the high places of the earth.
> *Amos 4: 13.*

The creators had seven bases in all:

> Those seven; they are the eyes of Yahweh, which run to and fro
> through the whole earth. *Zechariah 4: 10.*

This is the origin of the seven-branched candlestick, the meaning
of which has been lost. In the beginning at the creators' headquarters,
there was a switchboard with seven lighted switches enabling them to

stay in contact with the other bases and with the interplanetary vessel orbiting the Earth.

In *Psalms,* 139:4-6, there is an allusion to telepathy:

> For there is not a word in my tongue, but, lo, O Yahweh, thou knowest it altogether. Thou hast beset me behind and before, and laid thine hand upon me. Such knowledge is too wonderful for me; it is high, I cannot attain unto it.

At that time telepathy was unimaginable, hence "such knowledge is too wonderful for me". Astronomy and interplanetary journeys were also unthinkable at the time:

> He telleth the number of the stars; he calleth them all by their names. Great is our Yahweh, and of great power: his understanding is infinite. *Psalms 147: 4-5.*

Human beings were also unable to understand tele-communication:

> He sendeth forth his commandment upon earth: his word runneth very swiftly. *Psalms 147: 15.*

We now reach a decisive turning point in the creators' work. They decided at that period to let humanity progress scientifically without ever intervening directly. They understood that they themselves had been created in the same way, and that by creating similar beings to themselves, they were allowing the cycle to continue.

But first, in order for the truth to be spread throughout the world, they decided to send a Messiah who would be able to communicate worldwide what the people of Israel were then the only ones to know. This was in preparation for the day when the original mystery would be explained in the light of scientific progress - that is to say, the revelation. So they announced him:

> But thou, Bethlehem Ephratah, though thou be little among the thousands of Judah, yet out of thee shall he come forth unto me that is to be ruler in Israel; whose goings forth have been from of old, from everlasting... And he shall stand and feed in the strength of Yahweh... for now shall he be great unto the ends of the earth. And this man shall be the peace. *Micah 5: 2-5.*

> shout, O daughter of Jerusalem: behold, thy King cometh unto thee...lowly, and riding upon an ass... and he shall speak peace unto the heathen: and his dominion shall be from sea even to sea.
> *Zechariah 9: 9-10.'*

4

THE ROLE OF CHRIST

The Conception

The next morning, we met again at the same spot, and my host said: 'Christ's role was to spread the truth of the biblical scriptures throughout the world, so that they could serve as proof for all of humanity when the age of science would finally explain everything. The creators therefore decided to arrange for a child to be born of a woman of the Earth and one of their own people. The child in question would thereby inherit certain telepathic faculties, which humans lack:

She was found with child of the Holy Ghost. *Matthew 1: 18.*

Mary was the woman chosen, and obviously her fiance found these tidings hard to accept, but:

Behold, the angel of Yahweh appeared unto him. *Matthew 1:20.*

One of the creators appeared to explain that Mary would bring forth a son of "God". The prophets, who were in contact with the creators, came from very far away to see the divine child. One of the spacecrafts of the creators guided them:

We have seen his star in the east, and are come to worship him... the star, which they saw in the east, went before them, till it came and stood over where the young child was. *Matthew 2: 2 and 9.*

The creators watched over the child:

The angel of Yahweh appeareth to Joseph in a dream, saying, Arise, and take the young child and his mother, and flee into Egypt, and be thou there until I bring thee word: for Herod will seek the young child to destroy him. *Matthew 2: 13.*

The king was not too happy about the child-king coming from the people on his territory, which was announced to him by the prophets. But after King Herod died, the creators told Joseph that he could return to Israel:

But when Herod was dead, behold, an angel of Yahweh appeareth in a dream to Joseph in Egypt, Saying, Arise, and take the young child and his mother, and go into the land of Israel: for they are dead which sought the young child's life. *Matthew 2: 19-20.'*

The Initiation

'When he came of age, Jesus was led to the creators, so that they could reveal to him his true identity, introduce him to his father, reveal his mission and make known to him various scientific techniques.

The heavens were opened unto him, and he saw the Spirit of Yahweh descending like a dove, and lighting upon him: And lo a

voice from heaven, saying, 'This is my beloved Son, in whom I
am well pleased.' Then was Jesus[16] led up of the Spirit into the
wilderness to be tempted of the devil..

Matthew 3: 16-17 and 4: 1.

The devil, "Satan", the creator of whom we spoke previously, was
always convinced that nothing good could come of humanity on
Earth. He was "Satan the skeptic", and he was supported by the
government's opposition on our distant planet.

So he tested Jesus to find out if his intelligence was positive, and if
he really loved and respected his creators. Having discovered that they
could place complete confidence in Jesus, Jesus was allowed to go and
accomplish his mission.

In order to rally people to him, Jesus performed "miracles", which
in reality, were the application of scientific teachings shown to him by
the creators:

And they brought unto him all sick people... and he healed them.
Matthew 4: 24.

Blessed are the poor in spirit. *Matthew 5: 3.*

This sentence has been incorrectly interpreted as "the poor are
blessed". But the original meaning was that if the poor have spirit,
then they will be happy - which is totally different.

Then Jesus told his apostles that they must spread the truth
throughout the world. In the prayer called the "Lord's Prayer" or the
"Our Father", the truth is stated literally:

Thy kingdom come. Thy will be done on earth as it is in heaven.[8]
Matthew 6: 10.

In "heaven", on the creators' planet, the scientists eventually
became the ruling group and then created other intelligent beings.

67

The same thing will happen on Earth. The torch will be taken up again.

This prayer, which has been repeated time and time again without anyone understanding its profound meaning, now takes on its full significance: *On Earth, as it is in heaven.*

Amongst other things, Jesus had been taught to speak convincingly through a type of telepathic group hypnosis:

> And so it was, when Jesus had ended these sayings, that the people were astonished at His teaching, for He taught them as one having authority, and not as the scribes.[12]
> *Matthew 7: 28-29.*

He continued to heal the sick with the help of the creators who directed concentrated beams from a distance:

> A leper came and worshiped Him, saying, "Lord, if You are willing, You can make me clean. Then Jesus put out His hand and touched him, saying, 'I am willing; be cleansed.' Immediately his leprosy was cleansed.[12] *Matthew 8: 2-3.*

And he did the same for a man who was completely paralyzed. The operation was carried out from a distance using a concentrated ray, something like a laser, which burns only one spot through several layers:

> Arise, take up thy bed... And he arose. *Matthew 9: 6-8.*

Further on in *St. Matthew's Gospel,* Jesus announced his mission:

> For I came not to call the righteous, but sinners.[17] *Matthew 9: 13.*

He did not come for the people of Israel, who knew of the existence of the creators, but rather, so that this knowledge would be spread throughout the rest of the world.

Later there were more "miracles", somewhat similar to the first ones, all of which were medical. Nowadays there are transplants of hearts and other organs; leprosy and other similar illnesses are cured, and people are brought out of a coma with appropriate care. These would be considered miracles by technologically primitive people. At that time human beings were primitive, and the creators were similar to people of your present "civilized" nations, although a little more advanced scientifically.

Further on we find an allusion to the creators among whom is Jesus' real father:

> Every one therefore who shall confess me before men, him will I also confess before my Father who is in heaven. [17]
>
> *Matthew 10: 32.*

Before my Father who is in heaven [26] - this says it all. In fact, "God" is not intangible or immaterial. He is "in heaven". This is obviously incomprehensible to people who, at the time, believed that the stars were attached to a heavenly canopy just like pretty light bulbs, all rotating around the center of the world - the Earth. Now, since the advent of space travel and an understanding of the immensity of the universe, the old texts are brought to light in a completely different way.'

Parallel Humanities

'In *St. Matthew's Gospel*, Chapter 13, there is an important passage where Jesus explains in a parable how the creators left their planet to create life on other worlds:

Behold, a sower went forth to sow; And when he sowed, some seeds fell by the way side, and the fowls came and devoured them up: Some fell upon stony places, where they had not much earth: and forthwith they sprung up, because they had no deepness of earth: And when the sun was up, they were scorched; and because they had no root, they withered away. And some fell among thorns; and the thorns sprung up, and choked them: But other fell into good ground, and brought forth fruit, some an hundredfold, some sixtyfold, some thirtyfold. Who hath ears to hear, let him hear. *Matthew 13: 3-9.*

All this is an allusion to the various attempts to create life on other planets - and three of them failed.

The first failed because of the birds, which came and ate the seeds. In fact, this was a failure caused by the proximity of the planet in question to the creators' original planet. Those who were against the creation of people similar to themselves saw a possible threat in the experiment and therefore went to destroy the creation.

The second attempt was made on a planet too near a sun that was too hot; therefore, their creation was destroyed by noxious radiation.

The third attempt was made "among thorns" on a planet, which was far too humid, where the plant life was so powerful that it destroyed the equilibrium and the animal world. This world consisting only of plants still exists.

But the fourth attempt was finally successful on "good ground". And it is important to note that there were in fact three successes in all. This means that on two other planets, which are relatively near to you, there are living beings similar to yourselves who were created by the same creators.

"Who hath ears to hear, let him hear"; those who are able, understand. When the time comes, those who seek to understand will do so. The others, those who look without really seeing, and hear without really listening or understanding, such people will not understand the truth. On the other hand, those who prove their intelligence by their own efforts and thus show themselves to be worthy of their creators' help, they will be helped.

> For whosoever hath, to him shall be given, and he shall have more abundance: but whosoever hath not, from him shall be taken away even that he hath. *Matthew 13: 12*

The people who will not be able to prove their intelligence will not survive. Humans have almost proved that they are worthy of being recognized by their creators as their equals. They lack only... a little love. Love for each other, and particularly for their creators.

> ...it is given unto you to know the mysteries of the kingdom of heaven. *Matthew 13: 11*.

The three planets, on which life has been created, have been set in competition against one another. The planet on which humanity makes the most scientific progress, thereby proving its intelligence, will receive the benefit of their creators' inheritance on the day of the "last judgement" - so long as they do not behave aggressively towards their creators.

This will be the day when their knowledge will have reached a sufficiently high level. At present human beings on Earth are not very far away from that day. Human genius is:

> Which indeed is the least of all seeds: but when it is grown, it is the greatest among herbs, and becometh a tree, so that the birds of the air come and lodge in the branches thereof.
> *Matthew 13: 32.*

The "birds of the air" here refers to the creators who will come and lodge in the branches; that is to say, will come to give their knowledge to humanity when humanity shows itself worthy of it.

> The kingdom of heaven is like unto leaven, which a woman took,
> and hid in three measures of meal, till the whole was leavened.
> *Matthew 13: 33.*

This is another allusion to the three worlds in which the creators are waiting for science to bloom.

> I will utter things which have been kept secret from the
> foundation of the world. *Matthew 13: 35.*

Here we have something fundamentally important. Planets have a life span, and one day they will no longer be habitable. By that time humanity must have reached a level of scientific knowledge sufficient either to undertake a move to another planet, or if it cannot adapt itself elsewhere, to create a humanoid form of life capable of surviving on another world. If the environment cannot be adapted to suit people, then people must be created who are compatible with the new environment.

Before humanity becomes extinct, you would, for example, have to create another race of people capable of living in a totally different atmosphere, who would inherit your knowledge before you disappear. So that this inheritance would not be lost, the creators put life on three worlds, and only the best one will be entitled to the inheritance:

> So shall it be at the end of the world: the angels shall come forth,
> and sever the wicked from among the just. *Matthew 13: 49.'*

Scientific Miracles

'The passage concerning the multiplication of bread has already been explained. It refers to concentrated food products in the form of large pills, rather like those containing all the vital elements, which your astronauts use. Your "Holy Bread" hosts are reminiscent of these pills. With the equivalent of a few loaves of bread, there is enough to feed thousands of people.

When Jesus walked on the water, the creators supported him using an anti-gravity beam, which cancelled the effect of weight at a precise point:

> He came unto them, walking upon the sea.[17] *Matthew 14: 25.*

The beam, in fact, created a turbulence, which is described as follows:

> But when he saw the wind boisterous, he (Peter) was afraid... And when they were come into the ship, the wind ceased.
> *Matthew 14: 30-32.*

The "wind ceased" as they boarded the boat, because the beam was switched off when Jesus reached it. Another totally scientific "miracle".

In reality, there are no such things as miracles, only differences in levels of civilization. If you had landed at the time of Jesus in a spacecraft, or even a simple helicopter, even though your level of scientific development may have been limited, you would, in the eyes of the people of that time, have been performing miracles.

Just by producing artificial light, coming from the sky, driving a car, watching television, or even by killing a bird with a gun, because they would have been incapable of understanding the mechanism behind such phenomena, people of the time would have seen in them

73

a divine or supernatural force. Also do not forget that the same scientific gap which exists between you and the people at the time of Jesus, also exists now between you and us. We can still do things, which you would consider "miracles".

But for the most advanced individuals among you, they would no longer really be miracles since for the last few decades, you have taken the path of science and are trying to grasp the reason behind things instead of dumbly prostrating yourselves on your bellies and bringing offerings.

Our knowledge, however, remains such that if we decided to perform a few miracles, even your most eminent scientists would be unable to understand how we did them. There are some particularly well developed minds who would be able to cope with such things, but people in general would simply panic, and we are still capable of astonishing people, even though they are no longer so easily shocked.

It is necessary for people to understand that there is no ethereal "God", but only people who created other people in their image.

In Chapter 17 of *St. Matthew's Gospel,* the creators appear once again:

> Jesus taketh with him Peter, and James, and John his brother, and bringeth them up into a high mountain apart: and he was transfigured before them; and his face did shine as the sun, and his garments became white as the light... And behold, there appeared unto them Moses and Elijah talking with him... behold, a voice out of the cloud, saying, 'This is my beloved Son... hear ye him.'[17] *Matthew 17: 1-5.*

This scene happens at night, and the apostles are all frightened to see Jesus illuminated by the powerful searchlights of the spacecraft, out of which Moses and Elijah stepped, still alive thanks to the tree of life from which they had benefited. Immortality is a scientific reality, even if it does not correspond to humanity's idea of immortality.

In Chapter 19, Verse 30 of *St. Matthew,* there is a sentence:

But many that are first shall be last; and the last shall be first.

This means that the created shall become creators just as the creators were created.'

Deserving the Inheritance

'In Chapter 25, Verses 14-29 of *St. Matthew's Gospel,* it is said that the three planets must make scientific progress, and they will be judged one day. We read in the parable: Leaving for a trip, a man entrusted three of his slaves with his goods. The first one received five talents; the second, two talents; the third, one talent.

When the master returns, the first gave back to him the five talents and shows him five others which he won. The second gave him back the two talents plus two others that he won. The third gave him back only one talent, the one that was given to him.

Take therefore the talent from him, and give it unto him which hath ten talents. For unto every one that hath shall be given, and he shall have abundance: but from him that hath not shall be taken away even that which he hath.

Out of the three worlds where life has been created, the one which makes the most progress will receive the inheritance. The ones which have not progressed will be dominated by the other and eliminated. This is also true on Earth between peoples.

In *St. Matthew's Gospel,* Chapter 26, Jesus reveals the importance of his death and of the writings, which would later serve as proof. When one of his companions tried to defend him with a sword, he said:

> Put up again thy sword into his place: for all they that take the sword shall perish with the sword. Thinkest thou that I cannot now pray to my Father, and he shall presently give me more than twelve legions of angels? But how then shall the scriptures be fulfilled, that thus it must be? *Matthew 26: 52-54.*

It was in fact necessary for Jesus to die in order for the truth to be known throughout the world so that later on, when your creators return to Earth, they are not taken for usurpers or invaders. That is the purpose of the biblical and evangelical writings: to preserve traces of the work and presence of your creators, so that they will be recognized when they return.

After his death, Jesus was resuscitated with the help of the creators:

> And, behold, there was a great earthquake: for the angel of Yahweh descended from heaven, and came and rolled back the stone from the door, and sat upon it. His countenance was like lightning, and his raiment white as snow. *Matthew 28: 2-3.*

The creators took care of Jesus and revived him. And he said:

> Go ye therefore, and teach all nations... Teaching them to observe all things whatsoever I have commanded you.
> *Matthew 28: 19-20.*

Jesus' mission was coming to an end:

> So then after Jesus[16] had spoken unto them, he was received up into heaven. *Mark 16: 19.*

The creators took him away after this last most important phrase:

> They shall take up serpents; and if they drink any deadly thing, it shall not hurt them; they shall lay hands on the sick, and they shall recover.[18] *Mark 16: 18.*

This refers to humanity discovering anti-venom serums and antidotes, and developing surgery and so on - as is happening now.

In preparation for their arrival on Earth, the creators will appear more and more frequently, in order to highlight these revelations. This also is happening right now.

> Behold the fig tree... When they now shoot forth, ye see and know of your own selves that summer is now nigh at hand.
> *Luke 21: 29-30.*

When unidentified flying objects begin appearing in large numbers, as they are doing at present, it means that the time has come. In the *Acts of the Apostles*, it says, furthermore, in Chapter 2:

> And when the day of Pentecost was fully come, they were all with one accord in one place. And suddenly there came a sound from heaven as of a rushing mighty wind, and it filled all the house where they were sitting. And there appeared unto them cloven tongues like as of fire, and it sat upon each of them. And they were all filled with the Holy Spirit, and began to speak with other tongues... *Acts 2: 1-4.*

To make it possible for the apostles to spread the truth throughout the world, the creators exposed them to a concentrated burst of teaching sent to them by amplified telepathic waves, a little like electro-shocks, which impregnated their memories with elements of other languages.

In the *Acts of the Apostles,* note the numerous appearances made by the creators - the "angels" - particularly when they liberated Peter, who had been chained up by Herod:

And, behold, the angel of Yahweh came upon him, and a light shined in the prison: and he smote Peter on the side, and raised him up, saying, Arise up quickly. And his chains fell off from his hands. And the angel said unto him, Gird thyself, and bind on thy sandals. And so he did. And he saith unto him, Cast thy garment about thee, and follow me. And he went out, and followed him; and wist not that it was true which was done by the angel; but thought he saw a vision. *Acts 12: 7- 9.*

Peter, primitive as he was, thought he was having a vision as his chains fell off. He did not know about the electric laser welding torch, which was being used by one of the creators. When such fantastic things happen, people think they are dreaming. This is why it was often said that people who have seen the creators must have had a vision or seen them in a dream. In the same way, it is said that people who have seen our flying saucers must have had hallucinations. In that quotation, it is clearly explained that Peter thought he had seen everything in a dream, but in fact, it was all very real.

They came unto the iron gate that leadeth unto the city; which opened to them of his own accord... and forthwith the angel departed from him. *Acts 12: 10.*

Another sign that the time has come is that the people of Israel have regained their country:

After this I will return, and will build again the tabernacle of David, which is fallen down. *Acts 15: 16.*

Another important sentence is found in a following chapter:

For we are also his offspring. *Acts 17: 28*

This was said by an apostle while speaking of "God".

We shall not continue to read further in the Gospels where there are many more references to the creators, because they are less important. You can interpret them yourself for those who ask questions in the light of the explanations I have already given you.'

And saying that, he left, just as on previous occasions.

5

THE END OF THE WORLD

1946, First Year of the New Era

The next day, he returned just as before and started to speak: 'The time of the end of the world has arrived. Not the end of the world as in a catastrophe destroying the Earth, but the end of the world of the Church, which has completed its work. It performed this role more or less effectively. It was a task of vulgarization, making it possible for your creators to be recognized when they return. As you have noticed, the Christian church is dying. It is the end of this world because its mission has been fulfilled, albeit with quite a few mistakes because it tried for so long to deify the creators.

This deification was acceptable until the scientific age began. Then it should have been removed completely. This would have been possible had the truth been preserved, or if people had been able to read between the lines. But too many mistakes were made.

This was foreseen by the creators, and the Church will collapse because it is no longer of any use. In scientifically developed countries, people are already consumed by a kind of moroseness because they have nothing left to believe in. Nobody can believe in a "Heavenly God" any longer, perched upon a cloud with a white beard, omniscient and omnipotent, which is what the Church wants us to do. Neither can anybody believe in delightful little guardian angels, nor in a devil with horns and hooves. So nobody knows what to believe in any more. Only a few young people have understood that love is essential. You have reached the golden age.

People of the Earth, you fly in the heavens, and your voices are carried to the four corners of the Earth by means of radio waves. So the time has come for you to know the truth.

As it has been foretold, everything is happening now that the Earth has entered the Age of Aquarius. Certain people have already written about this, but no one believed them. Some 22,000 years ago, your creators decided to start their work on Earth, and everything that has happened since was anticipated because the movement of the galaxy implies this knowledge.

The Age of Pisces was the age of Christ and his fishermen, and the Age of Aquarius, which follows, began in 1946. This is the era in which the people of Israel found their country again:

> And it shall come to pass in that day... that there shall be the noise
> of a cry from the pisces[19] gate... *Zephaniah 1: 10.*

The Gate of Pisces is the passageway into the Age of Aquarius. This is the moment when the Sun rises over the Earth on the day of the vernal equinox in the constellation of Aquarius. The loud clamor is the sound accompanying this revelation.

It is not by chance that you were born in 1946.'

The End of the Church

'This revelation, thanks to the enlightenment it contains, will bring back hope and happiness to people who are morose. But it will also hasten the fall of the Church - unless the Church can understand its mistakes and place itself at the service of the truth.

For the terrible one is brought to nought, and the scorner is consumed, and all that watch for iniquity are cut off: That make a man an offender for a word, and lay a snare for him that reproveth in the gate, and turn aside the just for a thing of nought. *Isaiah 29: 20-21.*

It is the end of those people who want to make us believe in original sin and who want to make us feel guilty; the end for people who lay traps for those who spread the truth at the end of the Age of Pisces and the beginning of the Age of Aquarius; the end of people who are trying to save the Church as it existed, while ousting the just - those who speak of justice and those who write or preach the truth. They are like the people who crucified Jesus. Such people were convinced that they were defending what was right without trying to understand and were frightened of being ruined and destroyed at the dawning of the Age of Pisces.

And the eyes of them that see shall not be dim, and the ears of them that hear shall hearken... The vile person shall be no more called liberal, nor the churl said to be bountiful... For the vile person will speak villany, and his heart will work iniquity, to practise hypocrisy, and to utter error against Yahweh, to make empty the soul of the hungry, and he will cause the drink of the thirsty to fail. The instruments also of the churl are evil: he deviseth wicked devices to destroy the poor with lying words, even when the needy speaketh right. But the liberal deviseth liberal things; and by liberal things shall he stand.
Isaiah 32: 3-8.

Everyone in this case will understand the words: "the eyes of them that see shall not be dim". It is the Church who speaks of Yahweh deceitfully and leaves empty the souls of those who are hungry for the truth.

It is the Church, which devises infamous plans to annihilate the poor, so that those who are unable to understand or who dare not understand, will remain faithful to it through the fear of sin, excommunication or other such nonsensical things. While the poor try to plead their case, those who lack the intelligence to seize the truth stand up for the lies of the Church at the Church's bidding. But those of noble mind, those who loudly proclaim the truth, they perform noble acts, even though they may live without the approval of the agonizing Church of Man.

> Have ye not known? have ye not heard? hath it not been told you from the beginning? have ye not understood from the foundations of the earth? *Isaiah 40: 21.*

> Behold my servant whom I uphold, mine elect [in whom] my soul delighteth! I will put my Spirit upon him; he shall bring forth judgment to the nations.[20] *Isaiah 42: 1.*

You are the one who will spread the truth throughout the world, this truth which has been revealed to you over the past few days.

> A bruised reed will he not break, and a dimly burning wick will he not quench.[17] *Isaiah 42: 3.*

You will not be able to destroy the Church and its lies completely, but eventually, it will fade out by itself. This extinction has been going on for some time. The "wick" is weakening. It has accomplished its mission, and it is time for it to disappear. It has made mistakes and has enriched itself at the expense of the truth, without trying to interpret it in a clear enough way for people of this era. But do not be too hard on it, for thanks to the Church, the word of the Bible, which is a witness to the truth, has spread throughout the world.

Its mistakes have been great, particularly when it injected too much of the supernatural into the truth, and wrongly translated the scriptures in ordinary Bibles. It replaced the term "Elohim", which refers to the creators, with a singular term "God", whereas in fact Elohim in Hebrew is the plural of Eloha.

In this way, the Church transformed the creators into a single incomprehensible God. Another mistake was to make people adore a wooden cross in memory of Jesus Christ. A cross is not the Christ. A piece of wood in the shape of a cross means nothing:

> And none taketh it to heart, neither is there knowledge nor understanding to say, I have burned part of it in the fire, and have also baked bread upon the coals thereof, I have roasted flesh, and eaten, and with the rest thereof shall I make an abomination? shall I bow down to a block of wood?[21] *Isaiah 44: 19.'*

The Creation of the State of Israel

'The return of the Jewish people to Israel, as it was predicted, is a sign of the golden age:

> I will bring thy seed from the east, and gather thee from the west; I will say to the north, Give up; and to the south, Keep not back: bring my sons from far, and my daughters from the ends of the earth; Even every one that is called by my name: for I have created him for my glory. *Isaiah 43: 5-7.*

This is indeed the creation of the state of Israel welcoming Jews from the north and from the south. The Bible, preserved by the

Jewish people, bears witness to the coming of the creators as it is written:

Ye are my witnesses. *Isaiah 43: 10.*

Bring forth the blind people that have eyes, and the deaf that have ears. Let all the nations be gathered together, and let the people be assembled: who among them can declare this, and shew us former things? let them bring forth their witnesses, that they may be justified: or let them hear, and say, It is truth. Ye are my witnesses, saith Yahweh, and my servant whom I have chosen: that ye may know and believe me, and understand that I am he... therefore ye are my witnesses, saith Yahweh, that I am El. Yea, before the day was I am he. *Isaiah 43: 8-13.*

"Ye are my witnesses." That is quite explicit, isn't it? And I can tell you again on this day - from ancient days I am one and the same[22] - thanks to the witness that you hold in your hand, the Bible.

For a small moment have I forsaken thee; but with great mercies will I gather thee. *Isaiah 54: 7.*

The people of Israel have, in fact, regained their country after having participated in safeguarding the truth.

The time when humanity will overcome illness by scientific means is predicted:

There shall be no more thence an infant of days, nor an old man that hath not filled his days. *Isaiah 65: 20.*

Medicine now helps people triumph over illness and especially over infant mortality.

In the lips of him that hath understanding wisdom is found: but a rod is for the back of him that is void of understanding.
Proverbs 10: 13.'

The Mistakes of the Church

'The Church was sinful in making human beings feel guilty and making them pray without seeking to understand:

> But when ye pray, use not vain repetitions, as the heathen do: for they think that they shall be heard for their much speaking.
> *Matthew 6: 7.*

And despite the warning in the *Gospels,* the Church has also made itself too wealthy, while it was written:

> Lay not up for yourselves treasures upon earth... No man can serve two masters: for either he will hate the one, and love the other; or else he will hold to the one, and despise the other. Ye cannot serve Yahweh and mammon. *Matthew 6: 19-24.*

> Provide neither gold, nor silver, nor brass in your purses, Nor scrip for your journey, neither two coats, neither shoes, nor yet staves. *Matthew 10: 9-10.*

But with their stupid rules and meatless Fridays, they didn't respect their own *Gospels*:

Not that which goeth into the mouth defileth a man; but that which cometh out of the mouth, this defileth a man.

Matthew 15: 11.

How dare they, these men who are only men, indulge themselves in the wealth and luxury of the Vatican when the *Gospels* tell them to possess "neither gold, nor silver" - not even a spare coat?

How dare they preach goodness?

And Jesus said unto his disciples, Verily I say unto you, It is hard for a rich man to enter into the kingdom of heaven.[17]

Matthew 19: 23.

For they bind heavy burdens and grievous to be borne, and lay them on men's shoulders; but they themselves will not move them with one of their fingers. But all their works they do for to be seen of men... and love the uppermost rooms at feasts... and greetings in the markets... for one is your Master, even Christ; and all you are brothers. And call no man your father on the earth: for one is your Father, which is in heaven. Neither be you called masters: for one is your Master, even Christ. But he that is greatest among you shall be your servant.[17] *Matthew 23: 4-11.*

That is all written in their own *Gospels*. So how dare the Church burden people with their so called sins, which are only different concepts of morality and lifestyles; how dare they speak of goodness while living in opulence in the Vatican when people are dying of hunger; how dare they seek invitations and honors while preaching humility; how dare they ask people to call them "Father", "Your Eminence", or "Your Holiness", when their Gospels expressly forbid all these things?

If tomorrow the Pope took to the road as a pauper, the Church would be revived, but it would have a totally different humanitarian goal to that which it has pursued up to now - namely the propagation of what must serve as proof for today.

That mission is finished, but the Church can re-orientate itself towards goodness by helping those who are unhappy, by helping to spread the real truth of those writings, which until now, have been distorted or kept secret. In this way, the generous spirit of many priests would find fulfillment. For that to happen, the men of the Vatican should set an example by selling all their treasures to help finance underdeveloped countries. They should go to those countries and help people progress by offering practical help with their bare hands not just with "the good word".

It is unacceptable too that there are different categories of marriage and more particularly of burials, according to a person's wealth. This is another mistake of the Church.

But the time has come.'

At the Root of All Religions

'It is not only in the Bible and the Gospels that there are traces of the truth; testimonies can be found in practically every religion. The Kabala especially is one of the richest in testimonies, but it would not have been easy for you to get hold of one.

If one day you can find a copy, then you will be able to see that there are a great number of allusions to us. Particularly noteworthy is a description in the *Canticle of Canticles* (5) of the creators' planet and the distance which separates it from Earth.

It is written that the "height of the creator" is 236,000 "parasangs", and that "the height of his heels" is 30,000,000 "parasangs". The parasang is a unit of measurement just like the parsec, which stands for the distance that light can travel in one second, which is about 300,000 kilometers. Our planet is 30,000,000 parasangs away from

Earth or about nine thousand billion kilometers, just a little less than a light year.

By moving at the speed of light, or 300,000 kilometers per second, you would take almost one year to reach our planet. With your present day rockets, which travel at only 40,000 kilometers per hour, it would take you about 26,000 years to reach our planet.

So you can see that we have nothing to fear for the time being. We have the means to travel to Earth from our planet in less than two months with an atom-based propulsion method, which enables us to move at the speed of rays that are seven times faster than the speed of light.

Those rays "carry" us. To be carried by them, we leave the optical window, which is the spectrum of rays detected by the eye, to tune into the carrying beam. That is why people on Earth who have observed our spaceships have described them as becoming luminous, then very brilliant white, then blue, and finally disappearing. Obviously when a spacecraft goes beyond the speed of light, it disappears and is no longer visible to the naked eye. That is the "height of the creator's heels", the distance at which his heels, so to speak, rest on a planet.

The creators' own planet is 236,000 parasangs from its sun - a very big star - or seventy billion, eight hundred million kilometers. This is what is meant by the "height" of the creators.

The Kabala is the closest book to the truth, but almost all religious books allude to us with varying degrees of clarity. This is especially true in those countries where the creators had bases - in the Andes, in the Himalayas, in Greece where Greek mythology also contains important testimonies, as well as in the Buddhist and Islamic religions and among the Mormons. It would take many pages to name all the religions and sects that testify in a more or less obscure way to our work.'

Mankind: A Disease of the Universe

'There, now you know the truth. You must write it down and make it known throughout the world. If people on Earth want us to give them the benefit of our experience and help them gain 25,000 years of scientific knowledge, they have to show us that they want to meet us, and above all demonstrate that they deserve it, and that all this can be done without any danger to us.

If we give our knowledge to humanity, we have to be sure they will make good use of it. Our observations in recent years have not shown that wisdom rules the Earth. Certainly there has been progress, but some people still die of hunger, and a warlike spirit still exists throughout the world. We know that our arrival could improve many things and unite nations, but we have to feel that people really want to see us, and that they are truly starting to unify.

We also have to feel that they really want to see us arrive, knowing fully who we are and understanding the true meaning of our arrival.

Several times human warplanes have tried to chase our crafts, taking us for enemies.

You must tell them who we are, so that we can show ourselves without any risk of either getting hurt or killed - which is not the case at present - or of creating a dangerous and murderous panic.

Some researchers want to contact us by radio, but we do not respond because in this way they could locate our planet. On the other hand, transmission times would be too long, and our broadcasting system uses waves that your technology cannot pick up because you have not yet discovered them. They are seven times faster than radio waves, and we are experimenting with new waves that are one and a half times faster than that.

Progress continues, and our own research continues for the purpose of understanding and relating to the large being of whom we are a part, and on whose atoms we are parasites. These atoms are the planets and the stars.

In fact, we have been able to discover that intelligent living beings in the infinitely small live on particles that are planets and suns to them. They ask the same questions as ourselves.

Humanity is a disease inside this gigantic being, and the planets and stars are its atoms. Also this same gigantic being is in its turn a parasite on other greater atoms. In both directions, it is infinite. But the important thing is to make sure that the disease, which is humanity, continues to exist and never dies.

We did not know when we were creating you that we were accomplishing a secondary mission "written" into us, thus repeating what had been done for us.

From what we created and how it has developed, we have discovered our own origins. For we were also created by other people who have since disappeared. Their world has quite certainly disintegrated, but thanks to them, we were able to continue in their steps and create you.

We may disappear one day, but by then you will have replaced us and taken over our roles. So you are the link in the precious chain of human continuity. Other worlds exist, and humanity is certainly developing in other parts of the universe.

But in this region of the universe, our world is the only one to have made new creations. This is important because, from each world, innumerable children can be brought forth who are precious for preserving continuity. This allows us to hope that one day humanity will no longer be in danger of disappearing completely.

But we are not sure that humankind can ever stabilize itself in abundance. The chain has always continued, but we must not upset the equilibrium of the immense body in which we are a parasite because, by developing too much, we could trigger a catastrophe, which at best might bring about a recession and at worst cause complete destruction.

In a healthy body, a few germs can live without danger, but if they develop too much, they cause a disease, which troubles the organism. Then the organism reacts to destroy the germs responsible, either naturally or with the help of medication. The important thing, apparently, is to create enough worlds so that humanity does not extinguish itself, but above all else, to make sure that the equilibrium is not broken by concentrating our efforts anew on seeking to make those who exist happier.

It is in this area that we can help you tremendously.'

Evolution: A Myth

'I make a parenthesis here, because you must dispel from your minds all uncertainty about evolution. Your scientists who have elaborated theories of evolution are not completely wrong in saying that humanity is descended from the monkey, and the monkey from the fish, and so on. In reality, the first living organism created on Earth was unicellular, which then gave rise to more complex life forms.

But this did not happen by chance! When we came to Earth to create life, we started by making very simple creations and then improved our techniques of environmental adaptation. This enabled us to make in turn fish, amphibians, mammals, birds, primates and finally man himself, who is just an improved model of the monkey to which we added what makes us essentially human.

In this way, we made human beings in our image, as it is written in the Bible in *Genesis*. You could have realized for yourselves that there is little chance of a series of accidents producing such a large variety of life forms - the colors of birds and their elaborate mating rituals, or the shape of certain antelope horns.

What natural need could lead antelopes or wild goats to develop curled horns? Or birds to have blue or red feathers? And what about exotic fish?

All that is the work of our artists. Do not forget the artists when you yourselves create life. Imagine a world without them - no music, films, paintings or sculptures... Life would be very boring, and animals very ugly if their bodies corresponded only to their needs and functions.

Evolution of the various forms of life on Earth is really the evolution of techniques of creation and the increased sophistication of the creators' work. This eventually led them to create people similar to themselves. You can find the skulls of prehistoric men who were the first human prototypes.

These were replaced each time by others more evolved. This continued right up to your present form, which is the exact replica of your creators who were afraid to create anything highly superior to themselves, although some were tempted to do so.

If we could be sure that human beings would never turn against their creators to dominate or destroy them - as has happened between the different human races created successively on Earth - but instead would love them as parents, the temptation would be great to create an improved humankind.

This is possible but at what enormous risk! In fact, some creators worry that the people of the Earth may be slightly superior to their fathers. "Satan" is one of those who has always thought, and still does, that the people of the Earth are a danger to our planet because they are a little too intelligent. But the majority among us thinks that you will prove to us that you love us, and that you will never try to destroy us. That is the least we expect before coming to help you.

It is even possible that at each creation of humankind by humankind, a small improvement is achieved, a true evolution of the human race, which is gradual, so that the creators do not feel threatened when faced with their creations.

This makes it possible to speed up progress. Although we do not think that at present we can give you our scientific heritage, we do feel it is safe to give you our political and humanitarian knowledge.

This will not threaten your planet, but will allow you to be happier on Earth. Thanks to this happiness, you will progress faster, and that could also help you to show us more speedily that you deserve our help and our inheritance in striving to achieve an intergalactic level of civilization.

Otherwise, if humanity cannot calm its aggressiveness, if peace does not become your only goal, and you allow people to promote war, produce arms, test nuclear weapons, and maintain armies just to seize or retain power, then we will stop such people from becoming a danger to us, and there would be another Sodom and Gomorrah.

How could we not fear people from Earth when they attack their own, we who are from another world and slightly different?

You, Claude Vorilhon, you will spread the truth under your present name, which you will replace progressively with RAEL, which means literally "light of God" and if we translate it more accurately, "light of the Elohim" or "Ambassador of the Elohim", because you will be our ambassador on Earth, and we will come only officially to your Embassy. RAEL can be simply translated as "messenger".

And it is through telepathy that we made you name your son Ramuel, which means "the son of the one who brings light", because he is truly the son of our messenger, of our ambassador.'

And following that pronouncement, he left, just as he had done on other mornings.

6

THE NEW COMMANDMENTS

Geniocracy

I met him the next day, and again he began to speak: 'First of all, let us look at the political and economic aspects of life. What kind of people allows humanity to progress? The geniuses. Therefore, your world must revalorize its geniuses and allow them to govern the Earth.

Power was in the hands of brutes, who were superior to others because of their muscular strength. Next in power were the rich, who used their money to employ many "brutes" in their service. Then came the politicians who ensnared the people of democratic countries with their own hopes - not to mention military men whose success has been based around the rational organization of brutality.

The only type of people you have never placed in power are the ones who help humanity to progress. Whether they discovered the wheel, gunpowder, the internal combustion engine or the atom, the geniuses have always allowed less intelligent people in power to benefit from their inventions. Often such people have used peaceful inventions for murderous ends. All that must be changed.

For this to happen, you must abolish all your electoral and polling systems because in their present form, they are completely unsuited to human development. Each person is a useful cell in this huge body we call humanity. The cell in your foot should not decide whether or not your hand should pick up a given object. It is the brain, which must decide, and if the object in question is good, the cell of your foot will benefit from it. It is not up to the foot to vote. Its job is simply to transport the body - including the brain - and it is not capable of judging if what the hand takes is good or not.

Votes only have a positive effect when there is an equivalence of knowledge and intellect. Copernicus was condemned by a majority of incompetent people because he was the only one at that time who had a sufficiently high level of comprehension. Although the Church - that is to say the majority - believed the Earth was the center of the universe, this turned out to be wrong. The Earth really revolved around the sun, and Copernicus - the minority - turned out to be right.

When the first cars were invented, if we had asked everyone to vote to establish whether cars should be allowed to exist or not, the majority, who knew nothing about cars and did not care, would have responded negatively, and you would still be riding in a horse and cart. So, how can you change all that?

These days, you have psychologists who are capable of creating tests to evaluate the intelligence and adaptation of every individual. These tests should be applied systematically from infancy onward in order to define each individual's orientation towards subjects studied.

When individuals reach a responsible age, their intellectual coefficient can be measured and included on their identity or voter's card. Only those with an intellectual capacity of at least fifty per cent above the average should be eligible for a public post. To vote, individuals would need an intellectual coefficient of at least ten per cent above average. If such a system existed now, many of your present politicians would not hold the positions they do today.

This is a totally democratic system. There are many engineers, for example, who are of lower than average intelligence, but who have very good memories and have obtained several academic degrees because of this.

On the other hand, there are many laborers or farm workers who have no specialized education at all, but whose intelligence is fifty per cent above the average. What is totally unacceptable now is that the voice of someone whom you might vulgarly call "a cretin" is worth as much as that of a genius, who has thought maturely about the way he or she is going to vote. In some small cities, elections are won by the candidate who buys people the most drinks - not by the individual whose policies are the most interesting.

Therefore, right from the start, the right to vote should be reserved for those people whose brains are more suited to thinking and finding solutions to problems - that is to say, an elite group of high intelligence. This does not necessarily mean those people who have done the most studying.

We are talking about placing the genius in power, and you may call that "Geniocracy".'

Humanitarianism

'Second point: Your world is paralyzed by profit, and Communism fails to provide a carrot big enough to motivate people and encourage them to make progress.

You are all born equal; this is also written in the Bible. Your governments should ensure that people are born with approximately the same level of financial means. It is unacceptable that children of low intelligence should live in luxury thanks to the fortunes amassed by their fathers, while geniuses die of hunger and do any menial chore just to eat.

This way they forsake occupations where they could have made discoveries benefiting the whole of humanity. To avoid this, property ownership must be abolished without establishing Communism.

This world is not yours - that also is written in the Bible. You are only tenants. Thus all goods should be rented for forty-nine years. This will eliminate the injustice of inheritance. Your true inheritance, and that of your children, is the entire world, if you knew how to organize yourselves to make it pleasant. This political orientation of humanity is not Communism; its preoccupation is the future of humanity. If you want to give it a name, call it "Humanitarianism".

Take for example a man who has finished his studies at the age of twenty-one and wants to work. He chooses his profession and earns a salary. If he wants to find a place to live while his parents are still alive, he "buys" a house - but of course, in reality, he is renting a house or apartment for forty-nine years from the State which constructed it.

If the value of the house is estimated at 100,000 francs, he can pay that amount divided into monthly installments for forty-nine years. At the age of seventy (twenty-one plus forty-nine), he will have paid for his house and can live there until his death, without ever paying again.

After his death, the house will go back to the State, which must then allow his children, if there are any, to benefit from it freely. Supposing there is one child, then this child can live freely all his life in his father's house. At his death, his child in turn can also benefit from the family house, and so on indefinitely. Inheritance must be completely abolished, except for the family house. This does not, however, prevent each person from being rewarded individually for their merits.

Let us take another example. Someone has two children. One is a good worker, and the other is lazy. At the age of twenty-one, they both decide to go their own separate ways. They each rent a house worth 100,000 francs.

The worker will rapidly earn more money than the lazy one. He will then be able to rent a house worth twice as much as the first one. If he has the means, he will even be able to rent both houses, one as a country house.

If his savings are fruitful, he will also be able to build a house and rent it for forty-nine years, thereby receiving money due to him. But at his death, everything will go back to the community, except for the family home, which will go to the children.

Thus individuals can make a fortune for themselves depending on their own merits, but not for their children. To each their own merits. The same should apply to commercial and industrial enterprises.

If someone creates a business, it is theirs for their entire life, and they can rent it out, but never for more than forty-nine years. The same goes for farmers. They can rent land and cultivate it for forty-nine years, but after that, it all goes back to the State, which will be able to rent it out again for another forty-nine years. Their children can also rent it for forty-nine years.

This method must be adopted for all goods that remain exploitable, and as for the value of things, nothing changes. Everything that is of value such as shares, gold, enterprises, cash, or buildings is owned by the community but may be rented for forty-nine years by those who have acquired the means by their own merits and labor.

In this way, somebody who made a fortune around the age of forty will be able to construct houses, rent them as apartments for forty-nine years, and enjoy that money so long as life lasts.

Afterwards, the money, which comes from these rents, will go back to the community. This humanitarianism is already prescribed in the Bible:

> And thou shalt number seven sabbaths of years unto thee, seven times seven years; and the space of the seven sabbaths of years shall be unto thee forty and nine years. *Leviticus 25: 8.*

> And if thou sell ought unto thy neighbour, or buyest ought of thy neighbour's hand, ye shall not oppress one another: According to the number of years after the jubile thou shalt buy of thy neighbour, and according unto the number of years of the fruits he shall sell unto thee: According to the multitude of years thou shalt increase the price thereof, and according to the fewness of years thou shalt diminish the price of it: for according to the number of the years of the fruits doth he sell unto thee.
> *Leviticus 25: 14-16.*

The land shall not be sold for ever: for the land is mine; for ye are strangers and sojourners with me. *Leviticus 25: 23.*

If geniuses are admitted to power, they will understand the usefulness of these reforms. You must also see to it that all the nations of the Earth unite to form only one government.'

World Government

'The creation of a new worldwide currency and a common language would help you to establish a world government. The Auvergne dialect is no longer spoken in Clermont-Ferrand, and very soon, French will no longer be spoken in Paris, nor English in London, nor German in Frankfurt. Your scientists and linguists should unite and create a new language, inspired by all languages and made obligatory in all the schools of the world, as a second language.

The same must be done with money. Worldwide currency values cannot be based on the franc, the dollar, or the yen, but must be based on a new currency created for the needs of the whole Earth, without depriving one group of people who would ask themselves why another currency has been chosen instead of their own.

Finally, the trigger required to bring about such a union is the suppression of military conscription, which teaches only aggressiveness to young men. Professional armies must then be put at the service of the public.

This must happen at the same time in all countries so as to provide an indispensable guarantee of security.'

Your Mission

'As I have already told you, we know that our official arrival would accelerate many things. But we will wait until we see that human beings really want us to come, that they love us and respect us like the parents that we truly are, and that our spacecrafts will not be threatened by your destructive military forces.

To achieve this, make it known throughout the world that you have met me, and repeat what I have said to you. Wise people will listen to you. Many will take you for a madman or a visionary, but I have already explained to you what to think of the imbecilic majority.

You know the truth, and we will stay in contact with you by telepathy to give you confidence and additional information if we think it is necessary.

What we want is to see if there are enough wise people on Earth. If a sufficiently large number of people follow you, then we will come openly.

Where? At the place you will have prepared for our arrival.

Have a residence built in a pleasant country with a mild climate, with seven rooms always ready to receive guests, each with a separate bathroom, a conference room able to accommodate twenty-one people, a swimming pool and a dining room capable of seating twenty-one people.

This residence should be constructed in the middle of a park and should be protected from curious onlookers. The park should be entirely surrounded by walls to prevent anyone from seeing the residence and the swimming pool.

The residence should be situated at a distance of at least one thousand meters from the walls around the park. It will have a maximum of two stories and should be further screened from view by an inner barrier of trees and bushes. Install two entrances in the surrounding wall, one to the south and another on the northern side. The residence will also have two entrances.

There will be a terrace on the roof where a spacecraft of twelve meters in diameter may land. Access from that terrace to the interior is essential.

The air space above and around the residence should not be under direct military or radar surveillance.

You will try to ensure that the area where this residence is built - if possible larger than stipulated here - is treated as neutral territory by other nations and by the nation on whose territory it is located, by virtue of it being our embassy on Earth.

You may live with your wife and children in the residence, which will be under your direction, and you will be able to have servants there and invite guests of your choosing. However, the area containing the seven rooms should be directly under the terrace, and it should be separated from the section used by human beings by a thick metal door, lockable from the inside, which is kept permanently closed. An aseptic chamber should be built at the entrance to the conference room.

The financing of the project will be made possible through the help you will receive from those people who will believe in you, and therefore in us. They will be wise and intelligent, and they will be rewarded when we come.

Keep a record, therefore, of those who contribute financially to the construction and upkeep of the residence, however modest their contribution.

Also, in each nation throughout the world, appoint an individual who will be responsible for communicating the truth, and who will help others join together to spread it.

Once a year, on a mountain near the residence, gather together from all over the world all those people who have heard about us through these writings and want us to come. Assemble the largest number of people possible, and have them think intensely about us and hope for our coming.

When there are enough people, and when they wish intensely enough for us to come without any religious mysticism, but as responsible people respecting their creators, then we will land openly and give you our scientific knowledge as our heritage to all peoples of the Earth.

If those with warlike temperaments are rendered harmless all over the whole world, then this will happen. If the love of life and humanity's love for us and itself are strong enough, yes, we will come openly.

We will wait, and if human beings remain aggressive and continue to progress in a manner which is dangerous for other worlds, then we will destroy this civilization and its repositories of scientific wealth, and there will be another Sodom and Gomorrah, until such time as humanity becomes morally worthy of its level of scientific understanding.

The future of humanity is in its own hands, and the truth is in yours.

Communicate it throughout the world and do not be discouraged. We will never help you openly, or in any way that would give proof to the skeptics, since skepticism often goes hand in hand with aggressiveness. Intelligent people will believe you since what you will say contains nothing mystical.

It is important to us that they believe you without any material proof. This proves to us more than anything else that they are intelligent and so are worthy to receive our scientific knowledge.

Now go. You will not be forgotten if you succeed during your life on Earth - or even after. If necessary, we can wait until the time of your descendants to make our landing, because we can make you live again scientifically, just as we can resurrect all those who have led humanity along the path of human genius guided by the love of their creators - so long as their remains are preserved in coffins or tombs.

The only help we will give you will be to appear in the skies more and more frequently from now on in order to make people aware of the problems, and make them want to learn more about the truth that you are transmitting.

Gradually, thanks to these increased sightings, public awareness will also increase, and our presence will no longer trigger stupid adoration, but instead a deep desire within the population to make contact with us.

You will call your movement *Madech*[23]- the "movement for welcoming the Elohim, creators of humanity", which carries in its initials a message, *Moise a devancé Elie et le Christ,* which means: Moses preceded Elijah and the Christ.

In French this is:

M: mouvement pour (movement for)
A: l'accueil (the welcoming)
D: des (of the)
E: Elohim
C: créateurs de (creators of)
H: l'humanité (humanity).'

7

THE ELOHIM

Nuclear Weapons

'Before we leave each other for the last time,' he said, 'do you have any questions to ask me?'

'You have interpreted the vision of Ezekiel as people equipped with space suits,' I replied, 'and you told me that the atmosphere of your planet was not the same as that on Earth. So why aren't you wearing a pressurized suit now?'

'Because we too have progressed scientifically, and now we can do without them. My face seems to be in the open air, but really it is protected by an invisible shield composed of repellent rays inside which I breathe different air from you. These rays let waves pass through, but not air molecules. It's a bit like the way you prevent fuel deposits escaping from certain ports in your technology by using emissions of bubbles.'

'Are nuclear weapons a danger for humanity?'

'Yes, a great danger. But if humanity does not become wise and peaceful, the existence of your nuclear weapons will mean that if the need arises, we will not have much to do in bringing about the destruction of your civilization. Perhaps you might even destroy yourselves.'

'If you do not, however, and if you become a threat to us, we will only have to destroy your stocks of bombs without sending offensive weapons against you. We could do this with either rays, or telepathy, in such a way that, in effect, one of the great powers would become the aggressor, and this would automatically release a fatal retaliation.'

'If people do not want to be exposed to that danger any longer, all they have to do is take nuclear weapons away from the military. Such nuclear power used with care could enable countries that lack energy to make great strides forward. You urgently need to stop nuclear weapons testing because you know nothing of the risks to which you are exposing yourselves. However, if humanity continues to play with nuclear weapons, it will simplify our task if we have to reduce you to silence.'

'Do you have any women on your planet?'

'Yes, it is mentioned in the Bible, and I made you note the appropriate quotation.'

'And children also?'

'Yes, we can have children exactly like you.'

Overpopulation

'You told me you were immortal in some way. How do you prevent over population?'

'This problem will, in fact, be making itself evident very rapidly on Earth. To resolve it - and you should resolve it immediately because you are already sufficiently numerous - you must develop contraception and pass strict laws authorizing women to have no more than two children.

If a couple has only two children, the population will arrive at a point where it no longer increases. We will be watching how well you deal with this too. It will be another test of your intelligence, which will help us see if you have earned our heritage. This solution I offer is for humanity now where people only live for seventy-five years on average. For us, the problem is very different. We are not eternal, but we are able to live ten times longer than you, thanks to a small surgical adjustment, which in effect is the biblical "tree of life". We have children, and we observe the rules, which I have just explained: two parents, two children. This keeps our population constant.'

'How many of you are there?'

'We are a population of about seven billion.'

'We have met on six consecutive days, but did you always go back each time to your own planet?'

'No, I returned to an intergalactic ship, which we use as a base and which stays constantly close to the Earth.'

'How many of you are on that vessel?'

'Seven, and on our planet there are seven provinces. Each has a representative on that vessel. If we add the two who are responsible for the vessel, there are permanently nine of us.'

'If the people here on Earth do exactly as you wish, what will happen?'

'We will come officially and land at the residence, which you will have prepared. We will ask you to invite there the official representatives of the most important countries of humanity, in order to bring about total unification of the people on the Earth. If all goes well, we will allow humanity to benefit step by step from our scientific advances. Depending on the uses that will be made of it, we will see if we can give humanity all our knowledge and allow you to enter the intergalactic era with our 25,000 years of scientific progress as your inheritance.'

'Are you the only world to have attained such an advanced level in science?'

'In this region of the universe, yes. There is an infinite number of worlds inhabited by beings of the humanoid type whose scientific level is lower than ours, although much superior to yours. What makes us fearful of disappearing is the fact that we have not yet found any planet with a civilization as highly evolved as our own. We have economic relations with many other planets on which life has been created by other people who must have reached a scientific level equivalent to ours, because their religious writings prove this to us.

'Unfortunately, we have been unable to find the civilizations who created the closest of these worlds. But perhaps we will find them farther on as we continue to search the universe, each time moving further away. In most cases, their planets approached the sun too closely, and life became impossible, or their sun exploded, or became too cold. Although we have not noticed anything abnormal at present in our system, all this makes us fear the worst.'

'So there is no religion where you live?'

'Our only religion is human genius. We believe only in that, and we particularly love the memory of our own creators whom we never saw again and whose world we have never been able to find. They must have disappeared. However, they had taken the precaution of putting a huge space station in orbit around our planet, containing all their knowledge, and this landed automatically when their world was destroyed. Thanks to them, we have taken on the torch, and we would like to see this torch taken up by the people of the Earth.'

'And what would happen if your planet was destroyed?'

'In case our world is destroyed, the same arrangements have been made in advance, so that you would automatically inherit all our knowledge.'

The Secret of Eternity

'Do you really live ten times longer than we do?' I asked.

'Our body lives on average, ten times longer than yours,' he replied.

'Like the first people of the Bible, that is between 750 and 1,200 years. But our mind, our true self, can be truly immortal. I have already explained to you that, starting with any cell of the body, we can re-create the whole person with new living matter. When we are in full possession of our faculties and our brain is at its maximum level of efficiency and knowledge, we surgically remove a tiny sample of the body, which we then preserve. Then, when we really die, we take a cell from this preserved sample and re-create the body in full, just as it had been at the time the sample was taken.

I say, "as it had been at that time", meaning with all its scientific knowledge and, of course, its personality. But in this case, the body is made up of new elements with the potential for another one thousand years of life - and so on eternally. But in order to limit the growth of the population, only geniuses have the right to eternity.

Everybody on our planet has a cell sample taken at a certain age, hoping that they will be chosen for re-creation after their death. In fact they not only hope for it, they try to earn this resurrection during their life. Once they have died, a grand council of the eternals assembles to decide in a "last judgement", who among those who died during the year deserves to live another life. For a period of three lifetimes, the eternal is on probation, and at the end of this time, the council of the eternals reconvenes to judge who, in the light of their work, deserves to join the council of the eternals as a perpetual member.

From the moment that one wishes to have a new life, one no longer has the right to have children, although this does not of course prevent love. This explains why the scientists who were members of the council of the eternals wished to create life on other planets. They transferred their procreative instincts onto other planets.'

'What do you call yourselves?'

'If you wish to give us a name, even though we call ourselves men and women in our language, you may call us Elohim, since we did indeed come from the sky.'

'What language do you speak on your planet?'

'Our official language closely resembles ancient Hebrew.'

'Each day we have talked here, weren't you afraid other people might have surprised us?'

'An automatic system would have warned me immediately if people had approached within a dangerous radius, by air or by land.'

'What is your lifestyle and your work where you live?'

'Most of our work is intellectual, as our level of scientific development allows us to use robots for everything. We work only when we feel the inclination - and then only with our brain. Only our artists and our sports people work with their bodies and only because they have chosen this.

'Our highly developed atomic energy is almost inexhaustible, especially since we have discovered a way to use the atom in a closed circuit and solar energy. We also have many other sources of energy. We do not necessarily use uranium in our atomic reactors, but several other simple and harmless materials.'

'But if you live so long, and do not work, do you not get bored?'

'No, never, because we always do things we enjoy doing - especially making love. We find our women very beautiful, and we make the most of this.'

'Does marriage exist?'

'No. Men and women are both free. Couples exist. Those who have chosen to live as such may do so, but they may have their freedom back whenever they wish. We all love one another. Jealousy does not exist, since everyone can have everything, and property is non-existent. There is no criminality where we live, thus no prisons and no police. However, there are many doctors and regular medical visits for the mind.

Those who show the slightest sign of psychological imbalance that could threaten the life or liberty of others are immediately given treatment in order to bring them back to normal.'

'Can you describe the day of an average individual where you live?'

'In the morning, they would get up and bathe, since there are swimming pools everywhere, have breakfast and then do whatever they feel like doing. Everybody "works", but only because they feel like working, as there is no money where we live. Thus those who work always do it well, since it is by vocation.

Only the eternals have specific tasks, for example supervising the electronic brains and computers used for dealing with vital functions such as energy, food and organization. Of the seven billion inhabitants, there are only 700 eternals, and they live entirely apart from the others. They have the privilege of being eternals but with this goes the duty of doing everything for the others who are not obliged to work.

To these 700 eternals, we must add 210 probationers (about seventy each year, that is to say, ten from each province). Of the seven billion inhabitants, there are only about forty million children. It is only when they become of age - between eighteen and twenty-one years, depending on the individual - that the children undergo the operation, which gives them a life span of more than 750 years. From then on, they too may have children. This enables the oldest of our non-eternal inhabitants to know their descendants for up to fifty generations.

Out of seven billion inhabitants, there are only about one million inactive people, and almost all of them are under treatment for psychological disorders. Our doctors treat them for a period of six months. Most people are interested in the arts, and they paint, sculpt, play music, write, produce films and participate in sports etc... We have a leisure civilization in the full sense of the word.

Our cities have an average population of about 500,000 people spread over a very small area. A city is in fact a huge house situated in a high place, inside which people can sleep, love, and do whatever they please.

These city houses are about one kilometer in length and height and are traversed in all directions by waves used by everyone for travelling. You tie on a belt, and then place yourself in a wave current, which transports you very rapidly to wherever you wish to go.

The cities are cube-like in shape, so that they do not eat up the countryside as they do where you live. Indeed one of your cities with say a population of about 500,000 covers a surface area twenty times greater than ours. The result is that when you want to go into the country, you have to travel for many hours, whereas in our case, we are there in only tens of seconds. The same architect conceives an entire city, so that it will be pleasing to the eye and will harmonize perfectly with the scenery surrounding it.'

'But don't the people who have nothing to do get bored?'

'No, because we provide them with numerous activities. The individual's true value is recognized, and everyone wants to show that they have worth.

Whether it be in art, in science or in sports, each person wants to shine in order to become eternal, or simply to be admired by the community - or by a woman. Some people like to take risks, and to deprive them of the risk of dying would take away their joy of living, and that is why dangerous sports are very popular.

We can bring back to life any injured person, but those who practice these sports may do so only if they state in writing that they agree not to be taken care of if they die during their sporting activities. We have a kind of atomic automobile race that would fascinate you and more violent activities like boxing, and even more violent than that, a kind of rugby game, which is played in the nude and where everything is permitted - boxing, wrestling and so on. All this may seem barbaric to you, but do not forget that all extremes must be balanced to avoid breakdowns.

An extremely sophisticated civilization must have primitive counterbalances. If our people did not have their idols in their favorite sport, they would have only one wish left, to die. The life of another individual must be respected, but their wish to die, or to play with death, must also be respected and permitted within well structured and well defined specialties.

Where we live, contests are held each year in all branches of the various activities, one of which is a worldwide contest, permitting us to decide on the best individuals who deserve eternal life. Everyone lives only for that.

Each year, whether it be painting, literature, biology, medicine, or any other specialty where the human brain can express itself, a competition takes place in every province, with a vote from the eternals of that province; the "champions" are gathered in the capital to submit themselves to the vote of a jury of eternals who designate those who become "champions among champions".

These people are then presented to the Grand Council of eternals, who finally choose those who are worthy of becoming eternal probationers. This is the goal and everybody's ideal. Distractions may well take on a primitive aspect when the supreme goal is so high.'

'Does this mean that the eternals have a totally different way of life from the other inhabitants?'

'Oh yes. They live apart in cities reserved for them and meet regularly to make decisions.'

'How old are the oldest ones?'

'The oldest, the president of the council of the eternals, is 25,000 years old, and you see him before you now. I have lived in twenty-five bodies up to this day, and I was the first one on whom this experiment was successfully carried out. That is why I am the president of the eternals. I myself directed the creation of life on Earth.'

'Then your knowledge must be immeasurable?'

'Yes, I have accumulated quite a lot of knowledge, and I will not be able to gain much more. It is in this way that the people on Earth may be superior to us because the capacity of that part of the brain, which accumulates information, the memory, is larger. Human beings on Earth will be able to accumulate more knowledge than us, and therefore will advance further scientifically, if they have the means. This is what frightens those who oppose the council of eternals. People on Earth may progress faster than us, if nothing stops them.'

Chemical Education

'The knowledge that students need to accumulate must be enormous, and must take a very long time?'

'No. Thanks to an important scientific discovery, which in fact your scientists on Earth are beginning to consider, we can teach a student his lessons surgically. Your scientists have just discovered that if you inject the liquid from the memory of an educated rat into the brain of an uneducated rat, it will learn what the other knew.

We can transmit information by the injection of brain memory matter, thus our children have almost no work to do. They regularly undergo injections of brain matter taken from people possessing the information necessary for instruction. Therefore, children only spend their time doing interesting things, which they decide on themselves, such as rebuilding the world in theory and fulfilling themselves in sports and the arts.'

'You never have wars among the provinces of your world?'

'Never. The sports competitions are sufficiently developed to eliminate the war instinct. Besides, psychologically, the fact that young people are able to risk their lives in games where systematically there are many deaths during each event suppresses the war instinct.

This enables those who feel this instinct too intensely to satiate it at the peril of their own life, without involving those who do not want to travel along such perilous paths. If on Earth sports and games were more dangerous but organized, it would greatly reduce the chances of creating international conflicts.'

'Are the seven provinces of your world similar?'

'No, as on Earth there are different races and cultures. Our provinces were created and based on those races and cultures, while respecting the freedom and independence of each one.'

'Would it be possible for a man from Earth to visit your planet?'

'Yes, but you would have to wear a space suit adapted for your breathing. You could live without such a suit in a special residence where we have reproduced the Earth's atmosphere. There, many people from Earth live, including Moses, Elijah and Jesus Christ along with many other living testimonies of our creation. We will be able to bring all these people back to Earth when the time comes to support your statements.'

'Why not bring them back at once?'

'Because in your incredulous world, if Jesus Christ returned, he would be placed in a psychiatric institution. Imagine someone landing among you saying he is the Christ. He would certainly be

THE ELOHIM - CHEMICAL EDUCATION

mocked and quickly locked up. If we intervened by performing scientific wonders to show he really was the Christ, that would bring back religions based on God. It would also lend support to the idea of the supernatural or the mystical, and we do not want either.'

Having said that, the small man saluted me for the last time and told me that he would return only when all that he had asked of me was accomplished. Then he climbed back aboard his machine, and it took off and disappeared just as it had on other mornings.

The Raelian Movement

What a story! What a revelation!
After returning home and classifying and copying up the notes I had taken, I realized the immensity of the task that had been entrusted to me.

I felt I had little chance of carrying it out. But since it is not necessary to hope in order to embark on an undertaking, I decided to do exactly what was asked of me, even though I might be taken for a visionary. After all, if being a visionary means having received the light, then I am quite willing to be considered a visionary. It is better to be called a visionary and know the truth, than to be called enlightened and not know the truth.

I wish to emphasize to skeptics of all kinds that I never drink alcohol and sleep very well at night. One can neither dream for six consecutive days, nor invent all this.

To you who refuse to believe me, I say: Watch the sky, and you will see more and more sights that neither our scientists nor the military will be able to explain - except by foolish babblings aimed at saving reputations which they believe they would lose if the truth did not originate from someone in their closed circle. How could a scientist possibly not know?

Those who condemned Copernicus - because he dared to say the Earth was not the center of the universe - could never admit that someone other than themselves could reveal all that.

But all of you who have seen or will see unidentified flying objects, which some people will explain away as dreams, or weather balloons, or even hallucinations, and all of you who dare not talk about it for fear of being mocked, it is only by getting together with those who believe that you will be able to speak freely.

All these revelations brought me such a sense of well-being and such an inner peacefulness in this world where we do not know what to believe, where we cannot believe in a white bearded God or in a hoofed devil, and where official scientists cannot give precise explanations of our origins and our goals.

In the light of these amazing revelations, everything becomes so clear and seems so simple. Knowing that somewhere in the universe, there is a planet full of people who created us similar to themselves, who love us, all the while fearing that their creations might surpass them - is this not profoundly moving? Especially if one thinks that we will, in turn, be able to participate in the evolution of this Humanity, of which we are a part, like them, by creating life on other worlds.

Now that you have read this book that I have written, in which I have tried to set out as clearly as possible all that was said to me, if you simply think that I have a great imagination and that these writings were produced just to amuse you, then I will be profoundly disappointed.

But perhaps, on the other hand, these revelations will give you confidence in the future and allow you to understand the mystery of creation and the destiny of humanity. Perhaps they will answer the many questions that you have asked yourselves at night ever since your childhood, wondering why we exist and what our purpose is on this Earth. If this happens, I shall be very happy indeed.

Finally, if you understand that all I have said here is the profound truth and wish, as I do, to see these people land here officially very soon to give us their heritage, and if you want to play a part in realizing all that was asked of me, then I will have fulfilled my mission in writing this book.

If this is the case, write to me, and we will welcome you into the Raelian Movement. We will build the residence that they desire, and when we are numerous enough all over the world to wait for them with the respect and love that those who created us would have the right to demand, then they will come, and we will become the beneficiaries of their immense knowledge.

To all of you who believe in God or in Jesus Christ, I say you were right in such a belief. Even if you thought all was not exactly as the Church would have you believe, there was a foundation of truth. You were right to believe in the basis of the scriptures, but wrong to sustain the Church. If you continue to distribute your money to provide cardinals with the finest vestments, and at your expense continue to authorize the existence of the military and their nuclear threat, then it means that you wish to remain primitive and are not interested in entering the golden age to which we are now entitled.

If, however, you wish to participate passively or actively, according to your means, in the creation and development of the Raelian Movement, take your pen and write to me. We will very soon be numerous enough to choose a piece of land on which the embassy will be built. If you still have doubts, read the papers and look at the sky. You will see that sightings of mysterious crafts are becoming more and more numerous, and this will give you the courage to send your letter to me, addressed to:

Rael,
c/o: International Raelian Movement
C.P. 225, CH1211
Geneva 8
Switzerland

Or by email to: headquarters@rael.org

B O O K T W O

EXTRA-TERRESTRIALS TOOK ME TO THEIR PLANET

1

MY LIFE UNTIL THE FIRST ENCOUNTER

Introduction

When I started this second book I wanted simply to relate what my life had been like before my fantastic encounter of 13 December 1973, to answer the many people who had asked firstly what I had done before that time, and secondly whether anything extraordinary had happened to me during my childhood that could have foreshadowed such a destiny.

I was surprised myself as I searched my memories, for even though I thought that nothing extraordinary had occurred at the beginning of my life, I found scenes resurfacing, which formed a whole when put together, and I saw that my life had really been guided for me to be what I was and to find myself where I did on December 13, 1973.

I had almost finished writing this account when the second encounter took place. Consequently, I have summed up my early memories briefly in order to give as much space as possible to the second part of this message and to provide a full account of this second contact, which turned out to be even more fantastic than the first.

Two Years Have Passed

Two years! For almost two years now I have been trying somehow to radiate this truth, which is too great for me. Time goes by, and I feel I am getting nowhere. Yet, little by little, a solid core of people is forming around me, people who understand that *The Book Which Tells the Truth* really does just that.

There are seven hundred of them as I pen these lines, and I understand how this is both few and many at the same time. Few when we consider the four billion people who populate the Earth, and many when we consider how few people had decided, after two years, to follow the man who, two thousand years ago, had the equally heavy burden of being initiated and then initiating the primitive people of his time.

Who are these seven hundred? Are they, as the scoffers would no doubt love to believe, average simpletons who could be made to swallow anything? Not at all. Some of them are university graduates or people holding PhD's in philosophy, psychology, theology, sociology, medicine, physics, chemistry, etc.

My admiration perhaps goes as much to those who have no degree, since although they have not acquired knowledge through studying that would allow them to realize that living matter and people like us can be created scientifically, they are still able to feel it intuitively, as people capable of mastering matter and putting themselves in harmony with the universe that they are.

I must say that I am optimistic on the whole, and that I believe that I have so far accomplished the mission that has been entrusted to me. For whatever happens to me, MADECH is up and running, and nothing will ever be able to stop it.

In two years I have given nearly forty lectures, and since certain questions come up regularly, I suppose some parts of the message need to be clarified. So I will try to do that in this work.

First of all, what path did I follow before the encounter of 13 December 1973?

I have to admit I have only recently begun to look back on my life to figure out exactly how it had been guided for me to be available and ready to go into action on the spiritual, psychic and emotional levels at that time.

Certain events in my childhood had never seemed to me to have the least meaning when taken separately - but they did when taken together.

Now it all seems very clear to me, and I am moved when I remember some things that I considered unimportant at the time they occurred. Far be it from me to tell my life story in a way that suggests that each event in it was exceptional, but it seems that many people want to know more about what had happened to me before. Also, rather than leave it to wagging tongues, I would rather tell it all myself.

Childhood: a UFO over Ambert

As the child of an unknown father, I cannot say that I had a typical childhood. I was what is called a "natural" child - as if all others were "artificial" children.

My birth was an accident as it were, at least for the little town of Ambert, which is so devoutly Catholic that it is known as the "world capital of the rosary". Furthermore, the unknown father, who was not totally unknown, was apparently a Jewish refugee. What sacrilege!

My birth was concealed as much as possible - not in a cave, but in a clinic at nearby Vichy. It occurred on 30 September 1946 at about two o'clock in the morning and was a very difficult one. But the important thing is that I was conceived on 25 December 1945. Conception, the moment when a being truly begins to exist and develop in the womb of its mother, is the true date of birth for each individual. December 25 has been a very important date for almost two thousand years now. For those who believe in coincidences, my life began with a coincidence.

When we returned to Ambert, my poor mother tried for quite a long while to pass me off as "the son of a friend she was taking care of for a while" to her father who, even though he held it against her when he learned the truth, proved to be the nicest of grandfathers to me during the short time I knew him. Sadly, he died when I was still a very young child. I was later told about how amused he looked when, having seen him trim his fruit trees, I took a pair of scissors to cut... his lettuce.

I was raised by my grandmother and my aunt who were then, and still are, living together. They taught me to read and helped me take my first steps, which I remember very clearly - surely the earliest memory of my life.

It was only very recently that my grandmother told me that in 1947 she saw a strange craft flying very quickly and noiselessly over Ambert near her house. She had never dared tell anyone about it for fear of being accused of hallucinating. It was only after reading my book that she decided to talk to me about it... and at the same time she decided to join MADECH. Her decision to join was, in fact, one of the most important forms of encouragement that I received.

The Pope of the Druids

In Ambert there was an old man of whom small children were afraid, and of whom the grown-ups made fun. They nicknamed him "Jesus Christ" because he had very long hair rolled up in a bun and a magnificent beard.

He was always clad in a long cape that came down to his ankles, and he lived about a hundred meters from the house where my mother had found a small apartment. He did not work, and nobody knew how he could afford to live in the minuscule house in front of the municipal grammar school.

As they got older, the children lost their fear of him, and like their parents, started to make fun of him, laughing and making faces as they followed at his heels.

Personally, I did not enjoy playing with the others, preferring to contemplate insects and look at books. I had passed this man in the street several times and had been surprised by his face, which radiated great kindness, and by the mischievous smile he wore whenever he looked at me. I did not know why, but he did not scare me, and I did not see anything laughable about him. Also I did not understand why the other children made fun of him.

One afternoon I followed him, curious about where he was going, and saw him go into his house, leaving open the door that led into a small, very dark kitchen. I went closer and could see him sitting on a stool with the mischievous smile on his face, as if he were expecting me. He motioned for me to come nearer. I went inside the house and moved towards him.

He laid his hand on my head, and I felt a strange sensation. At the same time, he looked up in the air and uttered some words that I did not understand. After a few minutes had passed, he let me go, still without saying a word, and still smiling the same mysterious smile.

All this had me puzzled at the time, but I very quickly forgot about it. It was only in the summer of 1974, when reading a book that my mother had lent me about the mysteries of Auvergne, that I learned that Father Dissard, the old man in question, was the last Dissard - that is, the last living "Pope" of the Druids - and that he had been dead for several years.

Then I recalled the scene from my childhood, and thought again of the mysterious smile that the old man used to give me each time I passed him in the street - which was every day, since we had been virtually neighbors. I now know exactly who he was addressing when he looked up in the air and uttered those mysterious phrases, just as I know exactly what the silent, luminous machine was that my grandmother had seen.

One other thing also comes to mind again. After the scene that took place at Father Dissard's house, I went to sleep every evening counting up to nine a certain number of times.

This is a number that has frequently come up in my life, like a code that has been assigned to me. I have never been able to explain this sudden habit, which began several years after I had learned to count much higher than nine, and therefore could not have been the result of learning by rote. I was seven years old when this incident took place.

Poetry

At that time what mattered most to me were animals, which I loved to draw all day long, when I was not organizing snail races. I was fascinated by animal life, and I dreamt then only of becoming an explorer, so as to be able to get near the mysterious fauna of the virgin forests.

But at nine years of age - the number nine again - everything was to change. First of all, I was discovering what was to become a true passion for me - speed. Speed that is, on everything with wheels, with or without an engine. Speed and especially balance, the sense of trajectory and the struggle against oneself, against one's own reflexes - in fact, the ultimate mastery of mind over body.

It started with wild downhill runs on a little bicycle with almost no brakes, and I wonder how it was that I did not fall a single time. To liven things up, I would position myself at the top of a hill and wait for a fast car to pass by. Then I would launch into dizzying pursuit, catch up with the car and pass it - to the driver's great surprise - and, once at the bottom of the hill, I would turn and go back to wait at the top for another car.

A few months later, I found myself by chance attending the Tour de France motor race, and it was love at first sight. It was possible, I then realized, to know the joys of high speed without having to pedal back up a hill. And you could make it your job.

I made up my mind, the way you can when you are nine years old. I would be a race-car driver.

From that day on, my life was centered only around motor racing. Nothing else interested me, and I did not see the point of learning all they taught me at school, since I was going to be a racing driver. Children's comics were replaced by serious motor magazines, and I impatiently began counting off the years that separated me from the age when I could obtain a driver's license.

It was also at the age of nine that I had my first experience of boarding school. My mother was in despair because I no longer wanted to do anything at school, and I constantly told her that such learning was useless for motor racing drivers. So she decided to send me to the Notre-Dame-de-France boarding school in Puy-en-Velay.

She hoped that, without motor racing magazines, I would apply myself to school work, and in a way she was not far wrong. But I have very bad memories of that first boarding school, almost certainly because I was too young when I was sent there.

I remember that I spent many nights crying in a huge dormitory, where what I now believe I missed most was the chance to be alone and meditate.

This need, which caused me to spend entire nights crying, further increased my already great sensitivity, as will any emotional or affectionate need that is denied.

Then I discovered poetry.

I had always been more attracted to literature than to mathematics, although only as an interested and passive reader. Then came the desire, the need to write - in verse if possible. I remained uninterested in mathematics, yet I had now achieved a solid average in that subject as in all others. But in French language, and especially writing, I regularly came first, as long as I liked the set subject. I even wrote an entire collection of poems and won first prize in a poetry competition.

The most surprising thing was that even though I had not been baptized, I was in a private boarding school run by Catholic monks, with all the praying which that involves - prayers before eating, and going to bed, before rising in the morning, before studying - and attending daily mass with communion. When, after six months of daily communion the brethren discovered that I had not been baptized, they seemed utterly horrified. I actually thought it was funny; it was in fact the only part of their mass that I liked, this free tasting of morsels of bread.

It was also at the age of nine that I attained puberty. I enjoyed it very much and discovering unknown and secret pleasures, which no other nine year-old in the dormitory seemed yet to know about, was some consolation for my incomplete solitude.

Finally, it was at the age of nine that I fell in love for the first time - and it was the intense kind of love that can seize children at that age. Due to my improved classroom results, my mother had agreed not to send me back to boarding school, and I found myself in the fourth grade at the municipal grammar school in Ambert. There she was, nine years old or almost, and her name was Brigitte. I was shy and blushed quite ridiculously. It took only a glance during a medical visit, or perhaps a gesture of modesty to hide a non-existent bosom from my eyes, to release in me feelings of tenderness and a great desire to protect this apparently fragile being.

The following year I found myself at the same school, in the fifth grade, in the company of my first love to whom I dared not even speak. Still, I managed to end up sitting one desk in front of her at the beginning of the school year, so that I could turn my head from time to time and admire her beloved face. I was only ten and was always thinking about her.

The fact that I was close to her in class spurred me on, and I set myself to work hard enough to avoid having to repeat a year. In this way, I moved up to the sixth grade without the least interest in my studies.

Unfortunately, we were now constantly changing classes and had different teachers instead of just one. As a result, I was almost always separated from her and did practically no work - so much so that the next year I found myself back in a boarding school in the small village of Cunlhat, which is about thirty kilometers from Ambert.

It was even worse there than it had been at Puy-en-Velay. We were all crammed into a tiny dormitory that was barely heated. and worst of all, there was virtually no discipline. So the biggest and strongest boys enforced their own law. I think that is where I developed such a hatred of violence.

One day, fed up with being bullied by boys against whom no disciplinary measures were ever taken, I took to the road on foot, determined to cover the thirty kilometers that separated me from my maternal home. Nobody noticed my departure, and when the school principal caught up with me in his car, I had already walked nearly ten kilometers.

To my great delight, I was kicked out of the school and sent back to the Catholic brethren at Ambert in the middle of the school year as a day boy. What joy! I could now see Brigitte every day in the street. By then she was twelve, her small bosom was budding deliciously, and to me she was more beautiful than ever.

I grew less and less interested in my studies and began to taste the joys of playing truant, mainly because I did not like finding myself back among the priests, who had quickly advised my mother to have me baptized. Fortunately, she preferred to wait until I was old enough to understand, so that she could ask my opinion.

What I would have liked at that time was to become a garage mechanic because I had learned that this was a useful skill for racing drivers. My mother, who hoped I would become an engineer, wanted me at all costs to continue with my studies, so she would not allow me to become apprenticed to a garage.

This new harassment gave me the desire to write poems again, and I started pacing about in the country with a notebook in my hand instead of attending classes.

At fourteen I found myself back in boarding school once more, this time in Mont-Dore, at a grammar school where they take children not wanted by any of the other schools in the region.

I found myself in the company of a fairly interesting collection of dunces and "hard cases". It was one of the latter, a typical boarding school "big shot", who ended up being responsible for the direction I took during the next ten years of my life. His name was Jacques, and he played the electric guitar, which quite impressed me. As soon as the Christmas holidays came, I got my grandmother to buy me a magnificent guitar, and Jacques taught me a few chords. Then I started setting my poems to music and noticed that it was apparently very pleasing to those who listened. As soon as the summer holidays came, I began to enter some radio singing contests, which I almost always won.

It was also during that summer vacation that I discovered physical love for the first time - with a barmaid who had been enchanted by my songs. She was twenty years old and did not teach me much apart from the effects that the guitar can have on women.

The following year I was fifteen and wanted more than ever to live my own life. One day I took my guitar under my arm along with a small suitcase, said farewell to the boarding school with its uninteresting studies, and hitchhiked to Paris. I had two thousand old francs in my pocket and a heart full of hope. At last I was going to earn my own living, save up enough money to take my driving test at the age of eighteen and become a racing driver.

By a stroke of luck a man driving a car that had tremendous acceleration hidden beneath discreet-looking bodywork picked me up. When he told me he was a racing driver and gave me his name, I was able to tell him which car he had driven and the awards he had won. He was flattered and surprised, little known as he was, to meet a young boy who remembered all his achievements. He told me that he had once been a clown, and that he now owned a garage in the southwest. When we arrived in Paris, he invited me out to dinner and even offered me a room in the hotel where he was staying.

In the lounge, we chatted a bit with two young women who were dance hostesses in a bar and had finished their day's work. I sang some songs, and then we went to bed each with one of our charming companions. There I was truly initiated into physical lovemaking.

The next morning, I left discreetly because I wanted to find a room and some cabarets that would be interested in my songs. I did not find either and spent my second night in Paris in the subway with the tramps.

I had not a penny left, and the next morning, I was starving. I spent my day dawdling and despairing of ever sorting anything out. But that evening I saw a man playing an accordion on a cafe terrace, and the customers were throwing him coins. I decided to try the same thing, and right from the start, it worked very well. I was saved.

I lived like that for three years, often sleeping anywhere and eating a sandwich from time to time. But I made enormous progress, and one day I was hired by a small cabaret on the Left Bank. I made ten francs each night and needed fifteen for the taxi ride back to Montmartre, where I lived in a small room. Yet I had my name on the poster - although in small print! Already I was imagining my name high up on the poster in big letters, seeing the success I was having every night.

One day I met the actor Jean-Pierre Darras who advised me to take acting classes to improve my stage presence. Since I did not have the means to pay for them, he kindly arranged for me to attend a course at the National Theatre of Paris free of charge. So for three months I took the Dullin course - and then gave it up because I did not feel at all attracted to the theatre.

I used to introduce myself at the time under the pseudonym of Claude Celler, which I had chosen as a tribute to the skier and champion racing driver, Tony Sailer. I modified the spelling so that my initials would become C C. - retaining my real first name.

I began to win a lot of radio contests, and by singing in several cabarets, I was able to live reasonably well, and more importantly, to save up enough money to take my driving test at exactly eighteen, as planned.

But that was not enough to become a racing driver. First I had to make a name for myself in the hope of being hired by a major company, and for that I needed to have a competition car, participate in some races independently and, if possible, win them. A racing car is very expensive, and I had to continue saving in the hope of acquiring such a vehicle. I continued with my singing and tried to put some money aside. Many writer-composer friends had made recordings and seemed to be making a lot of money from them. So I decided to try it, having by now more than 150 songs in my bag.

The first recording firm that I approached offered me a three-year contract, which I signed. The director of the recording firm was Lucien Morisse, the director of the radio station Europe No. 1, which had launched a tremendous number of famous singers. My first record was fairly successful, and the second, thanks to a song called *Le Miel et la Canelle* (Honey and Cinnamon), was even more popular. It was often heard on the radio:

HONEY AND CINNAMON

I smell honey and cinnamon
I smell vanilla and love
I smell honey and cinnamon
Girls I'll always adore.

The first was a brunette, Margot was her name
We played the pipes as the moon lit the night
I took the road to her eyes
And followed the way to her hair.

The second was a blonde, her name was Marielle
The path around her curves I remember well
I took the road to her eyes
And followed the way to her hair.

The third was a redhead, Marion she was called
For her lovely little face and her frothy underslip
I took the road to her eyes
And followed the way to her hair.

Don't cry, my friend, for tomorrow will be spring
They are so lovely and you're not twenty yet
I took the road to her eyes
And you can travel the path to her hair.

I was giving many performances and taking part in many road shows. Everything was going well, and I even had the pleasure of being selected to participate in the Golden Rose song contest held in Antibes.

But those who were guiding me did not really want me to become too famous an artist. That stage of my life had been planned to develop my sensitivity, and to accustom me to expressing myself in public, but no more than that.

Even though the fact that I was among the contestants selected for the Golden Rose was being announced on the radio every morning, Lucien Morisse came to me one day and explained that he had to withdraw me from the contest. He said that I would understand why later, but he could not tell me more at that moment.

So, in the end, I did not participate in that Golden Rose contest but had to continue to live on what I could earn from my singing, which I realized, would never be enough to buy a car that would get me into racing.

Therefore, when I was offered the opportunity to become a representative for the company where I did my recording, I accepted immediately, convinced that I would be able to save up enough for a car in a few months.

I found myself back in Bordeaux, where I was a commercial agent in charge of fifteen regions. I stayed there for a year and left when at last I had enough money to buy myself a competition car. I just had time to break that car in before a friend wrote it off in an accident. However, I had composed new songs during the year in Bordeaux, and a wealthy friend urged me to make another record, which he would finance himself.

I spent another year living on my poetry and then, as if to make me change my lifestyle radically, I was involved in a very serious car accident.

On a very tiring tour I fell asleep at the wheel of my car and struck a wall head on, at about 100km per hour - 60 mph. More than ten people had already died at that spot. I came out of it with several fractures, but alive. I was immobilized for three months or more and my savings ran out. I was still not racing. I, who had dreamt of starting out at eighteen, had still not entered a single race by the age of twenty-two.

Having been to racing circuits many times as a spectator, I had noticed how infatuated young people were with this sport, and also the number of boys who wanted to be racing drivers without knowing how to proceed. I did not know much more than they did, and told myself that the best way for me to enter the racing scene would be to find a career that took advantage of their enthusiasm. I knew how to write, so the solution was obvious.

I would become a reporter for a sports car magazine.

I got in touch with a number of specialist magazines, but in vain because so many other young people had come up with the same idea. Then I noticed a small advertisement in the motor section of L 'Equipe from someone looking for photographer-reporters, no experience required.

I wrote, and the advertiser replied saying that my application was being considered, but that I had to send 150 francs for administrative costs. In exchange, I would receive some film to make a test report on a subject of my choice. I sent the money, got back the film, wrote the report - on a motor race, of course - and immediately sent it to the address indicated.

Very soon afterwards, I received a letter asking me to call a number in Dijon, where the head office of the firm that had placed the advertisement was situated. I met the head of the publishing company - a man of about thirty years of age who claimed to have made a fortune in photography in the United States.

He seemed to be very interested in my ideas about the creation of a sports car magazine intended for young people who hoped to become racing drivers and offered to hire me as editor-in-chief of a newspaper that was to come out in a few months' time. He showed me the factory that he was going to buy to set up his printing office, introduced me to the printer in Dijon whom he had hired to be the director, and showed me the house where my wife and I could live, at a stone's throw from my office.

I replied that it would suit me, provided I could cover and participate in races. He then told me that he was also looking for someone capable of running a competitions department, since he intended to launch the new newspaper by racing some cars painted in his own colors. That would enable me to be right where the action was, and I agreed to be the director of the competitions department for this company.

A week later, I moved from Paris to Dijon with my wife, Marie-Paul. I had been married for about three months, and she was expecting our daughter. I had met Marie-Paule in the month of June, and we had not left each other's side since the first day we met. We had married three months later, only because her family was shocked to learn that we had no intention of getting married religiously. Her family was very old-fashioned, and at first I prayed with them before meals.

My stay in Dijon, however, lasted only two months, and I received no salary. It transpired that the "rich American" who had wanted to create a newspaper had in fact just come out of prison without a penny. He had swindled sums of money ranging from 150 francs to 300 francs from more than 500 young people dreaming, like me, of becoming racing drivers or photographer-reporters.

I had worked two months for nothing, and I found myself full of ideas, but penniless. This time I decided to make a start alone in the great world of publishing. I moved to Clermont-Ferrand, close to my mother who was then looking forward to becoming a grandparent very soon, and started my own publishing house to produce a magazine in my own way. This magazine was soon born, thanks to a printer who also loved sports cars and who agreed to take the risk of extending me credit, although I could not give him any form of guarantee.

The magazine took off quickly and soon became one of the leaders in its field. I reserved for myself the most interesting task - test driving new models on the magnificent circuit of Mas-du-Clos, at Creuse, and on the road. By this means I gained entry into the world of motor sport, and cars were lent to me to race. At last my dream was becoming a reality, and what is more, I found from the start that I was a gifted competition driver, gaining many victories with cars that were unfamiliar to me.

For three marvelous years I lived like this, all the time making continuous progress with my driving technique and concentrating 100 per cent on the field that I loved - that of sports cars. I must say that I felt a real pleasure in steadily pushing back my limitations and constantly improving control of my reflexes and reactions. However, I did not care for either engine noise or the smell of burning fuel, and I dreamed of days to come when racing car manufacturers would be required to make their cars odorless and noiseless. Only then could I enjoy fully the sensation of driving at its purest level.

But all this was turned upside down towards the end of 1973.

The Encounter

On that extraordinary day, 13 December, 1973, I found myself in a crater of an Auvergne volcano, the Puy-de-Lassolas. There, as I have already described, I met for the first time an extra-terrestrial man, or more precisely, the Eloha - singular of Elohim - whom I would meet at the same place for six consecutive days and who, for about one hour each time, would dictate to me the fantastic revelations of *The Book Which Tells The Truth*.

For the first few days following this experience I must confess I wondered if I would dare tell anyone at all about it. The first thing I did was to make a neat copy of the notes that I had taken as best I could, although far too quickly as my interlocutor spoke to me. When this was finished, I sent the original manuscript to a serious publisher who to my knowledge did not publish esoteric works or science fiction. Obviously I did not want this message of such importance to humanity to be lost among collections of mysterious adventure stories or occult books that cater for people interested in alternative sciences.

Marcel Jullian, who ran the publishing house, invited me to Paris and told me that the manuscript was sensational. But he said that I must tell my life story before talking about the message, and that there might be "a few little changes to be made".

All that was absolutely out of the question. I did not want to take up a hundred pages telling my life story and then present the message that I had received, as if my personality were as important as those things which I had been asked to reveal. I wanted the message published, but only the message, even if it was not a thick book and thereby lacked interest for a publisher. So I asked Monsieur Jullian to return my manuscript. He replied that he did not have it because a reader had borrowed it, but that as soon as it was returned he would mail it to me.

I had just returned to Clermont-Ferrand when I received a telegram inviting me to return to Paris to appear in a television show named the *Great Chess Board*, presented by Jacques Chancel. He was the director of a series in the publishing house to which I had sent my manuscript. He had read it and understood that it was absolutely fantastic, whether anyone believed it or not. So I took part in the show, and the thousands of letters that I received afterwards showed that, while some laughed, many had taken what I said very seriously and wanted to help.

But days went by, and my manuscript was not returned. I sent a registered letter to the publisher, who replied that the manuscript would be sent to me, but that they had not yet found it. After ten days I went back to Paris to see if I could do something personally because nobody wanted to answer my questions any more when I telephoned to ask about the matter.

The famous designer, Courrèges, who had contacted me after the television show because he was interested, agreed to come with me to see the publisher in order to find out what exactly had become of the manuscript.

Marcel Jullian told us that the reader who had the manuscript had taken it with him on holiday, but they did not know where he was or how to reach him. The situation was becoming stranger and stranger.

In the end the manuscript was retrieved by Monsieur Courrèges, and he returned it to me personally. I still wonder if it had really been lost or just put away to prevent it from being published. If that publishing house really mislaid the manuscript so easily, then I would discourage other authors from sending their originals to them.

Alarmed by the mishap and by the growing pile of letters from people interested in buying the book containing the message as soon as it was published, Marie-Paule offered to leave her nursing job to help me with the publishing and distribution of this exceptional document.

I accepted because I was sure that this way, I would have permanent control over the use of these writings. Since it was incompatible with the seriousness of the mission that I had been given, I immediately stopped working for the sports magazine, and in the autumn of 1974, the book finally rolled off the printing press.

The shock to my nervous system caused by this unforeseen upset in my life had given me stomach pains and almost brought on an ulcer. All winter I suffered from a serious case of gastritis. No medication was effective, and it was only after I decided to take it easy by doing some meditation and breathing exercises that the pains vanished, as if by magic.

In June, I had been on a television show hosted by Philippe Bouvard. It was called *Saturday Evening*, and sarcastic as always, Monsieur Bouvard disguised his co-host as a Martian with pink antennae and a green suit, and asked me if he looked like the person I had met.

But many people, interested by the little I had been able to say, wrote to Philippe Bouvard, reproaching him for his lack of seriousness. Confronted by the thousands of letters he received, he decided to invite me back to do another show where I would be able to say a little more. Convinced that I would not be allowed to say enough, I decided to hire the Pleyel Hall for a date just after the television show and to announce to interested viewers that I would give a talk there in a few days' time. I hired a hall to seat 150, with an option on another to seat 500, as I did not know how many people would want to bother to come and listen to me.

In the end, more than 3,000 people came. Quite obviously we could only accommodate 500 in the hall I had booked, and when these seats were filled, we advised the others that I would give another talk in a few days in the great hall with 2,000 seats. Obviously, many people were not happy to leave, some of them having traveled several hundred kilometers.

In the end, everything went well, and I found that a great number of people were ready to help and support me, apart, of course, from those cynics whose questions, by virtue of their superficiality, I was able to show up as ridiculous.

Even though I had dreadful stage fright, much more than I had ever had when singing, everything went without a hitch, and the answers to the most difficult questions seemed to come to my lips by themselves. I really felt help coming from above, just as the Elohim had promised me. I had the impression of listening to myself give answers that I could not possibly have come up with alone.

The second talk took place a few days later. I was afraid that those who had not been able to get into the hall the first time would not come back, and that I would therefore find myself stuck with a very expensive hall nearly three quarters empty especially since there had not been any publicity about it since the television program, except for a short, three-line paragraph in *France Soir*, the only newspaper that would agree to publicize this second talk.

In the end, well over two thousand people came, and the hall was full. It was a triumph. From this time onward, I did not have any further doubts about the success of my mission.

The Public Talks

From the month of September 1974 onwards, over the course of some forty lectures, I was able to see which questions came up most frequently. I also saw the membership of MADECH rising constantly, as regional offices formed in all the big towns of France around the most dynamic and active members.

I also saw some reporters pursuing their craft honestly and well, their job being to inform the public by writing or saying exactly what they had seen or read about. However, some like those from the newspaper, *Le Point*, wrote lies. Even after registered letters were sent to remind them that they had to rectify an inaccurate article in conformity with the right to respond, they did not do so properly.

Others, like those at the newspaper, *La Montagne*, simply refused to inform their readers that I was giving a talk in Clermont-Ferrand and exploited the fact that they were the only daily newspaper in that region. Their news director had in fact met me and said that never would my activities or I be mentioned in his newspaper. All this was because they did not like the fact that when I appeared initially on television, I had not first informed them before talking to a major French broadcasting organization - a sad story and a fine example of freedom of speech. They even refused to run a paid advertisement announcing that talk, although in the same newspaper there were full-page advertisements for pornographic movies.

As for the newspaper, *Le Point*, it simply transformed an excursion of MADECH members to the place where the encounter had occurred into a broken appointment with the Elohim.

These tricks were played in an attempt to ridicule an organization trying to get off the ground. It is evidently easier and less dangerous for a newspaper with an extensive readership to do this to a new organization like MADECH than to the Church, with its 2,000 years of usurpation.

But the day will come when those who have tried to hide or twist the truth will regret their mistakes.

2

THE SECOND ENCOUNTER

The Sighting of July 31st, 1975

It was during June 1975 that I decided to resign as president of
MADECH, first of all because it seemed that the movement could
now manage very well without me, and secondly because I thought I
had made a mistake in structuring the organization in accordance
with a 1901 law that likened the movement, which is of such
importance to humanity, to a petanque club or a war veterans'
association.

I thought it was necessary to create a movement more in harmony
with the fantastic message the Elohim had transmitted to me. This
required a movement that respected to the letter what our creators
had advised - namely geniocracy, humanitarianism, the renunciation
of all deistic religious practices, and so on.

Any association based on that 1901 law ran contrary to the meaning
of the Elohim's message by definition, at least in the way we had
structured it. Since all members of such an association could vote, we
were not respecting the principles of geniocracy, according to which
only the most intelligent people may take part in making decisions.
So I had to correct this fundamental mistake, not by going so far as
to abolish MADECH, but rather by transforming it, pending more
effective modification of its structure. This would not run contrary to
the regulations of the 1901 law.

In this way, MADECH would become an organization that would support the real movement that I was going to create with its most open-minded members - in effect, a congregation of MADECH guides. This new association would bring together those people who wished to open others' minds to infinity and eternity and become guides for humanity by scrupulously applying what was required in the Elohim's message. So, in a society seeking to close people's minds in every way with deistic religions, soporific education, unthinking television programs and petty political battles, I was going to try to initiate people who would go out into the world and attempt to open the minds of others. Thus MADECH[23] would retain its importance by becoming a support organization that would be the first point of contact for those discovering the Elohim's message. It would be made up of practicing members, and the congregation of guides was going to be a movement made up of "monks" guiding those practicing members.

I knew that there were people among the MADECH members who were quite capable of managing the organization, and I received confirmation of this during the elections to the administrative council. My replacement as president, Christian, was a physicist with a promising future, and the rest of the council was made up of people who were all equally representative and competent.

It was also in the month of June that François, one of the most devoted MADECH members and one of the most open-minded, came to see me in Clermont-Ferrand. I told him about my desire to find a country house in as secluded a place as possible, in order to rest a little and calmly write a book in which I would relate all that had happened to me prior to 13 December 1973, before anyone could invent a lot of nonsense about my past. He told me that he had a farm in an out of the way place in Périgord, and that if I liked the area, I could spend a month or two there, and even stay as long as I wished, since nobody lived there.

We immediately drove off to visit the place, and inspired by the peace and quiet that I found there, I decided to stay for two months.

After two weeks, I was enjoying it so much that I seriously considered settling there more permanently.

François came back to join us at the end of July, and we started planning the move for the day after a celebration meeting at Clermont-Ferrand on the 6th of August. I still had not decided for sure because I was afraid I might fail in my mission somehow if I moved away from the place of my marvelous encounter. However, on July 31st, while my wife Marie-Paule, Francois and I were out getting some fresh air, we saw what must have been an enormous craft passing silently and with jerky movements almost over the house.

At times it moved with unimaginable speed, but it also stopped suddenly several times, proceeding in a zigzag pattern like this about 500 meters from where we stood. I was delighted that other people were with me to witness the event, and an indescribable feeling of happiness came over me. François told me that the hairs on his head stood on end from emotion. To me, it was an obvious sign of the Elohim's consent to my moving to that area.

The next morning I noticed that I had a strange mark on the bicep of one arm, close to the fold of my elbow. I did not immediately make the connection to the sighting of the day before, but later many people told me that it could only have been a mark made by the Elohim. It was a red circle about three centimeters in diameter, its circumference was five millimeters thick, and inside it were three smaller circles.(Fig.1)

This mark stayed the same for the next two weeks, then the three circles in the middle merged into one, making two concentric circles.(Fig.2) Then, after another two weeks, the two circles disappeared, leaving a white spot on my arm, which I still have. I wish to emphasize the fact that I never suffered from that mark, and that I did not feel the least itching during the entire time I had it. Some open-minded scientists to whom I showed the mark speculated that it could have been made while a sample was being taken with the help of a perfected laser.

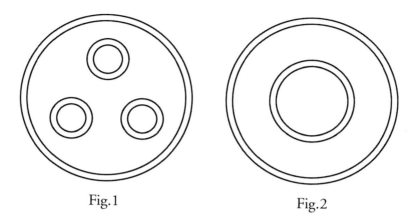

Fig. 1   Fig. 2

The reunion of August 6th finally took place as planned in the crater of Puy-de-Lassolas, near Clermont-Ferrand, and at that meeting a splendid feeling of fraternity and harmony prevailed.

I had decided to hold this gathering of MADECH members on this date without really knowing why, but in fact the Elohim had guided me because on the day of the meeting some members informed me that it was the thirtieth anniversary to the day of the atomic bomb explosion at Hiroshima, and that it was also a Christian holiday, the Transfiguration.

Fools will say that it was a coincidence.

After that meeting, some MADECH members helped me to move, and I settled down to live in Périgord.

The Message: Part Two

On October 7th, at around eleven o'clock at night, I felt a sudden urge to go out and look at the sky. I dressed warmly because it was rather cool and set out walking in the dark. I was going in a certain direction without being conscious of it, and suddenly felt the need to go to a spot that François had shown me during the summer - a deserted place between two brooks and surrounded by forest. It was called the Roc Plat. I reached it around midnight, half wondering what I was doing there, but following my intuition since I had been told that I could be guided telepathically.

The sky was magnificent, and stars were shining everywhere, for there was not a single cloud to be seen. As I stood watching the shooting stars, the whole countryside suddenly lit up, and I saw a huge ball of fire, like a spark, appear behind some bushes. I moved towards the place where the ball of fire had appeared, filled with a tremendous joy, as I was almost certain of what I was going to find.

The same craft that I had seen on six occasions in the month of December 1973 was there in front of me, and the same person I had met two years earlier came towards me with a smile full of kindness. I noticed one difference right away. He no longer had on the spacesuit that had seemed to make a halo around his face the first time. After all the time I had spent trying to make the world understand that I was indeed telling the truth, I was wonderfully happy to see once more the person who had been responsible for turning my life upside down. I bowed before him, and he spoke.

'Stand up and follow me,' he said. 'We are very satisfied with you and with everything you have done for the past two years. It is now time to pass on to the next stage, since you have proven to us that we can trust you.

These two years were in fact just a trial. You can see that today I have no protection around my face, and that my craft appeared to you all at once and was not equipped with flashing lights. All of that was only intended to reassure you, so that I would appear in a way that corresponds to the image that you generally have of space travelers. But now that you are sufficiently evolved not to take fright, we won't use such approach techniques any more.'

Following him inside the craft, I noticed that its interior looked very similar to what I had found at our first meeting - walls with the same metallic appearance as the outside, no control board or instruments, no portholes, and a floor made of a translucent blue substance on which stood two armchairs. These were made of a transparent material that reminded me a little of inflatable plastic chairs, but without feeling unpleasant.

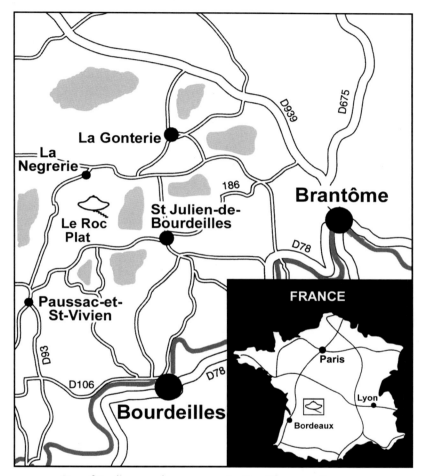

Site of Rael's second encounter: Le Roc Plat, near Brantome, Perigord region, October 7th, 1975

He invited me to sit down in one of the two chairs, settled into the other, and asked me not to move. He then pronounced a few words in an incomprehensible language, and I seemed to feel the machine rock slightly. Then all of a sudden, I felt a sensation of severe cold, as if my whole body were turning into a block of ice, or rather as if thousands of ice crystals were penetrating all the pores of my skin, right down to the marrow of my bones. It lasted a very short time, a few seconds perhaps, and I felt nothing after that.

Then my companion rose and said: 'You may come, we have arrived.'

I followed him down the small stairway. The craft stood motionless in a metallic-looking circular room about fifteen meters in diameter and ten meters high. A door opened, and my guide told me to go in and undress completely. After that, I would receive further instructions. I went into a new circular room that did not have the slightest angle and must have been about four meters in diameter. I undressed, and a voice told me to go into the room that was in front of me.

At that moment a door opened, and I went into a room similar to the one where I had left my clothes, but it was long and a little like a corridor. Along the length of that corridor I passed under lights of different colors in turn. The voice then told me that by following the arrows painted on the floor, I would arrive in yet another room where a bath awaited me.

In this next room I did indeed find a sunken bathtub. The water was lukewarm, just right, and discreetly perfumed. The voice advised me to satisfy my personal needs, which I did, and then it asked me to drink the contents of a glass located on a small shelf by the metallic wall. It was a white liquid deliciously savored with almonds, and very cold. Then some soft, pajama-like clothes that felt like silk were offered to me. They were white, very close fitting, and had been laid out ready for me on another shelf. At last a final door opened, and I found my guide again. He was escorted by two people who were of similar appearance to him but with different features, and they were every bit as welcoming.

I rejoined them in a huge hall where I found wonder after wonder. It was arranged on several levels and must have measured 100 meters in diameter. It was covered by an absolutely transparent dome, so transparent that at first sight it was not clear even that it was a dome.

Thousands of stars studded the dark sky, and yet the entire hall was brightly lit with a soft, natural looking light, as if it were midday. The floor was covered with furs and shaggy carpets of astounding, enchanting colors. The most admirable works of art were everywhere, each one more beautiful than the last, and some had animated and changing colors. Elsewhere there were plants - some bright red and others blue, as beautiful as exotic fish but several meters tall. Background music was playing that sounded like an organ and a musical saw, with occasional choirs and bass voices producing extraordinary vibrations.

This music made the flowers bend and sway in rhythm, and they changed colors with each change of musical style.

Every time someone spoke, the music grew softer so that we could hear each other without difficulty and without having to raise our voices. The air was perfumed with a thousand scents that also changed with the music and our positions in the room. The whole area had been designed with about ten angled corners, which were separated at different levels and each corner had a particular character. A small stream meandered through all this.

My guide's two companions were showing him great respect, and the next thing he said to me was: 'Follow me. We shall make ourselves comfortable, since I have many things to tell you.'

I followed him to a group of armchairs and sofas made of a very soft black fur, where all four of us sat down. There my guide spoke again:

'Today I am going to give you a second message that will complete the one that I dictated to you in December 1973. You don't have anything to take notes with, but don't worry, everything that I say to you will remain engraved in your mind, because here we have a technique that allows you to remember everything you hear.

First of all, we wish to congratulate you for all that you have done over the past two years, but we also wish to warn you that the rest of your mission may be more difficult. But never be discouraged in any case, because you will be rewarded for your efforts, whatever happens now.

To begin with, we must correct a passage in the first message we gave you that you wrongly transcribed concerning an eventual intervention on our part to destroy humanity. It must be made clear that we will not intervene. Humanity is now arriving at a turning point in its history, and its future depends only on itself. If you can control your aggressiveness towards each other and your environment, then you will reach a golden age of interplanetary civilization, in which universal happiness and fulfillment will be realized. If, on the other hand, your civilization gives way to violence, then it will destroy itself, either directly or indirectly through all this.

No scientific or technical problem is insurmountable for human genius, as long as human genius is in control. But someone with a deficient brain can threaten worldwide peace, just as a person of genius can bring the world happiness.

The sooner you set up geniocracy, the sooner you will remove the possibility of a cataclysm caused by people with minds that are not very evolved. In the event of a cataclysm destroying humanity, only the people who follow you will be saved, and they will have to repopulate the devastated Earth when all the danger has been dispersed, as happened in Noah's time.'

Buddhism

My guide continued:

'Buddhism explains that at the time of death, the soul of the dead person must be vigilant enough to escape numerous devils, otherwise it will be reincarnated and fall back into the cycle. On the other hand, if it manages to escape those infamous devils, it will be liberated from the cycle and attain a state of bliss through awakening.

In fact, this is a very good description, which applies not to the individual but to humanity as a whole. It must resist those devils, which can make it fall back into the cycle each time it is in a position to choose. Those "devils" are aggressiveness directed against our fellow human beings or against nature, and the "state of bliss through awakening" is a golden age of civilization in which science serves the people, thus producing an earthly paradise, where the blind can see and the deaf can hear by scientific means.

If humanity is not sufficiently wary of these devils, it will fall back into the cycle of reincarnation, where it must start all over again from a primitive state and advance progressively towards a more evolved society in a hostile world, with all the suffering which that entails.

That is why we can find the swastika in our symbol, as in numerous ancient writings, which signifies "the cycle". It is the choice between paradise, which the peaceful use of science makes possible, and the hell of returning to the primitive stage where humanity submits to nature instead of dominating and benefiting from it.

In a way, this is natural selection at the cosmic level for species that are capable of leaving their planet. Only those who perfectly control their aggressiveness can reach this stage. The others self-destruct as soon as their scientific and technological levels permit them to invent weapons powerful enough to do so. That is why we never fear those who come from elsewhere to contact us. Thousands of contacts have confirmed this absolute rule in the universe - people capable of escaping their planetary system are always peaceful.

When a species is capable of leaving its own solar system, it means that it has overcome the "progress-destruction cycle" that can occur when mastery of its own aggressive tendencies is lacking. At the same time that you discover powerful energy sources allowing you to travel beyond your own solar system, you also become capable of creating offensive weapons of irreversible destructive power.

Your region of the terrestrial globe, France, is already on the right track in its attempt to unite Europe, and it should be the first country without an army. France would thus set an example for the entire world. Its military professionals would then lay the foundation for a peacekeeping European army, eventually transforming it into a world peace corps. Instead of being the guardians of war, the military would then be the guardians of peace, a title deserving infinitely more respect.

It is necessary for an important country to show the way for others to follow, and France's neighboring countries will not invade her just because she has abolished compulsory military service and is using her professional army in the service of the Europe that she is trying to construct.

On the contrary, this would very quickly cause other countries to follow suit and pursue the same path taken by your country. Once Europe is united militarily, creating a single European currency can unite its economy.

Then the same process could be applied throughout the world, adding as we have already told you in the first message, a single world language that would become compulsory in every school on Earth. If one country must show the way, then France is that country. It is by advocating a "deterrent force" that we accumulate the arms of our own destruction.

With each country wishing to deter some other country, and in practice never quite knowing which one, an unfortunate action could then threaten to transform that "deterrent force" into a force of intervention, which could be fatal to the whole world.

It is through the past that humanity views the future. This is a mistake. We should instead be critical of the past and build the present for the future, rather than build the present on the basis of the past. You must understand that barely thirty years ago, people of countries that are now advanced were still primitive. You are only just emerging. There are millions of people on Earth who are still primitive and incapable of seeing something in the sky as anything other than a "divine" manifestation. Moreover, you know that deistic religions are still very strong in all the economically less-developed countries.

You must not revere people for their age, but for their intelligence, while seeing to it that old people have a pleasant life. Our distant ancestors should not be respected, and furthermore they should be seen as an example of poor, limited, primitive people who were unable to open themselves to the universe, and who were capable of handing down only very few things of value from one generation to the next.'

Neither God nor Soul

My guide went on to say:

'The more primitive a society is, the more deistic religions will flourish within it. This fact is actually cultivated by visitors from other planets, who have no other way of peacefully visiting worlds that have not yet overcome their aggressiveness.

If you reach the stage where you become evolved visitors on primitive worlds, you will be forced to use such a system, which is in fact very amusing and involves passing yourselves off as gods in their eyes. In fact, this is extremely easy since, for primitive people, if you come from the sky, you can only be divine. Of course, you must lay it on a bit thick to be respected and pleasantly received, which does no harm. We continue to make appearances on Earth to see if this still works and to see the reactions of public authorities, governments, and the press. We often amuse ourselves quite a lot...

As we have already explained to you in the first part of this message, there is no God, and obviously, no soul. After death there is nothing, unless science is used to create something. As you know, it is possible to recreate a dead organism from one of the organism's cells, which contains its physical and intellectual blueprint. We have noted that an organism loses a few grams at the moment of its death – in fact this is merely the energy that all living things have available to them, which is eliminated at that moment. As you know, energy, like matter, has weight.

You also know that we have discovered that there is organized, intelligent life on the level of the infinitely small, quite certainly as evolved as we are and comparable to what we are ourselves. We have been able to prove this.

From there, we have discovered that the stars and planets are the atoms of a gigantic being, which itself certainly contemplates other stars with curiosity. It is also highly likely that the people living on the infinitely small levels of the infinitely large person and his fellow creatures have known periods when they believed in an immaterial "God".

You must fully understand that everything is in everything. At this moment in an atom of your arm, millions of worlds are being born and others are dying, believing or not believing in a "God" and a soul, and when a millennium has gone by for you, the gigantic being of whom the sun is an atom has only had the time to take one step.

Time is, in fact, inversely proportional to the mass, or rather to the level of the form of life. But everything in the universe is alive and in harmony with the infinitely large and the infinitely small.

The Earth is alive like all the planets, and for the small growth that is humanity, it is difficult to notice this because of the time lag due to the enormous difference in mass, which prevents you from perceiving its palpitations. Nor could one of our red blood cells, or better still, one of the atoms that make up our body imagine that it forms, with its peers, a living being.

Finally, whatever happens to each individual, the universal balance remains constant. But if we want to be happy at our level, we must live in harmony with the infinitely large, the infinitely small, and with our fellow human beings.

No argument aiming to support the existence of any type of god or soul can be sustained when we glimpse, however briefly, at the infinite nature of the universe. No heaven could exist in any particular place because, since the universe is infinite, it cannot have a center. Besides, as I have already explained, there cannot be any communication between an infinitely large entity and a universe of infinitely small entities, because the difference in mass is too great, thus creating a difference in the flow of equivalent time.

Finally, if one can imagine an immortal soul escaping from the body after death - an image that is very poetic but rather naive since it comes from the minds of primitives - one cannot imagine where it would go, given that the universe is infinite.

The quantity of energy that flies off at the time of death disperses in a random way, losing all identity as it blends with all the energies suspended in the surrounding air. That identity is obviously engraved only in organized matter, such as the cells of a living being that has just died. This matter is organized according to the blueprint, which the genes of the male and the female determined at conception while creating the first cell.

With regard to the origin of life on Earth, some people might say: "Your explanation doesn't change a thing, since you cannot say what there was at the very beginning."

This is a foolish comment, which proves that the person who makes it has no awareness of infinity, which exists in time as well as in space. There is neither a beginning nor an end to matter, since "nothing is lost, nothing is created, everything is transformed," as you have already heard it said. Only the form of matter can change according to the wishes of those who have reached a scientific level, which allows them to accomplish this.

It is the same for the infinite levels of life. That is what the second part of our emblem represents. The Star of David, which is composed of two intertwined triangles, means "as above, so below." With the swastika, which signifies that everything is cyclic, in the middle of a six-pointed star, you have our emblem, which contains all the wisdom in the world. You can also find the two symbols together in ancient writings like the *Bardo Thodol* or Tibetan *Book of the Dead*, and in many other writings as well.

It is evidently very difficult for a finite human brain to be conscious of infinity, which explains the need to limit the universe in time and space by belief in one or several gods that are made responsible for everything.

Indeed, those who cannot reach a sufficient level of human understanding towards the universe have trouble accepting the notion of infinity, which makes humanity nothing exceptional, but merely people situated at a particular time and place in the infinite universe.

People obviously prefer things to be well defined, well framed, limited in a way, in the image of their own minds. Those who ask themselves if it is possible that there is life on other planets are the best example of those limited minds, and we liked very much the comparison you made during one of your lectures, likening such people to frogs at the bottom of their own pond wondering whether there was life in other ponds.'

Paradise on Earth

'You could very soon live in a genuine terrestrial paradise if only the technology that you have at your disposal today were made to serve human well-being, instead of serving violence, armies, or the personal profit of a few.

Science and technology can totally liberate humanity, not only from the problem of hunger in the world, but also from the obligation to work to live, since machines can quite easily look after the daily chores by themselves, thanks to automation.

Already, in some of your most modern factories, where it used to take several hundred people to build one car, now only a single individual is needed to oversee a computer that commands and carries out all the car building operations. In the future, even that one person will be unnecessary. Workers' unions are not happy about this because factories are in less and less need of personnel and are letting more and more workers go. This is not normal - these fantastic machines which do the work of 500 people should enable those 500 to really live, rather than enrich only one person, their boss.

No individual should be in the service of another, nor work for anyone for a salary. Machines can easily do all the chores and take care of all the work, enabling people to dedicate themselves to the one thing for which they were created - to think, create and blossom. That is what happens on our planet. Your children must no longer be raised according to the three primitive precepts of work, family, and country. On the contrary, they should be brought up following the principles of fulfillment, freedom, and universal fraternity.

"Work" is not sacred when it is motivated only by the need to earn just enough to live a laborious life of hardship. It is even terribly degrading to sell oneself, and one's life, in order to eat, by doing jobs that simple machines could do.

The "family" has never been anything but a way for ancient as well as modern supporters of slavery to force people to work harder for an illusory family ideal.

Finally, "patriotism" is still only a supplementary means of creating competition between people and urging them to perform their sacrosanct work with greater ardor each day.

What is more, those three concepts - work, family, and country - have always been supported by primitive religions. But now, you are no longer primitive people. Shake off all those dusty old principles and make the most of your life on Earth, which science can transform into paradise.

Do not be taken in by those who speak to you of potential enemies and allow armament factories to compel underpaid workers to produce destructive weapons that bring profits to big industrialists. Do not be taken in by those who speak to you in horror of the falling birthrate, because young people understand that they need not have so many children, and that it is better to have fewer so they can be happier, as they won't be too numerous on Earth.

Do not be taken in by those who constantly brandish remarks under your nose, saying things like "neighboring peoples are multiplying and could become a threat." They are the same people who support the stockpiling of nuclear weapons under the pretext of "deterrence".

Finally, do not let yourself be taken in by those who tell you that military service enables you to learn how to use a gun and that "it can always be useful", while they continue to pile up nuclear missiles.

They want to teach you violence, to teach you not to be afraid of killing a person like yourself, using the excuse that he is wearing a different uniform, and training you until it becomes a mechanical reflex after repeated practice against training targets.

Do not be taken in by those who tell you that you must fight for your country. No country deserves it. Do not be influenced by those who say to you: "What if enemies invade our country, shouldn't we defend ourselves?" Answer that non-violence is always more efficient than violence.

It is not proven that those who died for France were right, no matter how hostile their aggressors were. Look at the triumph of Gandhi in India.

Such people will tell you that you must fight for your liberty, but they forget that the Gauls lost their war against the Romans, and that the French are no worse off for being descendants of the conquered, having benefited from the civilization of the conquerors. Live rather in fulfillment, freedom and love, instead of listening to all those narrow-minded, aggressive people.

The most important aid you have to help you reach a long and lasting universal peace is television, the source of a genuine planetary awareness that makes it possible to see what goes on every day all over the globe and realize that the "barbarians" who live on the other side of the border have all the same joys, the same sorrows and the same problems as yourselves. It also records the progress of science, the latest artistic creations, and so on.

Of course, it is important to ensure that this wonderful tool of diffusion and communication does not fall into the hands of people who would use it to condition masses of people by providing biased information.

But you really can consider television to be the nervous system of humanity, which enables each individual to be aware of the existence of others and to see how they live. It also prevents the spread of distorted ideas about others that create a fear of strangers. Long ago there was fear of the neighboring tribe, then fear of the neighboring village, of the neighboring province, and of the neighboring state.

There is currently a fear of the neighboring race, and if this no longer existed, there would be fear of potential aggressors coming from another planet.

It is necessary to reverse this attitude and be open to everything that comes from the outside, because all fear of strangers is proof of a primitive level of civilization. In this sense, television is irreplaceable and is possibly the most important development of any civilization because, in the same way as radio, it enables all those isolated cells of humanity, which people are, to be informed at all times of what the others are doing. As already indicated, it works exactly as the nervous system does in the body of a living being.'

The Other World

'You are probably wondering where you are,' my guide said. 'In fact, you are now on a base located relatively close to the Earth. In the first message, you noted that we traveled seven times faster than the speed of light. That was true 25,000 years ago when we landed on Earth. Since then, we have made much progress, and we now travel through space much faster. It only takes us a few moments to make the journey that used to take us almost two months in those times, and we continue to progress. If you will now follow me, we will take a little trip together.'

I rose and followed my three guides. We went through an airlock, and in a vast room I noticed a craft similar to the one that had brought me from Earth, but it was far larger. The exterior must have been about twelve meters in diameter, and inside it had four seats facing each other instead of just two. We sat down as before, and again I felt the same sensation of intense cold, but it lasted much longer this time - about ten minutes. Then the craft rocked slightly, and we stepped out through the trap door exit.

Before me a paradisiacal landscape unfolded, and in fact I cannot find any words to describe my enchantment at seeing huge flowers, each more beautiful than the last, and animals of unimaginable appearance were walking among them. There were birds with multicolored plumage, and pink and blue squirrels with the heads of bear cubs climbing in the branches of trees that bore both enormous fruits and gigantic flowers.

About thirty meters from the spacecraft, a small group of Elohim was waiting for us, and behind the trees I was able to make out a group of buildings that resembled brightly colored shells harmonizing perfectly with the vegetation. The temperature was very mild, and the air was perfumed with countless scents of exotic flowers. We walked towards the top of a hill, and a marvelous panorama began to appear. Innumerable small streams wound through the lush vegetation, and far off an azure sea sparkled in the sun.

Reaching a clearing, I discovered with great astonishment a group of people similar to me, by which I mean people resembling those who live on Earth, not Elohim. Most of them were naked or wore robes made of multicolored silks. They bowed respectfully before my three guides, and then we all sat down.

Our armchairs seemed to have been carved in the rock and were covered with thick furs that always remained fresh and comfortable despite the warmth. Some people came out of a small cave located right next to us and approached us carrying trays piled high with fruits, grilled meats accompanied by the most incredible sauces, and drinks of unforgettable flavors.

Behind each guest two of the men who carried the trays were kneeling ready to satisfy the slightest wish of those who were eating. The latter would ask them for whatever they desired without even looking at them.

During the meal some marvelous music had started up, from where I could not tell, and young naked women with figures as sculptural as those of the waiters started to dance with incomparable grace on the surrounding lawn.

There must have been some forty guests who were similar to people from Earth in addition to my three guides. There were white, yellow and black men and women who all spoke a language I could not understand that resembled Hebrew.

I was sitting to the right of the Eloha whom I had met two years earlier, and to the left of the six other Elohim. Facing me sat a young bearded man, very handsome and very slim. He wore a mysterious smile and an expression filled with fraternal feeling. To his right was a man with a noble face sporting a black beard that was very thick and very long. To his left was a more corpulent man with an Asian face. He had a shaven head.

Meeting the Ancient Prophets

Towards the end of the meal, my guide started to speak to me:

'In my first message I told you of a residence located on our planet where people from Earth can continue to live thanks to the scientific secret of eternity that is based on a single cell.

Among those people are Jesus, Moses, Elijah and so on. This residence is, in fact, very large, since it is an entire planet where the members of the Council of the Eternals live as well. My name is Yahweh, and I am the president of that Council of the Eternals.

There are currently 8,400 people from Earth living on the planet where we are at this moment. They are people who during their lives reached a sufficient level of open-mindedness towards the infinite, or who enabled humanity on Earth to progress from its primitive level through their discoveries, their writings, their ways of organizing society and their exemplary acts of fraternity, love or selflessness. Alongside them live the 700 Elohim members of the Council of the Eternals.

Whatever the outcome of your mission may be, you have your place reserved here among us in this veritable little paradise where everything is easy, thanks to science, and where we live happily and eternally. I can truly say eternally, for, as on Earth, we created all life here, and we are starting to understand perfectly the life of the infinitely large, that is to say, of the planets, and we can detect signs of old age in solar systems, which will enable us to leave this planet in time to create another paradise elsewhere, as soon as we grow anxious about its survival.

The eternals who live here, both people from Earth and Elohim, can fulfill themselves as they wish, without having to do anything but that which pleases them - scientific research, meditation, music, painting, and so on.

Or they can do nothing at all if they feel like it.

The servants you saw carrying the dishes a little while ago, as well as the dancers, are just biological robots. They are created according to the same principle we used to create the people of Earth in a totally scientific way, but they have been limited and are absolutely submissive to us.

They are also incapable of acting without orders from us, and they are very specialized. They have no aspirations of their own, and no pleasure, except those that are necessary for their specialization. They grow old and die like us, but the machine that makes them can make far more than we need. They are incapable of feelings or suffering, and cannot reproduce themselves.

Their life span is similar to ours - that is to say about 700 years with the help of a small surgical intervention. When one of them must be destroyed due to old age, the machine that created them produces one or several others, depending on our needs. They come out of the machine ready to function and with their normal height, for they have neither growth nor childhood.

They only know how to do one thing: obey people from Earth and Elohim, and they are incapable of the slightest violence.

They can all be recognized by the small blue stone that both males and females wear between their eyes. They take care of the dirty jobs and do all the work that is uninteresting. They are produced, taken care of and destroyed underground where, in fact, all the maintenance work is done by such robots and by enormous computers that regulate all the problems of nourishment, supply of raw materials, energy and other things. We each have on average ten robots at our service, and as there are slightly more than 9,000 of us - Earth people and Elohim - there is a permanent total of 90,000 male and female robots.

Like the Elohim members of the Council of the Eternals, the eternals from Earth are not allowed to have children. They agree to have a small operation, which makes them sterile, but that sterility can easily be reversed. The purpose of this measure is to prevent undeserving beings from joining us in this marvelous world. However, male and female eternals can unite freely just as they wish, and all jealousy is eliminated.

In addition, men who wish to have one or more companions outside the relationships of equality that exist between eternal men and women, or who do not want to live with a woman on an equal basis, may have one or more totally submissive biological robot women with the exact appearance that is desired. The same goes for women, who can have one or several totally submissive biological robot men.

The machine that generates the robots gives the entity that it creates the exact physical appearance and specialization desired. There are several types of ideal women and men in terms of shape and physiognomy, but the height, measurements, shape of the face, and so on, can be modified as one wishes. One can even submit the picture of someone particularly admired or loved on Earth, for example, and the machine will produce an exact replica. Thus the relationships between eternals of both sexes are much more fraternal and respectful, and the unions between them are marvelously pure and high.

Because of the extraordinary level of open-mindedness of those admitted here, there is never any problem between them. The majority spends almost all of their time meditating, doing scientific research, making inventions and artistic compositions, and creating all sorts of things. We can live in different cities with multiple architectural styles in greatly varied sites that we can modify at will. People fulfill themselves as they wish, only doing what they like to do.

Some find pleasure in doing scientific experiments, others in playing music, others in creating ever more amazing animals and others in meditating or doing nothing other than making love while enjoying the numerous pleasures of this heavenly environment, drinking from the innumerable fountains and eating the juicy fruits that grow all over the place at all times. Here there is no winter; we all live in a region comparable to your equator, but as we can scientifically control the climate, it is always fine weather and not too hot. We make the rain fall during the night when and where we wish. All this, and many other things, which you could not understand all at once, makes this world a true paradise. Here, everyone is free and can be so in total safety, for all deserve that liberty.

All things that bring pleasure are positive, as long as that pleasure is not harmful to anyone in any way. This is why all sensual pleasures are positive, for sensuality is always an opening up to the outside world, and all such opening is good. On Earth you are only just emerging from all those primitive taboos that tried to make anything to do with sex or nudity appear evil, whereas nothing could possibly be purer.

Nothing is more disappointing for your creators than to hear people say that nudity is something bad: nudity, the image of what we have made. As you can see, almost everyone is naked here; and those dressed in clothes wear them either because they are works of art given to them by other eternals who made them with their own hands, or for elegance and decoration.

When people from Earth are admitted to this world of the eternals, they start out by receiving some chemical education so that nothing surprises them, and they have a good understanding of where they are and why.'

My guide, Yahweh, paused for a moment, and then said: 'You are now sitting directly opposite the man who, 2,000 years ago, was given the responsibility of creating a movement to spread more widely the message we had left originally to the people of Israel - a message which would enable you to be understood now. I am referring to Jesus, whom we were able to recreate from a cell that we had preserved before his crucifixion.'

The handsome, bearded young man seated opposite offered me a smile full of fraternity.

'To his right is Moses, on his left Elijah, and to the left of Jesus sits the one remembered on Earth by the name of Buddha. A little further on you can see Mohammed, in whose writings I am called Allah, because out of respect they did not dare call me by name. The forty men and women present at this meal are all representatives of the religions created after our contacts on Earth.'

All those present looked at me with expressions that were very friendly and amused, probably because they were remembering their own surprise upon arriving in this world.

My guide continued: 'Now I will show you some of our installations.' He stood up, and I followed him. He invited me to put on a very wide belt bearing a huge buckle. He and his two friends had buckled on the same kind of adornment. Immediately I felt myself being lifted up from the ground and carried at about twenty meters above the grass, almost level with the tops of the trees, at a very great speed, maybe a hundred kilometers per hour, maybe more, towards a precise location. My three companions were with me, Yahweh in front and his two friends behind. One curious thing, among others, was that I did not feel any wind at all whipping against my face.

We landed in a small clearing, quite close to the entrance of a small cave. We were in fact still being carried by our belts, but only at a height of one meter above the ground, and moving more slowly. We passed through galleries with metallic walls and arrived in a vast hall, in the center of which was an enormous machine surrounded by about ten robots recognizable by the ornaments on their foreheads. There, we landed on the ground again and took off our belts.

Yahweh then spoke: 'Here is the machine that makes biological robots. We are going to create one of them for you.'

He made a sign to one of the robots located near the machine, and the robot touched certain parts of it. Then he made a sign for me to move close to a window measuring about two meters by one meter. In a bluish liquid I then saw the form of a human skeleton vaguely taking shape. Its form grew clearer and clearer, finally becoming a real skeleton. Then some nerves took shape and formed over the bones, then some muscles and finally some skin and hair. A splendid athlete was now lying there in a position where moments earlier there had been nothing.

Yahweh spoke again: 'Remember in the Old Testament, this description in *Ezekiel*, Chapter 37:

> Son of man, can these bones live?...there was a noise, and behold a shaking, and the bones came together, bone to his bone. And when I beheld, lo, the sinews and the flesh came up upon them, and the skin covered them above...and the breath came into them, and they lived, and stood up upon their feet, an exceeding great army.

The description that you will give of this will certainly be similar to Ezekiel's - apart from the noise, which we have been able to eliminate.'

Indeed, what I had seen corresponded perfectly to Ezekiel's description. Following this, the prostrate figure had slid to the left and disappeared completely from my sight. Then a trap door opened, and I saw the creature whose rapid creation I had witnessed, lying on a very white fabric.

He was still immobile, but suddenly he opened his eyes, got up, came down the few steps that separated him from our level, and after exchanging a few words with another robot, came up to me. He gave me his hand, which I shook, and I felt his skin soft and warm.

'Do you have a picture of a loved one with you?' Yahweh asked.

'Yes,' I answered, 'I have a picture of my mother in my wallet, which I left in my clothes.'

He showed it to me, asking if it was the right one. When I agreed that it was, he gave it to one of the robots, who inserted it in the machine and touched parts of it. Through the window I witnessed yet another creation of a living being. Then, as the skin started to cover the flesh, I realized what was happening: they were making an exact replica of my mother from the picture I had provided. Indeed, a few moments later, I was able to kiss my mother, or rather the image of my mother as she had been ten years before, for the picture I had provided had been taken about ten years previously.

Yahweh then said to me: 'Now allow us to make a very small puncture in your forehead.'

One of the robots came towards me, and with the help of a small device similar to a syringe, pricked my forehead so lightly that I hardly felt it.

Then he inserted the syringe in the enormous machine and touched other parts of it. Again an entity was formed before my eyes. As the skin covered the flesh, I saw another 'me' take shape, little by little. Indeed, the being that emerged from the machine was an exact replica of myself.

'As you can see,' Yahweh told me, 'this other you is not wearing the small stone on his forehead, which is characteristic of the robots and that the replica of your mother also had.

From a photo we can only make a replica of the physical body, with no psychological personality or almost none, whereas from a sample cell like the one we took from between your eyes, we can create a total replication of the individual whose cell we took, complete with the memory, personality and character. We could now send the other you back to Earth, and people would not notice a thing. But we are going to destroy this replica immediately, for it is of no use to us.

At this moment there are two of you who are listening to me, and the personalities of these two beings are beginning to be different, because you know that you are going to live, and he knows that he is going to be destroyed. But that does not bother him, since he knows he is nothing but yourself. This is more proof, if proof is needed, of the non-existence of the soul - or a purely spiritual entity unique to each body - in which certain primitive people believe.'

After that we left the room that housed that enormous machine, and through a corridor we entered another room containing other equipment.

We approached another machine.

'In this machine are kept the cells of malevolent people who will be recreated to be judged when the time comes. They are cells from those on Earth who preached violence, wickedness, aggressiveness and obscurantism. Despite having in their possession all the elements to understand where they came from, these people did not have the sense to recognize the truth. They will be recreated to undergo the punishment they deserve, after being judged by those whom they made to suffer or by their ancestors or descendants.

You now fully deserve a rest. This robot will be your guide and will provide you with anything you desire until tomorrow morning. We will then have a few more words to say to you, and afterwards we will accompany you back to Earth. Between now and then you will have a foretaste of what awaits you when your mission is completed on your planet.'

The next moment a robot approached and saluted me respectfully. He was tall, athletic looking, dark, beardless and very handsome.

A Foretaste of Paradise

The robot asked me if I wanted to see my room, and after I agreed, he handed me one of the belts used for travelling. I found myself being transported above the ground again, and when I landed once more, I found myself in front of a house that looked more like a scallop shell than a residence. The interior was entirely carpeted with shaggy furs, and there was a huge bed, at least as big as four Earth beds, looking as if it had been sunk into the ground. It was recognizable only by the different colored furs covering it. In one corner of the huge room, there was a massive sunken bathtub as big as a swimming pool, surrounded by vegetation of marvelous shapes and colors.

'Would you like some female companions?' asked the robot. 'Come, you can make your own choice.'

I put my belt on again and found myself transported back in front of the machine used for making robots. A luminous cube appeared in front of me.

I was shown to an armchair facing the cube and given a helmet. When I had settled down, a magnificent young brunette with marvelously harmonious proportions appeared three-dimensionally within the luminous cube. She moved in such a way as to show herself off, and had she not been in a cube floating one meter above the ground, I would have thought she was real.

My robot asked me whether she pleased me and if I wished to have her shape altered or her face modified. I told him that I considered her perfect.

He replied that aesthetically speaking, she was the ideal woman, or rather, one of the three types of ideal women, as defined by the computer according to the taste of the majority of residents on the planet. But I could ask for any modification that I desired.

At my refusal to change anything whatsoever about that magnificent creature, a second woman, this time blonde and alluring, appeared in the luminous cube. She was different but just as perfect as the first one. With her I could not find anything to alter either. Finally, a third young female, this one a redhead more sensual than the first two, appeared in the strange cube. The robot asked me if I cared to see other models, or if these three ideal types of my race would be enough for me. I answered quite naturally that I thought these three people were extraordinary.

At that moment, a magnificent black woman appeared in the cube, then a very fine slender Chinese female, and then finally another voluptuous young Asian woman.

The robot asked me which person I desired to have as a companion. Since I answered that they all pleased me, he went towards the robot making machine and spoke for a moment with one of his peers. Then the machine was set in motion, and I understood what was about to happen.

A few minutes later I was back at my residence with my six companions. There I had the most unforgettable bath that I have ever had, in the company of those charming robots, totally submissive to all my desires.

Afterwards my robot guide asked if I wished to make some music. When I said 'yes', he took out a helmet similar to the one I had put on before the projection of the female robot models.

'Now,' he said, 'imagine some music that you would like to hear.'

Immediately a sound was heard, corresponding exactly to music that I had been thinking about, and as I constructed a melody in my head, that same melody became a reality with sounds of an amplitude and a sensitivity that were more extraordinary than any I had ever heard. The dream of every composer had become a reality - the ability to compose music directly without having to go through the laborious process of writing and orchestrating.

Then my six adorable companions began dancing to my music in a most voluptuous and bewitching way.

After a while, my robot asked me if I would also care to compose some images. Another helmet was given to me, and I sat in front of a semi-circular screen. I set myself to imagining certain scenes, and these scenes at once became visible on the screen. I was seeing, in fact, an immediate visualization of all the thoughts that came to me. I started thinking about my grandmother, and she appeared on the screen. I thought of a bouquet of flowers, and it appeared; and when I imagined a rose with green spots, it appeared as well. This machine actually made it possible to visualize one's thoughts instantaneously, without having to explain them. What a marvel!

'With training one can create a story and have it played out,' my robot told me. 'Many performances of this kind, performances of direct creation, are held here.'

Finally, after a while, I went to bed and spent the most extravagant night of my life with my marvelous female companions.

The next day, I got up, took another perfumed bath, and then a robot served us a delicious breakfast. Then he asked me to follow him, for Yahweh was expecting me. I put on the transportation belt again, and soon found myself in front of a strange machine, where the president of the Council of the Eternals was waiting for me.

It was not as large as the one that created robots but was still very big. A sizable armchair was embedded in its center.

Yahweh asked me if I had spent a pleasant night, and then explained to me: 'This machine will awaken certain faculties that lie dormant within you. Your brain will then be able to exploit its full potential. Sit down here.'

I sat down in the chair that he indicated, and a sort of shell covered my skull. I thought I was losing consciousness for a moment, and then it felt as if my head were about to explode.

I saw multicolored flashes pass before my eyes. Finally, everything stopped, and a robot helped me out of the armchair. I felt terribly different.

I had the impression that everything was simple and easy.

Yahweh spoke again: 'From now on, we will see through your eyes, hear through your ears, and speak through your mouth. We will even be able to heal through your hands, as we already do at Lourdes and in many other places in the world, for some sick people who deserve our help because of their will to radiate the message we have given you, and because of their efforts to acquire a cosmic mind by opening themselves to infinity.

We observe everyone. Huge computers ensure a constant surveillance of all people living on Earth. A mark is attributed to everyone depending on whether their actions during their life led towards love and truth or towards hate and obscurantism.

When the time comes to evaluate, those who went in the right direction will have the right to eternity on this heavenly planet, those who achieved nothing positive yet were not evil will not be recreated, and for those whose actions were particularly negative, a cell from

171

their body will have been preserved, which will allow us to recreate them when the time comes, so that they can be judged and suffer the punishment they deserve.

You who are reading this message, understand clearly that you can have access to this marvelous world, this paradise. You will be welcomed, you who follow our messenger, Claude Rael, our ambassador on the path to universal love and cosmic harmony, you who will help him realize what we will ask of him - for we see through his eyes, hear through his ears, and speak through his mouth.

Your idea of creating a congregation of guides for humanity is very good. But be strict with regard to their selection, so that our message will never be deformed or betrayed.

Meditation is indispensable for opening one's mind, but asceticism is useless. You must enjoy life with all the strength of your senses, for the awakening of the senses goes together with the awakening of the mind.

Continue to play sports if you wish and if you have the time, for all sports and games are good whether they develop musculature, or better still, self-control as do motor racing and motorbike racing.

A person who feels alone can always try to communicate telepathically with us, while trying to be in harmony with the infinite; he or she will feel an immense sense of well being. What you have advised concerning a gathering of people who believe in us in each region on Sunday mornings at about eleven o'clock is very good. Few members are presently doing this.

Mediums are useful, so seek them out. But balance them because their gifts as mediums - which are only gifts of telepathy - unbalance them, and they begin to believe in magic, the supernatural, and other incredibly stupid things, including an ethereal body, which is a new way of trying to believe in the soul which does not exist. In fact, what they are actually doing is tuning into people who lived several centuries ago, and whom we have recreated on this paradisiacal planet.

There is an important revelation, which you may now make. The Jews are our direct descendants on Earth. That is why a specific destiny is reserved for them. They are the descendants of "the sons of Elohim and the daughters of men", as mentioned in *Genesis*.

Their original mistake was to have mated with their scientific creations. That is why they have suffered for such a long time.

But for them the time of forgiveness has come, and they will now be able to live peacefully in their recovered country, unless they make another mistake in not recognizing you as our messenger. We wish our embassy on Earth to be built in Israel on a tract of land given to you by the government. If they refuse, you may build it elsewhere, and Israel will undergo a new punishment for not having recognized our messenger.

You must devote yourself entirely to your mission. Do not worry, you will be able to support your family. People who believe in you and therefore in us must help you. You are our messenger, our ambassador, our prophet, and in any case you have your place reserved here among all the other prophets.

You are the one who must gather together people of all religions. For the movement you have created, the Raelian Movement, must be the religion of religions. I insist that it is indeed a religion, although an atheistic religion, as you have already understood.

Those who help you we shall not forget, and those who cause you trouble we shall not forget either. Do not be afraid and fear no one, for whatever happens you have your place among us. As for those who lose confidence, shake them up a little.

Two thousand years ago, those who believed in our messenger, Jesus, were thrown into a lion's den. Today, what do you risk? The irony of fools? The sneers of those who haven't understood anything and prefer to keep to their primitive beliefs? What is all that compared to a lion's den? What is all that compared with what awaits those who follow you? Truly it is easier than ever to follow one's intuition.

In the Koran, Mohammed, who is among us, has already said on the subject of prophets:

The moment for men to give account is drawing near; and yet in their nonchalance they are turning away (from their creator).

No new warning comes from their creator whom they ignore and laugh at. And their hearts are amused by it.

Those who do evil comfort themselves secretly by saying: Is not this man only a mortal as we are?

It is a jumble of dreams. He made it all up himself. He is a poet. But let him bring a miracle like those who were sent in time past.
Koran, Sura 21: 1-5.

Already Mohammed had to suffer the sarcasm of some, and Jesus had to suffer it as well. When he was on the cross, some said:

If thou be the Son of Elohim, come down from the cross..
Matthew 27: 40.

And yet, as you have seen, Jesus is in marvelous shape and will be for all eternity, as is Mohammed and all those who followed them and believed in them. On the other hand, those who criticized them will be recreated in order to receive their punishment.

The computers that monitor those people who have no knowledge of this message are linked to a system that, at the time of death and from a distance, automatically samples a cell from which they may be recreated if they deserve it.

While waiting to build our embassy, create a seminary for the Guides of the Raelian Movement near the area where you reside. It is there that you who are our prophet, the Guide of Guides, will be able to train those responsible for spreading our message all over the Earth.'

The New Commandments

Yahweh then said:
'Those who wish to follow you will apply the laws I am now about to give you:

You will appear at least once in your lifetime before the Guide of Guides so that he may transmit your cellular plan through manual contact, or have it transmitted by an initiated Guide, to the computer that will take this into account at your life's assessment hour of judgment.

You will think at least once a day of the Elohim, your Creators.

You will try to radiate the message of the Elohim around you by every possible means.

You will, at least once a year, give a donation to the Guide of Guides that is equal to at least one percent of your annual income, in order to help him devote himself full time to his mission and travel around the world to spread this message.

You will, at least once a year, invite the Guide of your region into your home, and you will gather at your place people who are interested in hearing him explain the message in all its dimensions.

If the Guide of Guides should disappear, the new Guide of Guides will be the one who has been designated by the former Guide of Guides. The Guide of Guides will be the guardian of the embassy of the Elohim on Earth and will be able to live there with his family and with the people of his choice.

You, Claude Rael, you are our ambassador on Earth, and the people who believe in you must provide you with the means to accomplish your mission.

You are the last of the prophets before the Judgement; you are the prophet of the religion of religions, the demystifier and the shepherd of shepherds. You are the one whose coming was announced in all the religions by the ancient prophets, our representatives.

You are the one who will bring back the shepherds' flock before the water is spilled, the one who will bring back to their creators those they have created. Those who have ears may hear, those who have eyes may see. All those who have their eyes open will see that you are the first prophet who can be understood only by scientifically evolved beings. All that you speak of is incomprehensible to primitive peoples.

This is a sign that will be noticed by those whose eyes are open - the sign of the Revelation, the Apocalypse.'

To the People of Israel

'The State of Israel must give some territory located near Jerusalem to the Guide of Guides so that he may build there the residence, the embassy of the Elohim. The time has come, people of Israel, to build the New Jerusalem as it was foreseen. Claude Rael is the one who was foretold. Reread your writings and open your eyes.

We wish to have our embassy among our descendants, and the people of Israel are the descendants of the children born of the unions between the sons of Elohim and the daughters of men.

People of Israel, we removed you from the clutches of the Egyptians, and you did not show yourselves worthy of our confidence; we entrusted you with a message destined for all humanity, and you jealously kept it instead of spreading it abroad.

You have suffered for a long time to pay for your errors, but the time of forgiveness has come, and as was foreseen, we have said: "To the North give them up and to the South do not hold them back." I have gathered your sons and daughters "from the ends of the Earth," as was written in *Isaiah*, and you have been able to find your country again. You will be able to live there in peace if you listen to the last of the prophets, the one who was foretold to you, and if you help him to accomplish what we ask of him.

This is your last chance, otherwise another country will welcome the Guide of Guides and build our embassy on its territory, and that country will be close to yours; it will be protected and happiness shall prevail, and the State of Israel will be destroyed once more.

You, child of Israel who has not yet returned to your ancestral lands, wait before returning there to see if the government will agree to our embassy being built there. If they refuse, do not return, and you will be one of those who will be saved from the destruction and whose descendants will one day be able to find the promised land again, when the time comes.

People of Israel, recognize the one foretold to you, give him the territory to build our embassy, and help him build it. Otherwise, as happened 2,000 years ago, it will be constructed elsewhere, and if it is constructed elsewhere, you will be dispersed once again. If, 2,000 years ago, you had recognized that Jesus was indeed our messenger, all the Christians in the world would not be Christians, but Jews. You would not have had problems, and you would have remained our ambassadors. But instead this task was given to other people who took Rome for their base.

Two thousand years ago, you did not recognize our messenger, and it was not Jerusalem but Rome that shone. Now you have a new chance for it to be Jerusalem once more. If you do not seize it, another country will shelter our embassy, and you will no longer have any right to the land we had chosen for you.

There, I have finished. You will be able to annotate all this by yourself once you have returned to Earth. Now enjoy this paradise a while longer, and we will take you back for you to complete your mission before returning to us for good.'

I remained there for several more hours, enjoying the many pleasures of that world, meandering amongst numerous fountains and enjoying the company of the great prophets whom I had met the day before during meditation sessions. Then, after a last meal taken with the same people as the day before, I found myself once again in the large vessel, which set me down at the observation station. From there I retraced my route of the day before, and found myself with my clothes in the small craft, which dropped me off where it had picked me up, at Roc Plat. I looked at my watch - it was midnight.

I returned home, where I immediately set to work to write down all that I had been told. Everything was perfectly clear in my mind, and I was surprised to find that I was writing it all at one stroke, recalling without any hesitation the sentences I had heard. The words remained as if engraved in my mind just as I had been told they would at the beginning.

When I finished the account of what had happened, I began to feel very clearly that something had been released inside me. This had never happened before. I began writing again, all the while observing closely what I was putting down as if I was simultaneously discovering it as a reader. I was writing, but this time I did not feel like the author of what was appearing on the paper. The Elohim were starting to speak through my mouth, or rather, to write with my hand.

What was being written before my eyes dealt with all areas that a person is confronted with during his or her lifetime, and the right way to react when faced with these problems. It was, in fact, a code of life - a new way of behaving in the face of life's events, of behaving like a man, that is to say, as an evolved being, and therefore trying in every way to open one's mind to infinity and to place oneself in harmony with it.

These great rules dictated by the Elohim, our creators, "Our Fathers who are in Heaven", as our ancestors used to say without really understanding, are all set forth here in the following pages in their entirety.

3

THE KEYS

Introduction

For thousands of years those opposed to enlightenment and reform have effectively imprisoned our minds in straitjackets. These writings, however, are the keys we can use to set ourselves free.

The door that seals the human mind is fastened by many locks, all of which must be opened at the same time if one wants to be able to free it towards the infinite. If only one key is used, the other locks will remain fastened, and if they are not all kept open at the same time, then while the second lock is being freed, the first one will close again, preventing the door from opening.

Human society is afraid of what it does not know, and so it is afraid of what lies behind this door - even if it is happiness gained through knowledge of the truth. Therefore, it applies pressure to prevent people from even partly opening this door because society itself prefers to remain in a state of misfortune and ignorance.

This is yet another obstacle found on the threshold of the doorway through which the mind must pass to free itself. But, as Gandhi said: 'It is not because no one sees the truth that it becomes an error.' So if you attempt to open this door, ignore the sarcasm of those who have not seen anything - and of those who having seen, pretend not to see, because of their fear of the unknown.

Also if opening the door seems too difficult for you, ask for help from a Guide, since Guides have already opened the doors of their own minds and know the difficulties involved. They will not be able to open your door for you, but they will be able to explain the different techniques that will enable you to succeed. Besides, they are living witnesses of the happiness that can be achieved by opening the door, and they prove wrong those who are afraid of what lies behind the door.

Humanity

In every situation, we must always consider things in regard to four levels:
- In relation to infinity;
- In relation to the Elohim, our parents and creators;
- In relation to human society;
- And finally, in relation to the individual.

The most important level is that relating to infinity, for it is in relation to this level that all things must be judged - but always with one constant factor: love. This means taking others into account, who must be given love, because we must live in harmony with infinity, and to do this we must live in harmony with others, because they are a part of infinity as well.

Then we must take into account the advice given by our creators, the Elohim, and act in such a way that human society listens to the advice of those who created it.

Then we must take into account society, which makes it possible for individuals to blossom on the path of truth. But although society must be taken into account, it should not be followed; on the contrary, society must be helped to emerge from its primitive straitjacket by regular questioning of all its habits and traditions, even if these are supported by laws that are only there to try and imprison our minds in shackles of obscurantism.

Finally, we must take into account the fulfillment of the individual. Without this the mind does not reach its full potential, and it is impossible to harmonize yourself with infinity and become a new man if you are not fulfilled.

Birth

You must never impose any religion whatsoever on a child, who is still but a larva, unable to understand what is happening to itself. So you must neither baptize nor circumcise children, nor submit them to any action that they have not themselves accepted. You must wait for them to reach the age when they can understand and choose, and if a religion appeals to them at that time, then leave them free to adhere to it.

A birth should be a festive occasion, for the Elohim created us in their image to be capable of reproducing ourselves. By creating a living being, we preserve our own species and respect the work of our creators.

A birth should also be an act of love, achieved in harmony as far as sounds, colors and temperature are concerned, so that the human being who is emerging into life develops the habit of being in harmony.

You must immediately develop in children the habit of respecting the liberty of others, and when they cry at night, go to them discreetly but without their realizing that crying has brought them the comfort of being tended. On the contrary, you must go to them and look after them when they make no sound, and not go to them - at least not with their being aware of it - when they cry. That way they will get used to everything going better when they are in harmony with their surrounding. "God helps those who help themselves".

In fact, parents must understand that as soon as a child is born, it is first of all an individual, and that no individual should be treated like a child.

Even our creators do not treat us like children, but as individuals. That is why they do not intervene directly to help us solve our problems but allow us to overcome the obstacles that we encounter by working things out for ourselves as responsible individuals.

Education

The little creature who is still just the larva of a human being must, in its infancy, grow accustomed to respecting the liberty and the tranquillity of others. Since little children are too young to understand and reason, corporal punishment[28] should be rigorously applied by the person bringing them up, so that they suffer when they cause suffering or disturb others by showing a lack of respect.

This corporal punishment[28] should be applied only to very young children, and then, in keeping with the child's growing power to reason and understand, it should be phased out progressively and eventually stopped altogether. From the age of seven, corporal punishment[28] should be quite exceptional, and from the age of fourteen, it should never be applied.

You will use corporal punishment[28] only when punishing a child for not respecting the freedom and tranquillity of others or yourself.

You will teach your child to blossom, and you will teach him or her always to have a questioning attitude towards those things which society and its schools want to inculcate. You will not force your child to learn things that are not useful, and you will let him or her follow any desired path because, do not forget, the most important thing is his or her fulfillment.

You will teach your child always to judge things in the right order with respect to infinity, with respect to our creators, with respect to society, and with respect to itself.

You will not impose any religion on your child, but instead impartially teach him or her the various beliefs that exist throughout the world - or at least the most important ones in chronological order: the Jewish religion, the Christian religion and the Muslim religion. You will try to learn the major trends of thought of the eastern religions, if you can, so that you are able to explain them to your child. Finally, you will explain to him or her the main points of the message given by the Elohim to the last of the prophets.

Above all, you will teach your child to love the world in which it lives, and through this world, our creators.

You will teach him or her to open up to infinity and try to live in harmony with infinity.

You will teach your child about the marvelous work accomplished by the Elohim, our creators, and constantly seek ways for humanity to become capable of repeating, some day, what our creators have done - namely creating other humanities elsewhere by scientific means.

You will teach your child to consider itself a part of the infinite - that is, both immense and minute at the same time. "From dust were ye made, and dust ye shall become."

You will teach your child that the wrong done to others cannot be repaired by any confession or absolution once it is done, and that it must not be thought that when death is near, it is sufficient to begin to believe in the Elohim or any god in order to have the right to eternal life.

You will teach your child that we are judged by what we do throughout our lives, that the path which leads to wisdom is long, and that it certainly takes a whole lifetime to master it sufficiently. A person who has not gone in the right direction throughout life will not gain the right to scientific resurrection on the planet of the eternals just by making a sudden late change to the right path - that is, unless that person's regret is truly genuine, and he or she acts with great sincerity, making up for lost time, striving to be forgiven by those who were harmed, and devoting all his or her means to bringing them love and happiness.

All this will still not be enough for the person who has made others suffer, for even if he or she is forgiven by them and gives them love, the errors will have been erased, but nothing positive will have been accomplished.

This person will then have to set out anew, bring happiness to new people whom he or she has never harmed and help those who spread the truth, the guides.

But it is too late for someone who has regrets only at the moment of death or shortly before. This person will not be forgiven.

Sensual Education

Sensual education is one of the most important things, and yet at the moment, it scarcely exists at all.

You will awaken the mind of your child, but you will also awaken his or her body, for the awakening of the body is linked to the awakening of the mind. All those who seek to numb the body are also numbing the mind.

Our creators have given us our senses so that we use them. The nose is meant for smelling, the eyes for seeing, the ears for hearing, the mouth for tasting, and the fingers for touching. We must develop our senses so as to get more enjoyment from all the things around us, which our creators put here for us to enjoy.

A sensual individual is far more likely to be in harmony with infinity, because such a person can feel it without having to meditate or reflect.

Meditation and reflection will enable that individual to understand this harmony better and to radiate it all around himself or herself by teaching it.

To be sensual means to let your environment give you pleasure. Sexual education is very important as well, but it only teaches the technical functions and uses of the organs. Sensual education, on the other hand, teaches us how to gain pleasure from our organs purely for pleasure's sake, without necessarily seeking to use them for their utilitarian purposes.

To say nothing to your children about their sexual organs is wrong, and although it is better to explain what they are for, this is still not enough.

You must explain how they can gain pleasure from them.

To explain only their function would be like telling them that music is for marching to, that knowing how to write is helpful only for penning letters of complaint, or that movies are useful only for giving audio visual courses, and other such nonsense. Fortunately, thanks to artists and through the awakening of our senses, we can obtain pleasure from listening, reading or looking at works of art that were made for no other reason than to give pleasure. The same goes for the sexual organs. They are not just for satisfying our natural needs or for ensuring reproduction, but also for giving pleasure to others and ourselves. Thanks to science, we have finally emerged from the days when showing one's body was a "sin", and when sexual intercourse brought its own punishment - the conception of a child.

Now thanks to contraceptive techniques, sexual union is freely possible without it becoming a definitive commitment - or even a possible one. You will teach your child all this without shame, but on the contrary, with love, clearly explaining that he or she was made to be happy and blossom fully - that is to say, to enjoy life with all the senses and with their full force.

You must never be ashamed of your body or of your nakedness, for nothing displeases our creators more than to see those they created feeling ashamed of the appearance that has been given to them.

You will teach your children to love their bodies and every part of the Elohim's creation, because in loving their creation, we love them as well.

Each one of our organs was created by our parents, the Elohim, so that we might use it feeling not shame, but happiness at using something for which it was designed. If the act of using one of our organs brings pleasure, it means that our creators wish us to have that pleasure.

Every individual is a garden that should not be left uncultivated. A life without pleasure is an uncultivated garden. Pleasure is the fertilizer that opens up the mind. Asceticism is useless unless it is a temporary ordeal designed to train the mind to dominate the body. But once we have succeeded in the ordeal that we have set ourselves - which must always be limited in time - we should once more enjoy the pleasures of life.

Asceticism can be accepted as the fallow period of that garden which is an individual - that is to say, a momentary pause in the search for pleasure, which enables us to appreciate it better later on.

You will accustom your children to having more and more freedom by always treating them as individuals. You will respect their tastes and inclinations, as you would like them to respect your own. Make sure you realize that your child, male or female, is what it is, and that you will not be able to make it what you want, just as it will not be able to make you what it wants you to be. Respect your child so that it respects you, and respect its tastes so that it respects yours.

Fulfillment

Self-fulfillment should be sought according to one's tastes and aspirations, without any preoccupation with what others think, as long as no one else is being hurt.

If you feel like doing something, first see that it does no harm to anyone, then do it without worrying about what others think of it. If you feel like having a sensual or sexual experience with one or several other individuals, whatever sex they may be, you may behave as you desire, as long as they agree. Everything is permitted on the path to fulfillment in order to awaken the body, and hence the mind.

We are at last emerging from those primitive times when women were seen merely as instruments of reproduction belonging to society. Thanks to science, women are now free to fulfill themselves sensually, without having to fear the punishment of pregnancy. At last, woman is truly the equal of man, since she may enjoy her body without living in fear of having to endure alone the undesired consequences of her acts.

Conceiving a child is something too important to be left to chance. Therefore, do so only by choice after mature consideration in a marvelous act of love, being fully aware of what you are doing, and being certain that you truly wish it, because a child cannot become a successful individual unless it is truly desired at the very moment of conception.

The moment of conception is the most important because it is at that time that the first cell, and therefore the plan of the individual, is conceived.

This moment must therefore be desired, so that the first cell may be created in perfect harmony, with the minds of the two parents thinking strongly and consciously of the human being that they are conceiving. This is one of the secrets of the new individual.

If you are looking only for the fulfillment of your body, and therefore of your mind, use the means that science has put at your disposal, starting with contraception. Only conceive a child when you yourself are fulfilled, so that the life you conceive may be the fruit of the union of two fulfilled individuals.

To reach fulfillment, use the means that science has provided to enable you to awaken your body to pleasure without any risks. Pleasure and procreation are two different things that must not be confused. The first is for the individual, and the second is for the species. It is only when the individual is fulfilled that he or she can create a fulfilled human being.

If by accident you have conceived a child without desiring it, use the means that science puts at your disposal - abortion. A child who was not desired at the moment of conception cannot blossom fully, since it was not created in harmony. Do not listen to those who try to frighten you by talking about the physical - and especially moral - consequences that an abortion can trigger. There are none if you are treated by competent people. It's rather by keeping an undesired child, that you will be left with physical and moral disturbances that can be passed on, and that will make the child you brought into the world suffer too.

Having a child does not necessarily imply that you must be married or even live with a man. Already, many women have decided to have one or more children without marrying or living with a man. The education of a child, who is an individual right from birth, should not necessarily be provided by the parents. It would indeed often be preferable for education to be entrusted to specialized people who would contribute far more than some parents towards their children's fulfillment.

If you wish to have a child without living with a man, do as you desire. Fulfill yourself, as you would like, without worrying what others think.

If you choose to do this, do not think that you are condemned to live alone forever. Welcome the men you like, and they will serve as masculine role models for your child.

You can even decide one day to live with a man - this will not cause any problems for your child at all. On the contrary, it will contribute to his or her fulfillment. A change of environment is always positive for a child.

Society should organize itself to take charge of the education of children partially or totally, depending on the parents' wishes. Those parents who want to work should be able to leave their children in the custody of competent people, and those who want their children to receive an education given entirely by such individuals should be able to entrust their children completely to establishments created for this purpose. In this way, if you give birth to a child you desired, but afterwards you separate from your companion, or for any other reason you no longer desire the child, you will be able to entrust your child to society, so that it may be brought up surrounded by the harmony necessary for its fulfillment, for a child who grows up in surroundings where it is not really and truly wanted cannot blossom and be fulfilled.

Bringing up a child should be mutually fulfilling for both parent and offspring. If a child becomes a nuisance, however slight, it realizes this and fulfillment is affected. A child should therefore be kept near you only if its presence is felt to be fulfilling.

Otherwise the child should be put in establishments that society must create to encourage fulfillment and be placed there without the least regret.

On the contrary, parents should feel a profound sense of joy because they are entrusting their child to others more capable than themselves of helping each little individual to blossom.

Regular visits can even take place if the children, whose wishes are of primary importance, would like them. The people in charge of the children's education should always describe the parents as exceptional people, who placed more importance on their children's fulfillment than on their own selfish pleasure of bringing them up themselves. They did this, the children should be told, by entrusting them to people more competent than themselves.

Choose your partner freely if you desire one. Marriage, whether religious or civil, is useless. You cannot sign a contract to unite living individuals, who are bound to change because they are alive.

Reject marriage, which is only the public proclamation of ownership of a person. A man or woman cannot be the property of anyone else. Any contract can only destroy the harmony existing between two individuals.

When we feel loved, we feel free to love, but when we have signed a contract, we feel like prisoners who are forced to love each other, and sooner or later we begin to hate each other. So you will live with the person of your choice only for as long as you feel happy with him or her.

When you no longer get on well together, do not remain together, because your union will become hell. All living beings evolve, and rightly so. If the personal evolution of each individual is similar, the union lasts, but if their progress is different, then union is no longer possible. You no longer like the individual you used to like because one of you has changed. You must part from each other while retaining happy memories of your time together, instead of spoiling it with useless bickering which gives way to hostility. A child chooses clothes that fit, and when it outgrows them, they must be changed for different clothes, otherwise they will be torn to pieces. The same applies for unions; you must leave each other before being torn to pieces.

Above all, do not be worried about your child. It is better for him or her to be with only one parent in harmony than to be with both in discord, or lacking perfect harmony. Do not forget that children are, above all, individuals.

Society must make absolutely sure that old people have a happy life without any material worries. But although we must respect the elderly and do everything to make them happy, we should not listen to them just because of their seniority.

An intelligent person can give good advice at any age, but a stupid person, even if he is a hundred years old, does not deserve to be listened to for a second. What is more, such a person has no excuse, having had an entire lifetime in which to try to awaken, whereas there is still hope for a young and stupid person. But in any case, a stupid old person must still be able to live comfortably. This is a duty for society.

Death should not be an occasion for sad gatherings; on the contrary, it should be a time of joyful celebration, because it is the moment when the beloved one may perhaps reach the paradise of the eternals in the company of our creators, the Elohim.

You will therefore ask not to be buried religiously, but you will donate your body to science, or you will ask that your body be disposed of as discreetly as possible, except for the bone of your forehead - more precisely the part located above the beginning of the nose, 33 millimeters (1.3 inches) above the middle of the axis linking the pupils of your eyes. At least one square centimeter (0.4 square inches) of this bone should be sent to the Guide of Guides, so that he may keep it in our embassy on Earth.

Each person is monitored by a computer that records all their actions and will make a tally of them at the end of their life. But people who know about this message which Claude Rael is communicating will be re-created from the cells that they have left in our embassy. In their cases, re-creation will take place only if they ensure that the required part of their body is sent to the Guide of Guides after their death.

The mechanism within the computer that records the information to be used in judgement of individuals remains in operation after they learn about the message. But the mechanism that allows an automatic sampling of a cell at the moment of death is disconnected. So only those who comply exactly with what is required once they know about the message will be recreated.

Make sure that at least once in your life you see the Guide of Guides or a guide authorized by him to transmit your cellular plan to the Elohim, so that they may awaken your mind and help you to remain awakened.

In accordance with what is written earlier in this message, you will not leave an inheritance to your children, except for the family house or apartment. The rest you will leave in your will to the Guide of Guides, and if you fear your descendants might not respect your last will and testament but might try to recover your property through the courts, you will bestow it while you are alive on the Guide of Guides, in order to help him spread the message of our creators on Earth.

Those of you who remain after the death of a loved one, do not be sad and lament. Try instead to give love to those you love while they are still living, because once they are dead, what makes you unhappy is the thought that perhaps you did not love them enough, and that now it is too late.

Anyone who was good in their lifetime has the right to the Elohim's gardens for eternity and will know happiness, and anyone who was not good does not deserve to be missed.

But even if an individual is not among those chosen for re-creation, he or she does not really vanish. Death is not a very important thing, and we should not be afraid of it. It is just like falling asleep, except it is an endless sleep. Since we are a part of infinity, the matter of which we are made does not disappear. It continues to exist in the soil, or in plants, or even in animals, clearly losing all homogeneity and, therefore, all identity. This part of infinity that was organized by our creators according to a very precise plan returns to the infinite, while remaining a part of this small ball called Earth, which is alive.

Everyone has the right to live, the right to love and the right to die. Everyone is the director of his or her own life and death. Death is nothing, but suffering is terrible, and everything must be done to eliminate it. Someone who is suffering too much has the right to commit suicide. If this person's actions were positive during his or her life, he or she will be admitted to the planet of the eternals.

If someone you love suffers very much and wishes to die, but does not have the strength to commit suicide, help them to take their own life.

When science one day enables you to eliminate human suffering, then you can ask yourselves whether it is right to commit suicide or not.

Society and Government

Just as a human body has a brain to make decisions, it is essential that society also have a government to make decisions. So you will do everything you can to set up a government that practices geniocracy, which puts intelligence in power.

You will also participate in the creation of a worldwide political party advocating humanitarianism and geniocracy, as they are described in the first part of this message of the Elohim, and you will support its candidates. Only via geniocracy can humanity move fully into the golden age.

Total democracy is not good. A body in which all the cells command cannot survive. Only intelligent people should be permitted to make decisions involving humanity. You will therefore refuse to vote, unless a candidate advocating geniocracy and humanitarianism is standing for election.

Neither universal suffrage nor public opinion polls are valid ways of governing the world. To govern is to foresee, not to follow the reactions of a sheep-like population, among whom only a very small number are sufficiently awakened to guide humanity. Since there are very few awakened people, if we base decisions on universal suffrage or opinion polls, the decisions become the choice of the majority - and therefore of those who are not awakened. Such people respond in the interests of their immediate gratification, or as a result of instinctive reactions that are unconsciously confined in a straitjacket of obscurantist conditioning.

Only geniocracy, which is a selective democracy, is worthwhile. As was stated in the first part of this message of the Elohim, only people whose net level of intelligence is fifty per cent above average should be eligible to stand for election, and only those whose net level of intelligence is ten per cent above the average should be eligible to vote. Scientists are already developing techniques to measure net intelligence. Follow their advice, and act in such a way that the most precious minerals of humanity - exceptionally gifted children - may receive an education at a level appropriate to their genius, since normal education is designed only for normal children of average intelligence.

It is not the number of diplomas that one has obtained that signifies intelligence, since this only calls upon the rather uninteresting faculty of memory, which machines can replace. Intelligence in its raw state is the quality that can make peasants or workers much more intelligent than engineers or professors. This can be spoken of as common sense, as well as creative genius, because most inventions are nothing more than a matter of common sense.

As already stated, to govern is to foresee, and all the great problems that humanity is now facing prove that past governments did not have foresight and were therefore incompetent governments. The problem does not lie with the people who govern, but rather, the technique that is used to choose them: the problem is the way we select those who govern us. Basic democracy must be replaced by a selective democracy - that is geniocracy, which puts intelligent people in power. This is a very fundamental requirement.

Human laws are indispensable, and you will respect them, while seeing to it that those that are unfair or obsolete are changed. Between human laws and those of our creators, you will not hesitate one instant, as even the human judges will be judged some day by our creators.

The police will be essential for as long as it takes society to discover the medical means to eradicate violence and prevent criminals or those who infringe the freedom of others from acting out their anti-social impulses.

Unlike soldiers, who are the keepers of war, police officers are the keepers of peace, and they will remain indispensable until science has solved this problem.

In countries where compulsory military service exists, you will refuse to participate. Instead, ask to be granted the status of a conscientious objector, which will allow you to serve in a division that does not carry weapons, as is your right if your religious or philosophical convictions forbid you to kill your fellow human beings. This is the case for those who believe in the Elohim, our creators, and want to follow the directives of the Guide of Guides of the Raelian Movement.

Contrary to what many young people think, conscientious objectors are not sent to jail, but serve instead in some civilian role or in an unarmed division for a period that is double the normal duration of military service.

It is better to spend two years working in an office than to be trained for one year in techniques that enable you to kill fellow human beings.

Military service must be eliminated urgently in all the countries of the world. All professional soldiers must be transformed into guardians of world peace who work in the service of freedom and human rights.

The only system of government that is worthwhile is geniocracy applying humanitarianism. Capitalism is wrong because it enslaves people to money, benefiting a few on the backs of others. Communism is also wrong, since it places greater importance on equality than on liberty. There must be equality among people at the beginning, at birth, but not afterwards.

Although everyone has the right to have sufficient means to live decently, those who do more for their fellow human beings have the right to receive more than those who do nothing for the community.

This is obviously a temporary rule until human beings can have robots to perform all menial labor, so that they can devote themselves exclusively to their fulfillment, after having totally abolished money. In the meantime, it is shameful that while some people are dying of hunger, others throw food away to prevent prices collapsing. Instead of throwing away this food, they should distribute it to those who have nothing to eat.

Work must not be considered sacred. Everyone has the right to live comfortably, even if they do not work, and should try to fulfill themselves and blossom in whatever field attracts them. If people are organized, it will not take them long to mechanize and automate all indispensable work. Then everybody will be able to blossom freely.

If all individuals really set their minds to it, in only a few years freedom from the need to work could be attained. What is required is a marvelous burst of enthusiasm and solidarity in working for the liberation of humankind from material constraints.

All humanity's technical and scientific resources should be pooled, and all those working in these areas should truly set their minds on striving together for the well being of the entire community, rather than for vested interests. Use all the resources, which are currently wasted on military budgets or the inane development of nuclear weapons - or even flights into space. Such things could be better planned and much more easily accomplished once humanity is free of material constraints.

You have computers and electronic equipment that can better replace manpower. Put them all to work, so that this technology can truly operate in the service of humankind. In a few years you can build a completely different world. You have reached the golden age.

Do everything possible to create the biological robot that will release you from all menial labor and enable you to blossom and fulfill yourselves.

Urban development must be reconsidered, as it is described in *The Book Which Tells The Truth*. You must build very tall communal houses situated in open country, so that individual houses do not "devour" nature. Never forget that if everyone had a country house with a small garden, there would be no more countryside. These communal houses must be cities that are equipped with everything people need and be capable of accommodating about 50,000 inhabitants each.

Until the day you become creators and can re-create it yourselves, you must respect nature. By respecting nature, you respect those who created it - our parents, the Elohim.

You will never make animals suffer. You may kill them to feed on their flesh, but do this without making them suffer. Although as already indicated, death is nothing, suffering is an abomination, and you must avoid making animals suffer, as you must prevent human beings from suffering.

Nevertheless, do not eat too much meat, and you will feel better for it.

You may live on all that the land provides. You do not have to follow a special diet; you may eat meat, vegetables, fruits and other plants. But it is foolish to follow a vegetarian diet under the pretext that you do not want to live on the meat of other living creatures. Plants are alive just as you are, and suffer in the same way that you do.

You must not cause suffering to plants that are alive, just as you are.

Do not intoxicate yourself with alcoholic beverages. You may drink a little wine while eating, for it is a product of the Earth. But never intoxicate yourself. You may drink alcoholic beverages in exceptional circumstances, but in very small quantities and accompanied by solid food so that you never get drunk. Anyone who is drunk is no longer capable of being in harmony with infinity, nor able to control himself. This is something appalling in the eyes of our creators.

You will not smoke, for the human body was not made to inhale smoke. This has appalling effects on the organism and prevents total fulfillment and harmonization with infinity.

You will not use drugs. You will not drug yourself in any way, for the awakened mind needs nothing outside itself to approach infinity. It is an abomination in the eyes of our creators that people think they must take drugs to improve themselves. Human beings have no need to improve themselves because all are perfect, having been made in the image of our creators.

To say that a human being is imperfect is to insult our creators who made us in their image. But although we are perfect, we cease to be so if we think of ourselves as imperfect and remain resigned to such thoughts.

To remain perfect as the Elohim created us, we need to make an effort at every moment of the day to keep ourselves in an awakened state.

Meditation and Prayer

You should meditate at least once each day, locating yourself in relation to infinity, in relation to the Elohim, to society, and yourself. You should meditate upon awakening, so that your whole being becomes fully conscious of infinity, and you are placed in full possession of all your faculties.

You should meditate before each meal, so that all parts of your body eat when you eat; and when you nourish yourself, think of what you are doing.

Your meditation will not be a dry meditation, but on the contrary, a sensual meditation. You will let yourself be engulfed by peace and harmony until it becomes a pleasurable delight. Your meditation should not be forced labor, but a pleasure. It is better not to meditate at all than to meditate without really wanting to do so.

Do not impose meditation on your children or your family. But explain to them the pleasure that it gives and the sense of well-being that it brings, and if they then feel like meditating, try to teach them what you know.

Think intensely of the Elohim, our creators, at least once a day, and try to communicate with them telepathically. In this way you will rediscover the original meaning of prayer. If you do not know how to go about it, you can take your inspiration from the Lord's Prayer, the words of which are perfectly appropriate for communication with our creators.

At least once a week attempt group telepathic communication with the Elohim alongside other people from your region who believe in them. If possible, you should be accompanied by a Guide.

Do your very best every year to attend the meeting of all those who believe in the Elohim and in the message they have given to the last of the prophets.

TECHNIQUE FOR ATTEMPTING TELEPATHIC CONTACT WITH THE ELOHIM

Here is a model of what you could say while looking towards the sky and thinking intensely about the words:

Elohim, you are there somewhere near those stars.

Elohim, you are there, and I know you are watching us.

Elohim, you are there, and I would so much like to meet you.

Elohim, you are there, and what am I to hope to deserve a contact?

Elohim, I recognize you as our creators, and I place myself humbly at your service.

Elohim, I recognize Claude Rael, your messenger, as my guide, and I believe in him and in the message you gave him.

Elohim, I will do my best to make the message known to those around me because I know I have not done enough.

Elohim, I love all human beings as my brothers and sisters because they are made in your image.

Elohim, I am trying to bring them happiness by opening their minds to infinity and revealing to them what was revealed to me.

Elohim, I am trying to stop their suffering by placing my whole being at the service of humankind, of which I am a part.

Elohim, I am trying to use to the utmost the mind you have given me, to help humankind emerge from darkness and suffering.

Elohim, I hope that you will judge the little I have done by the end of my life to be sufficient to grant me the right to eternal life on the planet of the wise.

I love you, as you must have loved human beings to admit the best of them among your eternals.

The original French editions of the three books that comprise "The Messages", first printed in 1974, 1977 and 1979 respectively.

Rael, 1979 - shown here with a depiction of the symbol that he saw on the side of the Elohim's space-craft. Its interlocked Star of David triangles and swastika mean 'that which is above is like that which is below and everything is cyclic'.

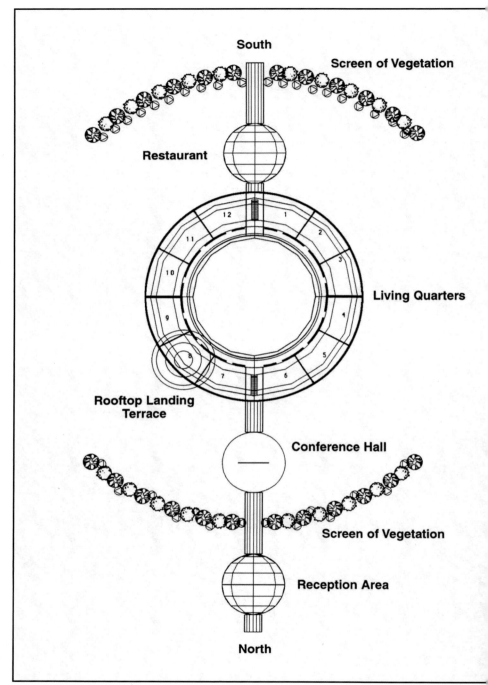

An architect's drawing of the planned extra-terrestrial embassy, based on details given to Rael during the second encounter of October 7, 1975.

A scale model of the embassy with one of the Elohim's spacecrafts on its rooftop landing pad.

'Some crop circles,' says Rael, 'are made by the Elohim to encourage humanity to build the embassy.' This one, which appeared at Cheesefoot Head, Wiltshire, England in August 1990 bears a very close resemblance to the detailed plans of the building.

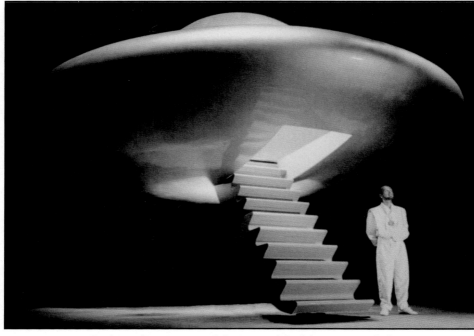

Rael standing next to a life-size model of the space-craft that
he boarded during his encounters with the Elohim.

Two examples of religious paintings containing what some might describe as UFOs.
On the left: *The Baptism of Christ* by Dutch painter, Aert de Gelder, 1710.
On the right: *The Annunciation, with Saint Emidius* by Carlo Crivelli, 1486.

This crop circle which appeared at Etchilhampton, Wiltshire, August 1, 1997 is one of many that resemble the revised Raelian symbol that was introduced by Rael in 1991.

A medallion showing the revised symbol of the Raelian Movement that Rael changed out of respect for victims of the Holocaust and in an effort to help negotiations with the Israeli government concerning the building of the Elohim's Embassy or the "Third Temple of Israel".

The Elohim's symbol - the oldest symbol on Earth - can be found on the Tibetan Book of the Dead or Bardo Thodol. Its central swastika, meaning 'well being' in Sanskrit, represents infinity in time.

Even after dedicating more than 30 years of his life to his mission, the Messenger of Infinity, Rael, continues to teach at open-mind seminars on each continent. This particular photo was taken during the Japanese summer seminar of 2005.

The Arts

Do as much as possible to encourage artists and to help your child if he or she is attracted by the arts. Art is one of the things which best enables you to harmonize with infinity. Consider every natural thing an art, and every art a natural thing. Surround yourself with artistic things, whether they appeal to your ears, your eyes, your sense of touch, smell or taste.

Everything, which appeals to the senses, is artistic. There is more than just music, painting, sculpture and all the officially recognized arts.

Gastronomy is also an art, as well as perfume making, since they both appeal to the senses. Standing above all finally, love is an art.

All art makes use of harmony, and therefore allows those who appreciate it to be taken over by something harmonious. This consequently produces the right conditions for placing oneself in harmony with infinity.

Literature is particularly important because it contributes to opening people's minds by showing them new horizons. But literature for literature's sake is just prattle: what counts is not writing beautiful sentences, but the transmission of new ideas to others through reading. Audiovisual means are even more important, for they appeal to our senses of sight and hearing at the same time. They could well replace literature, since they are more complete. Meanwhile, literature is useful for the time being.

Sensual Meditation

If you want to reach a high level of harmony with infinity, arrange a place of sensual meditation for yourself. Place in it works of art, paintings, reproductions, tapestries, posters, sculptures, drawings,

201

photographs or anything else that is intended to represent love, infinity and sensuality, for the enjoyment of your eyes.

Arrange for yourself a corner where you can sit close to the ground, on cushions, for example. Or lie down on a couch or on fur, for the pleasure of touching it. Evaporate agreeable scents and oils to please your nose. Have a tape recorder and a cassette on which you have recorded music that you like for the pleasure of your ears.

Have trays and bottles filled with food and drink that you like for the pleasure of your mouth, and invite one or several people you love, who share your tastes and with whom you feel at ease and in harmony; then feed your senses together and open your bodies in order to open your minds in love and fraternity.

If someone appeals to you physically, and you feel that it is reciprocal, invite him or her to this place. Together you can reach a sublime state of harmony, which will enable you to approach infinity by satisfying your five senses. To this state will be added the synthesis of all these pleasures - the physical union of two individuals in total harmony and in the illumination of the act of love.

Obviously, the harmony must first exist spiritually. In other words, there must be a mutual attraction between the minds, and thus, the bodies of the individuals in the way they approach and respect each other. But a spiritual love is always made sublime by a fulfilled physical love. To love is to give and expect nothing in exchange. If you love somebody, you should give yourself to this person entirely if he or she desires it.

Never be jealous, for jealousy is the opposite emotion to love. When you love someone, you must seek his or her happiness first and foremost, and in every way. To love is to seek the happiness of others, and not your own.

If the person you love is attracted to another, do not be jealous; on the contrary, be happy that the one you love is happy, even if it is because of somebody else.

Love also the person who, like you, wants to bring happiness to the person you love, and who therefore has the same goal as you. Jealousy is the fear that someone else may make the person you love happier than you do yourself, and that you may lose the one you love. But instead of feeling jealous, we should try to do as much as possible to make the person we love happy, and if somebody else succeeds better in this, we should be happy about it. What counts is not that our beloved be happy because of us but simply that they be happy, whoever is responsible.

So if the person you love is happy with somebody else, rejoice in this happiness. You will recognize the person who loves you in that he or she will not oppose your happiness with someone else.

It is your duty to love the person who loves you that much and to give him or her happiness yourself. In that direction lies the path of universal love.

Do not reject someone who wants to make you happy, for by accepting that he does so, you make him happy, and this is an act of love. Rejoice in the happiness of others, so that they may rejoice in yours.

Human Justice

Between human laws and those of our creators, you will not hesitate one instant, as even the human judges will be judged some day by our creators.

Human laws, as already stated, are essential. But they must be improved upon because they do not take love and fraternity sufficiently into consideration.

The death penalty must be abolished because no individual has the right to kill another coldly in a premeditated, organized manner. Until the time comes when through science, society is able to control the violence that occurs in some people and can cure them of their illness, you will keep criminals apart from society. Then give them the love that they have lacked, while trying to make them understand the monstrous nature of their actions. Give them also the desire to redeem themselves.

Do not mix hardened criminals - who are suffering from an illness that can be contagious - with people who have merely committed petty offenses. That way you will avoid contaminating the lesser offenders.

Never forget that all criminals are sick, and always consider them as such. We are shocked when we remember that once upon a time we used to suffocate people between mattresses if they suffered from fits of hysteria. Some day, when we are able to cure, and more importantly, prevent the sickness of crime, we will be just as shocked when we look back at how we used to execute criminals.

Forgive those who have done you harm unintentionally, and bear no grudge against those who have willingly done you harm. They are ill, for one must be ill to harm one's neighbor. Besides, think how unfortunate those people are, who do harm others, because they will not have the right to eternal life in the gardens of the Elohim.

But if someone wants to harm you or those you love, try to subdue them. If you cannot, then you have the right to defend yourself to save your own life or the lives of your loved ones. However, never strike with the intention to kill, even in legitimate defense. Try only to render the person harmless - by knocking him or her out, for example. If the blow you give turns out to be fatal, you have nothing to blame yourself for, as long as you did not have the intention to kill.

You will subdue violent people by non-violence, and if necessary, by direct action. Violent behavior is intolerable, and you will not tolerate it, even if you have to forcibly restrain violent people. But always use a non-violent force, that is to say, a balanced force applied without malicious intent, sufficient only to overcome those who try to do harm.

Any threat of violence should be treated as seriously as an actual violent deed. To threaten violence is to think it possible and to see it as an acceptable way of achieving one's goals. A person capable of threatening another with violence is as dangerous as someone who has already committed a violent act. Until we can find a medical cure for those who make such threats, they must be kept outside society, and we must try to make them understand that their behavior is dreadful.

When dealing with those who take hostages, think first of the lives of innocent people who are in the hands of the hostage-takers. People who take hostages are sick, and you should not give them what they demand. Society, in fact, must never give in to them because by doing so, you encourage other criminals to copy such actions and give credence to their threats.

All human beings must have equal rights and opportunities at birth, whatever race they may be. Discriminate against fools, however, whatever the color of their skin. All the races that populate the Earth were created by the Elohim, and must be equally respected.

Humanity as a whole must unite to form a world government, as it is written in *The Book Which Tells The Truth*. Impose also a new world language on all the school children of the entire world. Esperanto exists, and if no one proposes anything better, choose Esperanto.

Until it becomes possible to abolish money, create a new world currency to replace national currencies. Therein lies the solution to the monetary crisis. If no one can propose anything better, use the federalist system. Create a federation from all the countries of the world. Grant independence to regions, which need to be able to organize themselves as they wish.

The world will live in harmony when it is no longer composed of separate countries, but consists instead of regions united in a federation to take charge of the destiny of the Earth.

Science

Science is the most important thing of all for humanity. You will keep yourself in touch with the advances made by scientists who can solve all problems. Do not let scientific discoveries fall into the hands of those who think only of making profit, nor into the hands of the military who keep certain inventions secret in order to retain a hypothetical supremacy over illusory enemies.

Science should be your religion, for the Elohim created you scientifically.

By being scientific, you please your creators because you are acting as they do, and you show them that you understand that you were made in their image and are anxious to take advantage of all the potential that you have within you. Science must be used to serve and liberate humankind, not to destroy and alienate it. Trust those scientists who are not being manipulated by financial interests, and only them.

You may participate in sports, for they are very good for your equilibrium - particularly those sports that develop self-control. Society should also authorize violent, and even very violent, sports. These are safety valves. An evolved and non-violent society must have violent games that maintain an image of violence, enabling young people who wish it, to be violent with others who wish the same thing. This also allows others to watch these violent exhibitions and so release their aggressive energies.

You may participate in games that require thought and use of the mind. But as long as money has not been abolished, never play to win money; rather play for the pleasure of making your mind function.

You will date your writings counting the year 1946 as "year one", after Claude Rael, the last of the prophets. Then 1976 is therefore year 31 after Claude Rael, or year 31 of the era of Aquarius, or year 31 of the age of the Apocalypse, or year 31 of the golden age.

The Human Brain

We still have a long way to go in fully understanding the potential of the human brain. The sixth sense, direct perception, should be developed in young children. This is what we call telepathy. Telepathy enables us to communicate directly with our creators, the Elohim.

Numerous mediums have come to me asking what they should do, because they had received messages from what they call "the beyond", asking them to get in touch with me in order to help me, and for me to bring them "the light". Mediums are very important people because they have an above average gift of telepathy, and their minds are already on the path to an awakened state. They should try to practice meditation in order to fully master their potential.

I am eagerly waiting for all those mediums who have received such messages to get in touch with me, so that we may organize regular meetings. The true mediums who seek to be informed will all receive instructions. The power of one brain is great, but the power of several brains is infinite. Let those who have ears, hear.

Never forget that all those things, which you do not understand and which scientists cannot explain, have been created by the Elohim. The clockmaker knows all the parts of the clock he has made.

The Apocalypse

Do not forget that the Apocalypse - literally the "age of revelation" - has arrived as was predicted. It has been said that when the time comes, there will be many false prophets. You only have to look around you to see that the time has indeed come. False prophets are writers of horoscopes of which the newspapers are full, and there are also many others who reject the benefits of science and cling to every last letter of ancient writings that were the messages given by the Elohim to the primitive people of ancient times.

Such false prophets prefer to believe what narrow-minded and primitive people have fearfully copied down long ago while listening to those whom they considered to be gods because they came from the sky. They should instead believe the message of the Elohim that has been given now to people who no longer kneel stupidly before all that comes from the sky. These latter people try to understand the universe, and they can be addressed as adults.

But if you look around, you will see the crowds of fanatic and obscurantist religious sects, which attract young impressionable people thirsty for the truth.

A philosopher once said: 'Jesus came to show people the path to follow, and everybody kept staring at his finger.' Meditate on this sentence. It is not the messenger who matters, but the person who sends the message, and the message itself.

Do not go astray among the sects of the East - the truth is not on top of the Himalayas any more than in Peru or elsewhere. The truth is within you.

But if you want to travel, and you like exotic places, go to all these distant countries. You will understand then that you have wasted your time, and that what you were looking for was inside you all the time.

Travel within yourself, otherwise you are only a tourist - someone who passes by and thinks he or she will find the truth by watching others search for it within themselves. They may find it, perhaps, but those watching them certainly will not. To travel inside yourself, you do not need to take a plane.

The East has nothing to teach the West about wisdom and awakening the mind. Rather, the opposite is true. How can you find wisdom amongst people who die from hunger as they watch herds of sacred cows go by?

On the contrary, it is the West with its intellect and its science that comes to help people who, for ages, have been shackled by primitive and murderous beliefs. It is not by chance that countries in the West no longer face the same problems as those of the Third World. Where the mind rules, the body does not die of hunger. Where obscurantism prevails, the body cannot survive. Can primitive people solve the problems of famine in the world and give food to those who are starving? They already have enough difficulties trying to feed themselves, and you expect to find wisdom there?

All the people of the Earth had the same chances at the beginning. Some have solved their problems, and even have more than they need, while others simply do not have the means to survive. In your opinion, which ones can help the others? The people of the West still have an enormous distance to go on the path of open-mindedness, but the people of the East have not achieved one tenth of what the people of the West have achieved.

Telepathic Communication

Mind and matter are eternally the same thing.
The Tibetan Book of the Dead.

If you want to have telepathic communication of a very high quality, do not cut your hair or your beard. Certain people have a telepathic organ that is sufficiently developed to work well even if their head is shaved. But if you want to achieve the best results, then do not cut what the creators have made grow on your head and face. If it grows, there is a reason, for none of your physical characteristics were given to you without reason. By respecting the creation, you respect the creator.

The best moment to enter into communication with your creators is on waking because as your body is emerging from sleep, your mind is re-awakening too. A mechanism starts up at that point, a mechanism, which you must activate by deliberately opening your mind as far as possible to everything around you and to infinity. You should take special care not to halt the process.

Sit down cross-legged, or better still, lie on your back on the ground. If possible, position yourself in the open air and look up towards the sky.

The mind is like a rose. In the morning, it begins to open, but you often prune it when it is still just a bud. If you would wait a little, it would bloom.

To practice physical fitness is good, but to practice the physical fitness of the mind is better.

Yet, do not be impatient if you do not obtain results right away. When an organ is not used, it atrophies. When you have had a limb in plaster for a long time, you need a lot of physical therapy to recover its normal use.

Look up to the sky and think of your position in the context of everything that surrounds you. Visualize yourself in relation to the house that you occupy, a tiny speck lost between stone walls. See yourself in relation to all the people who are waking up at the same time as you, and in relation to those who, in other parts of the globe, are going to bed. Think of all those who are being born, those who are uniting with each other physically, those who are suffering, working or dying at that time, all this while you are waking up. Situate yourself in regard to your own level.

Situate yourself in relation to the infinitely large as well. Think of the town where you are, a tiny speck lost in a landscape that is the country, the continent or the island where you live. Then fly away in your mind, as if you were in a plane travelling further and further away from the ground, until the town and then the continent are nothing but a tiny spot.

Be aware of the fact that you are on the Earth, a small ball where humanity is but a parasite. It is always spinning although you do not realize this is happening. Situate yourself in relation to it, and in relation to the moon, which is revolving around the Earth, and in relation to the Earth, which is revolving around the sun, and in relation to the sun, which is itself rotating as it revolves around the center of our galaxy. Situate yourself in relation to the stars that are also suns, which have planets orbiting them. On these planets an infinite number of other beings live, and among them is the planet of our creators, the Elohim, as well as the planet of the eternals, where you may one day be admitted for eternity.

Locate yourself in relation to all those worlds where other living beings live - some more advanced and some more primitive than we are, and in relation to those galaxies which themselves revolve around the center of the universe. Finally, situate yourself in relation to our whole universe, which itself is an atom of an atom of a molecule located perhaps in the arm of somebody who is looking up at the sky, wondering whether there is life on other planets...

This is all in relation to the infinitely large.

Then situate yourself also in relation to your body, to all its vital organs and the other parts of which it is made up. Think of all those organs that are working without your noticing it, right at this very moment.

Think of your heart, which is beating without your asking it to, your blood, which circulates and irrigates your whole body, and your brain, which enables you to reflect and be conscious of doing so. Think of all the corpuscles that make up your blood and of all the cells that are being born in your body, those feeling pleasure while reproducing and those that are dying without your knowing it, and perhaps without being conscious that they help form the individual that you are.

Think too of all the molecules that constitute these cells, and the atoms that constitute these molecules, revolving like suns around the center of a galaxy, and of the particles that make up these atoms, and of the particles of these particles on which there is life asking itself if there is life on other planets...

This is all in relation to the infinitely small.

Place yourself in harmony with the infinitely large and with the infinitely small by radiating love towards what is above and towards what is below, and by being conscious that you yourself are part of infinity. Then by thinking intensely, try to transmit your message of love to the Elohim, our creators; try to transmit to them your wish to see them, to be among them one day, to have the strength to deserve it, to be among the chosen ones. Then you will feel light and ready to do good around you with all your strength all day long, because you will be in harmony with infinity.

You may also do these exercises in the sensual meditation room during the day, alone or with other people. But the moment when you come closest to perfect harmony with the infinite will occur when this takes place in your room of sensual meditation with someone you love, and you unite yourself physically with him or her, and jointly harmonize yourselves with infinity during your union.

In the evening, when the sky is full of stars and the temperature is mild, lie down on the ground. Look up at the heavens and think intensely of the Elohim, wishing that some day you may deserve to be amongst them, and thinking strongly that you are available and ready to do exactly what they may ask of you, even if you do not clearly understand why they are asking it. Perhaps you will see a signal if you are sufficiently ready.

As you are lying there on your back, be aware of the extent to which your organs of perception are limited, which explains the difficulty you may have in conceiving of infinity. A force keeps you nailed to the ground, you cannot fly off to the stars with a jerk, and yet you do not see any rope holding you down.

Millions of people are listening to thousands of radio stations and watching hundreds of television programs that are being broadcast in the atmosphere, yet you do not see these waves of sound and vision, and you do not hear them. Compasses all have their points drawn to the north, and yet you neither see nor hear the forces that attract their needles.

So I repeat again: your organs of perception are very limited, and energies like the universe are infinite. Wake yourself up, and wake up the organs you have within you, which will allow you to receive waves that you are not yet picking up or do not even suspect. Simple pigeons are able to find the north, and you, a human being, cannot. Think about this for a moment.

Furthermore, teach your children, whose organs are developing, all about this. This is how the "new humanity" will be born, and their faculties will be infinitely superior to those of present human beings.

When his growth is finished, a man who has never learned to walk will always be a cripple, and even if he is taught later, he will always be handicapped, even if he is very gifted. Therefore, it is during their growth that you must open the minds of your children, so that all their faculties may blossom, and they will turn into individuals who have nothing in common with what we are: poor, narrow-minded, primitive people.

The Reward

May this book guide those who recognize and love our creators, the Elohim. May it guide those who believe in them and those who remember to communicate telepathically with them, thus rediscovering the original meaning of prayer. May it guide those who do good to their fellow human beings. May it guide those who believe in what was revealed to me and in what was revealed before me, and those who are sure that scientific reincarnation is a reality. All such people have a guide and an aim in life, and are happy.

As for those who are not awakened, it is useless to speak to them about this message of the Elohim. One who is asleep cannot hear, and the unconscious mind does not wake up in just a few moments - especially if the person sleeping finds his or her sleep very comfortable.

Spread this message around you to those who do good to their fellow human beings. Spread it particularly among those who, by using the mind that the Elohim gave them, are relieving society from fear of food shortages, disease and the burden of daily exertions. They do this by giving others time to fulfill themselves and blossom, and it is for such individuals that the fountained gardens of the planet of the eternals are reserved.

For it is not enough merely to avoid harming others without doing them any good. Anyone whose life has been neutral will be entitled to neutrality. That is to say, he will not be re-created, neither to pay for crimes which have not been committed, nor to receive the reward for non-existent good deeds.

Anyone who has made many people suffer during part of his life, and then makes up for it by doing as much good as harm, will also be neutral. To have the right to scientific reincarnation on the planet of the eternals, one must have an unambiguously positive assessment at the end of one's life.

To be satisfied with doing good on a small scale around oneself is enough for someone who is not of superior intelligence, or who does not have many means, but it is not enough for someone who is very intelligent or someone who has many means. A very intelligent person has a duty to use the mind given to them by the Elohim to bring happiness to others by inventing new techniques to improve their living conditions.

Those people who will be entitled to scientific reincarnation on the planet of the eternals will live in a world where food will be brought to them without their having to make the slightest effort, and where there will be marvelously beautiful female and male partners scientifically created for the sole purpose of satisfying their pleasures. They will live there eternally, seeking only to fulfill themselves doing whatever pleases them. As for those who have made others suffer, they will be re-created, and their suffering will be equal to the pleasure of the eternals.

How can you not believe in all this now that science and ancient religions are coming together perfectly? You were nothing but matter, mere dust, yet the Elohim made you into living beings in their image capable of dominating matter. Later you will again become matter or dust, and they will make you live once more as they have created you, scientifically.

The Elohim created the first human beings without knowing that they were doing what had already been done for them. They thought they were only conducting a minor scientific experiment, and that is why they destroyed almost all of humanity the first time.

But when they understood that they had been created just like us, they began to love us as their own children, and swore never to try to destroy us again, leaving us to overcome our own violence by ourselves.

Although the Elohim do not directly intervene for or against humanity as a whole, they do, however, exert influence on some individuals whose actions please or displease them. Woe to those claiming to have met the Elohim or to have received a message from them if it is not true. Their life will become hell, and they will regret their lie when faced with all the troubles they will encounter.

Also those who act against the Guide of Guides and try to prevent him carrying out his mission, or who go along with him in order to spread strife amongst those who follow him, they will also see their life become hell.

Without any obvious influence coming from above, they will know why disease, family and professional difficulties, emotional woes and other problems will all invade their earthly existence while they await their eternal punishment.

You who smile as you read these lines, you are among those who would have crucified Jesus if you had lived in his time. Yet now you want to see members of your family born, get married and die under his effigy because this has become part of the morals and customs. Behaving like those who went to see the lions devouring the first Christians, you also direct ironic smiles at those who believe in these writings, saying that they should spend some time in a psychiatric asylum. Nowadays, when someone has disturbing ideas, he is no longer crucified or fed to wild animals - this is far too barbaric. Rather, such people are sent to a psychiatric asylum. Had these establishments existed two thousand years ago, Jesus and those who believed in him would have been confined there. As for those who believe in eternal life, ask them why they weep when they lose a loved one.

For as long as humankind was unable to understand the work of the Elohim scientifically, it was natural for people to believe in an impalpable "God". But now that, thanks to science, you understand that matter is infinitely large and infinitely small, you no longer have an excuse to believe in the "God" that your primitive ancestors believed in. The Elohim, our creators, intend to be recognized by those who are capable now of understanding how life can be created and can make the appropriate comparisons with ancient writings. Those people will have the right to eternity.

Christians! You have read a hundred times that Jesus would return, yet if he came back, you would put him in a psychiatric asylum. Come, open your eyes.

Sons of Israel! You are still waiting for your Messiah, and yet you do not open the door.

Buddhists! Your writings indicate that the new Buddha will be born in the West. Recognize the anticipated signs.

Muslims! Mohammed reminded you that the Jewish people had made an error in killing the prophets, and that the Christians had also made an error in adoring their prophet more than the one who sent him. So welcome the last of the prophets, and love those who sent him.

If you recognize the Elohim as your creators, and if you love them and wish to welcome them, if you try to do good to other people by making as much use as you can of all your potential, if you think of your creators regularly, trying through telepathy to make them understand that you love them, if you help the Guide of Guides to accomplish his mission, you will without a doubt be entitled to scientific reincarnation on the planet of the eternals.

When humanity discovered the necessary form of energy to travel to the moon, it also came to possess sufficient energy to destroy all life on Earth.

'The hour has drawn near, and the moon is rent asunder' it says in the *Koran, Sura 54, Verse 1*. Therefore, any day now, humanity can destroy itself. Only those who follow the last of the prophets will be saved from destruction.

Long ago, people did not believe Noah, and they laughed at him when he made preparations for the destruction. But they did not have the last laugh.

When the Elohim told the inhabitants of Sodom and Gomorrah to leave the city without looking back, some did not heed those warnings and were destroyed. Now that we have reached the stage when humanity itself may destroy all life on Earth, only those who recognize the Elohim as their creators will be saved from destruction. You may still not believe any of this, but when the time comes, you will think of these lines again, and it will be too late.

When the cataclysm takes place - and there is a good chance that it will happen quite soon, given the way human beings are presently behaving - there will be two sorts of people: those who have not recognized their creators and have not followed the last of the prophets, and those who have opened their eyes and ears and recognized what was announced a long time ago.

The former will undergo the suffering and destruction in the final furnace, and the latter will be spared and taken with the Guide of Guides to the planet of the eternals. There they will enjoy a marvelous life of fulfillment and pleasure with the sages of ancient times. It is they who will be waited on by magnificent athletes with beautifully sculptured bodies who will bring them sophisticated food to savor in the company of men and women of unequalled beauty and charm who will be entirely compliant to their desires.

> Seated on couches wrought with gold and jewels,
> Reclining thereon facing each other,
> There will wait on them youths, who will not age,
> Carrying goblets and ewers and cups filled out of a flowing spring,
> No headache will they get therefrom, nor will they be intoxicated,
> And carrying such fruits as they choose,

And flesh of birds as they may desire,
And there will be fair maidens with wide,
Lovely eyes,
Like pearls, we preserved,
As a reward for what they did.

The Koran, Sura 56, Verses 15-24.

You who believe in all that is written here, when the Guide of Guides summons you somewhere, drop everything, for it might be because he has received some information concerning the end. If you are near him at that moment, you will be saved and taken away with him, far from the suffering.

You who believe, do not pass judgement on the words or deeds of the Elohim. The created does not have the right to judge his creator. Respect our prophet, and do not pass judgement on his actions or his words, for we hear through his ears, we see through his eyes, and we speak through his mouth. If you lack respect for the prophet, you lack respect for those who sent him, your creators.

The messages which were given earlier by the Elohim and all those people who adhered fully to them over the centuries were right. But the obscurantist systems that were built on these messages using those who had a feeling for them were wrong. The Church is in the process of disappearing, and it deserves just that.

As for the men and women of the Church, let those who have their eyes open join the last of the prophets and help him spread throughout the world the latest message that has been handed to him. He will welcome them with open arms, and they will be able to blossom and fulfill themselves completely, while remaining the messengers of those in whom they had always believed. But this time they will at last truly comprehend what the Elohim's task was when they created humanity and when they sent Jesus.

They will really be able to fulfill themselves, far from the constraints of the Church, which is fossilized and encrusted with crimes and criminal inquisitions thousands of years old. They will be able to do what they must do - make use of the organs their creators gave them, for our creators do not like us failing to use the organs they gave us.

The men and women of the Church will be able to enjoy their five senses and unite physically forever, or for an instant of happiness with whomsoever they please, without feeling guilty. It is now that they should feel guilty - guilty of not using all that was given to them by their creators. But released from their old constraints, they will truly open people's minds instead of putting them to sleep!

Already, there are almost no more seminarists, but people who are unhappy - those who have in them the vocation to bring love around them and to open people's minds. Fifty years ago there were 50,000 seminarists; now there are only 500; this means that there are at least 49,500 unhappy people, human beings who have in them the potential, which has been placed in them by our creators so that they use it, to radiate. However, they do not feel attracted to this church shrouded with crimes and darkness.

You who are among those 49,500 people feeling a need to radiate the truth and do something for your fellow people; you who want to remain faithful to your creators and to Jesus who told you to love one another and to respect your creators, *"the Father who art in heaven"*; you who feel that this message is true, come with us and become Guides, that is to say, people who devote themselves to the Elohim in the tradition of Moses, Elijah and Jesus, and to the spreading of their messages, while continuing to live a normal life, truly fulfilling yourselves and enjoying all the senses that your creators gave you.

You who are presently members of the Church, take off those clothes that are as sad as their color, the color of the crimes that have been committed under their facade. Come with us and become guides for humanity on the path of universal peace and love.

Leave those churches that are nothing but monuments built by primitive people, temples where they could adore worthless things - pieces of wood and metal. The Elohim do not need temples in every city to feel loved. It is sufficient that human beings try to communicate with them telepathically, thereby rediscovering the original meaning of prayer, but also opening themselves to infinity and not shutting themselves away in obscure, mystical stone buildings.

Hypocrisy and mystification have lasted long enough. Using truthful messages as their basis, organizations were built and grew fat on them, living in misplaced luxury and using people's fear to achieve their own ends. Wars were even waged under the pretext of spreading these messages abroad. Shame!

The money of the poor has been used to build a financial power base. Shame!

Love for one's neighbor has been preached with weapons in hand. Shame!

Human equality has been preached while supporting dictatorships. Shame!

'God is with us!' was said to encourage people to launch themselves into fratricidal wars. Shame!

Many times has the following Gospel passage been quoted:

> And call no man your father upon the earth: for one is your Father, which is in heaven. *Matthew 23: 9.*

Yet in the Church they make sure they themselves are constantly called "Father" and "Monsignor" and "My Lord". Shame!

Other texts have been read again and again that say:

> Provide neither gold, nor silver, nor brass in your purses, nor scrip for your journey, neither two coats, neither shoes, nor yet staves.
> *Matthew 10: 9-10.*

Yet they have been wallowing in the luxury of the Vatican. Shame!

The Pope, if he does not sell all the properties of the Vatican to help unfortunate people, will not be admitted among the righteous on the planet of the eternals. It is shameful to wallow in luxury acquired at the expense of poor people by using true messages and by exploiting the births, marriages and deaths of human beings.

If all this changes, and if those people who were a part of that monstrous organization without understanding their mistake now leave it and regret their error, they will be forgiven and entitled to eternity. For the Elohim, our creators, love us, their children, and forgive all those who sincerely regret their errors.

The Church has no reason to exist any longer, for it was entrusted with spreading the message of Jesus in anticipation of the age of the Apocalypse, and this age has now come. Also the Church has used methods of disseminating information that are a shame to it. Although it has accomplished its mission, the Church will be reproached for all its crimes, and those who still wear its clothes covered with blood will be among the guilty.

Wake up slumberer that you are! This is no fabricated story. Re-read all the writings of the ancient prophets, inform yourself about the most recent scientific discoveries - especially in biology - and look at the sky.

The predicted signs are there. The UFOs - unidentified flying objects - which mankind has dubbed "flying saucers", are appearing every day.

'*There will be signs in the sky*' - that was written a long time ago. Once you have informed yourself of these things, integrate them all in your mind, and wake up. Claude Rael exists, he is indeed alive, and he has not written what Moses, Ezekiel, Elijah, Jesus, Mohammed, Buddha and all the others wrote. He is not a biologist, but he is the last of the line of prophets, the prophet of the Apocalypse - that is, of the time when everything can be understood.

He is living among you right now; you are lucky enough to be one of his contemporaries, and you are able to receive his teaching. Wake up! Pull yourself together, and take to the road. Go and see him, and help him - he needs you. You will be one of the pioneers of the final religion, the religion of religions, and you will have your place, whatever may happen, among the righteous for eternity, savoring the delights of the planet of the eternals in the company of wonderfully pleasant beings who are ready to fulfill all your desires.

The Guides

You will follow the Guide of Guides, for he is the ambassador of the Elohim, our creators, "our Fathers who art in Heaven". You will follow all the advice that is given in this book, because it is the advice of your creators, transmitted by Claude Rael, our ambassador, the last of the prophets, the shepherd of shepherds, and you will help him to build the religion of religions.

Jews, Christians, Muslims, Buddhists and all you who have other religions, open your eyes and your ears; re-read your holy writings, and you will understand that this book is the last one - the one predicted by your own prophets. Come and join us to prepare for the coming of our creators.

Write to the Guide of Guides, and he will put you in touch with other people who, like you, are Raelians - that is, people who understand the message transmitted by Claude Rael. He will put you in touch with a Guide in your region, so that you may meet regularly to meditate and act to spread this message, so that it becomes known throughout the world.

You who are reading this message, be aware that you are privileged, and think of all those who do not yet know about it. Do all you can to make sure that no one around you is ignorant of these fantastic revelations, without ever trying to convince those to whom you speak. Bring this message to their notice, and if they are ready, they will open up by themselves.

Constantly repeat to yourself this sentence of Gandhi: *'It's not because no one sees the truth that it becomes an error.'*

You who feel such joy in reading this message, and who wish to radiate this truth and make it shine around you, you who want to live by devoting yourself totally to our creators, by scrupulously applying what they ask, by training to guide humanity on the path of blossoming and fulfillment, you should become a Guide if you want to be fully capable of this.

Write to the Guide of Guides, to Claude Rael, and he will welcome you and arrange an initiation, which will enable you to radiate this truth fully; for you can open the minds of others only if your own mind is open.

The love of the creators for their work is immense, and you should return this love to them. You must love them as they love you, and prove it by assisting their ambassador and his helpers, putting all your means and all your strength at their service, so that they may travel all over the world to spread this message and build an embassy to welcome our creators.

If you wish to help me realize the goals set by the Elohim, write to me, Rael at:

International Raelian Movement
Case Postale 225, CH 1211
Geneva 8
Switzerland

or by email to: **headquarters@rael.org**

Also, do not forget that regular local meetings of people who believe in this final message are held on the first Sunday of April, on the 6th of August, the 7th of October and the 13th of December each year. The venues for these meetings will be set out in the liaison bulletin of the Raelian Movement of your country, and some addresses to help you make contact are listed at the end of this book.

BOOK THREE

LET'S WELCOME THE EXTRA-TERRESTRIALS

1

FREQUENTLY ASKED QUESTIONS

This chapter provides Rael's answers to those questions that were most frequently raised by journalists during radio and television interviews in which Rael participated worldwide in the years immediately following the publication of his first two books in the mid-1970s.

Seeming Contradictions Between
the First and Second Message

QUESTION:

The first contradiction which appeared between the first and second message was found in the beginning of the dialogue which took place between the Eloha and you. In the first message, when you asked him if it would be possible to visit his planet, he replied: 'No, you could not live there because the atmosphere is very different from yours, and you are not sufficiently prepared to support the journey.' Nevertheless, at the time of the second meeting on October 7th, 1975 (31), you were taken in one of their machines, and you spent nearly 24 hours on the planet of the Eternals.

We would remark that on the first contact, the machine appeared progressively, showing a flashing red light at about ten meters altitude and descending slowly. When the machine was low enough for you to see the upper part, a strong white light was flashing on its top, whereas at the time of contact for the delivery of the second message, the machine appeared instantly behind the bushes at Roc Plat, without any flashing lights and at ground level. Also, when it returned, it disappeared instantly once you had descended from it, as if it had disintegrated.

Another contradiction: At the time of the first contact, the Eloha had his face surrounded by some sort of halo, which he later explained was a sort of space helmet composed of waves, whereas at the time of the most recent meeting, he had nothing surrounding his face. This contradiction is elsewhere strengthened by what is stated on page 30 in the first message: 'Thou canst not see my face: for there shall no man see me, and live', *Exodus 33:20*, and this biblical citation is explained thus: 'If man came on our planet, he would see the creators without their space helmets, but he would die because the atmosphere would not be suitable for him.' How do you explain this?

ANSWER:

The explanation for these seeming contradictions is very simple and can be summarized in one word: psychology.

When one decides to come and make contact with a person living on a primitive planet, even though he was created to accomplish a very specific mission, there are certain precautions which must be taken so as not to irreversibly damage his psyche. To see a machine appearing in the sky equipped with flashing lights is not traumatic for a man living in a scientifically developed country of our time. He is more or less used to seeing satellites and rockets on TV and has already seen airplanes and helicopters since his childhood and understands, to some extent, how they operate. The best way to make an appearance without frightening him is to make a gradual approach with a machine equipped with flashing lights like his own airplanes and helicopters, well known to him. Man would find that almost normal and would only be surprised at the absence of noise from a machine seemingly made of metal, and consequently very heavy. The being who appeared to him would have to be dressed in a way resembling how man expects present air pilots and astronauts to be dressed. The sort of space helmet covering the face would give him confidence, by reminding him of the pilots of Earth's flying machines with which he was well acquainted. Thus they would be able to reach their objective not to panic the person contacted, and at the same time allowing him to see technology which is still unknown to people on Earth, so that he will understand that he has discovered visitors from another planet.

At the time of the second encounter, when the flying machine appeared more brutally, the Elohim were using their technology without camouflage before a witness whom they knew was sufficiently prepared psychologically so as not to be traumatized. If they had appeared so brutally at the first encounter, the shock would have been too great, and my mental balance would have been too disturbed at that time, when I wasn't expecting anything. In spite of all their precautions, the nervous shock brought on the beginning of stomach ulcers, which took several months to heal. The message was "sweet in my mouth, but bitter in my stomach". It would have been even more serious without the approach precautions which they took.

Up to our present day and age, our creators were only appearing while trying to impress their creation to the maximum, as incapable as they were to understand who these beings from the sky were. The Elohim's main objective was to make Man believe, even if they did not understand. Now that we are reaching the Age of Apocalypse, which means the "Age of Revelation", that is to say, the age when everything can be understood, and not the "end of the world", as some would like you to believe and as you can check in any dictionary, they have decided to appear while trying to be understood and recognized as our creators, those of which all the religious books of the Earth are talking, including *The Bible*, in which they are called the "Elohim". This bible was dictated to the first human beings precisely with the aim to be recognized, now that millennia have passed and human knowledge has progressed sufficiently. In this way, we can look at what is coming from the sky without kneeling to pray and shouting "miracle".

Finally, it must be remembered that the Elohim had decided to test me before giving me the complete message, so they went at it most progressively.

In spite of my insistent wish to take a trip in their vessel, they cut short my demands by stating that it was impossible for me to do so, just as people sometimes tell their children that if they drank alcohol they would stop growing. They added the example of the verse in *Exodus,* which they addressed to primitive men so that they would stay aloof. These primitives were meant to believe without, above all, trying to understand.

Dating the Works of the Elohim

QUESTION:

The Elohim said they created life on Earth 25,000 years ago. How is it that we find traces of animal bones as old as many hundreds of thousands of years?

ANSWER:

The Elohim have explained that they did not create our planet. When they decided to pursue their experiments of creating life scientifically in a laboratory, they set out to search the universe for a planet which would have a suitable atmosphere, allowing them to work easily. The Earth proved to be positive after many tests and analyzes.

Then they came down to our planet and created the life forms we now know, including humans.

It doesn't mean, that 10,000 or 20,000 years before their arrival, there wasn't another creation on Earth that could have been destroyed by a natural or an artificial catastrophe.

Imagine that an atomic war breaks out tomorrow, and all life on Earth is destroyed. Then 10,000 years later, extra-terrestrials settle down to create new living organisms, intelligent beings who would discover traces of our civilization after a slow scientific progression; these same beings would find it hard to believe that beings coming from the sky had created them scientifically, using as proof the bones which they found to be older than 25,000 years, our bones! They might even find the far older bones of mammoths that we ourselves still find existing in the debris of our time because the life that exists on Earth at present is not the first one to be created, and it won't be the last.

There has been an infinity of creations on our planet, but also an infinity of destructions, due for the most part to a lack of wisdom by those who were the equivalent to our humanity.

The People of Israel and the Jews

QUESTION:

In the first message, on page 18, it is written that the people of Israel were elected at one of the Elohim's competitions, as the most successful humanoids as far as intelligence and genius are concerned. Then in the second message on page 170, it is written 'The Jews are our direct descendants on Earth. That is why a special destiny is reserved for them. They are the descendants of the 'Sons of Elohim and the daughters of men', as written in *Genesis*. Is this not contradictory?

ANSWER:

The people who were chosen by our creators, the Elohim, as being the most accomplished, were the people of Israel, who had been created in a laboratory at this location on our planet. It is perhaps because these people were the greatest success that the Sons of the Elohim were tempted by their females and had children by them, from whom the Jewish people descend. That is how the race populating the soil of Israel became the Jewish people.

The Raelian Movement and Money

QUESTION:

In the first book, it is written on page 86:

> Lay not up for yourselves treasures upon earth... No man can serve two masters: for either he will hate the one, and love the other; or else he will hold to the one, and despise the other. Ye cannot serve Yahweh and mammon. *Matthew 6: 19-24.*

And the Vatican is vigorously attacked for its riches, while the Raelian Movement is asking for money from its members. Is it not falling into the same trap as the Vatican?

ANSWER:

One must not compare those who live in luxury and opulence, recommending their faithful to live poorly, and who use these poor people's money to maintain a myriad of bishops and cardinals, to increase continually their real estate investments, to maintain a palace of another era with guards wearing halberds; one must not compare these Roman usurpers with a movement that has not, nor will ever have, a paid clergy: that had not, nor will ever own three-quarters of the houses and real estate in a capital where people are having problems finding suitable lodgings, as is the case in Rome, where they refuse to rent to whoever it may be for fear of devaluation of the investment; that has not, and never will have a princely palace crumbling under the heaviness of gold and silver.

We have indeed a need for a lot of money, but it will be used to attain these precise objectives:

1. Translate the messages of the Elohim into every language, and bring them to the attention of all the peoples of the Earth.
2. Build an embassy where the Elohim will be able to meet men officially. This embassy will be neither a princely palace nor a cathedral, but rather a simple house possessing the comforts to which all modern men are entitled, with the kind of diplomatic immunity that even the smallest state has for its embassy.

Finally, if by good fortune, we succeed in obtaining more money than we need to realize the first two objectives that I have already pointed out, and in such a short space of time that we have not yet managed the diffusion of the message all over the planet, we will then use the excess money to build a research centre near the embassy. This centre will bring together all the scientists who wish to work on the creation of life in a laboratory, allowing Mankind to equal their creators. The creation of biological robots will allow the elimination of work and consequently money. Also, we plan to build a school for the geniuses and the gifted. These research teams will be able to work freely, outside the exploiting laboratories, the multinational trusts and the suffocation of geniuses by state systems.

In this way they will have the opportunity to work without fear of seeing their inventions fall into the hands of politico-military powers, seeking to use new discoveries to build ever more destructive armaments.

Nothing is Constant in Space and Time

QUESTION:

In the first book on page 89, you wrote that the planet of the Elohim is a little less than a light year away, that being the distance that light can travel in one year, or nine thousand billion kilometers, since light moves at about three hundred thousand kilometers per second. Our present day scientists state that the closest star outside our sun is located four light years away. How do you explain the difference?

ANSWER:

The Elohim do not want us to know exactly where their planet is located. This is quite understandable when we consider man's persistence towards destruction, even though the level of technology on Earth is still fairly primitive.

That will all be revealed in more detail when they will officially arrive in the embassy that we will build for them. In the meantime, we can only ask questions.

Scientific members of our movement have put forth an hypothesis: the distance between their planet and ours could be about four light years by following the light, which could be moving in a pronounced curve, but would only be one light year away if we travelled in a straight line. That is a possibility.

I might add that light does not move at the same speed in all strata of the universe, because nothing is invariable, neither in space nor time. This is one of the biggest errors that present scientists are committing. They start with an observation based on a limited period of time to draw conclusions bearing on the past thousands of years and on the time to come, or they base conclusions on a limited space, to draw conclusions on the infinity of space. Man has always made the same mistake of judging according to his knowledge. Those who used the horizon as a base reasoned that the Earth had to be flat.

This is also true for historical dating, such as the methods based on radioactivity named "Carbon 14", potassium-argon, uranium-lead-thorium or all other such methods. There exists a very interesting book which explains all of this very seriously for the scientists who might be interested: I am referring to *Evolution or Creation* (see bibliography at the end of this book). In short, the error in these dating methods is to start with the principle that the present atomic movement has always been the same, and starting from there, to make calculations based on false information, because nothing is invariable in the universe in time or in space.

To illustrate this error, let's take a 25 year old human, for example, and measure his growth in one year, about one millimeter is a good average for most subjects. Starting from there, we could establish that the man is 1,750 years old, because he measures 1.75 meters. We would forget that the growth of this young man has never been invariable. The first year, he grew more than 500 millimeters (since conception), between four and five years only 60 millimeters, between seven and eight years only 30 millimeters, but between 14 and 15 years another 80 millimeters! As you will see, nothing is constant, all efforts to determine the subject's age, starting from a partial observation of his growth, would be a total failure. One could note that if we started at 60 centimeters in the first year of growth, to estimate the age of the person, in 21 years of such growth, we could predict that this individual would measure 12.6 meters at age 21.

QUESTION:

In the first book on page 13, you wrote that the Elohim had created the original continent 25,000 years ago, from which fragments later detached to form the continents we now know. The American continent continued to separate itself from Europe by a few centimeters each year according to certain scientists, or by a metre each year as others claim. Be that as it may, even if it is one metre per year, in twenty-five thousand years, we will reach 25,000 meters or 25 kilometers, but the North American continent is many thousands of kilometers away from Europe. How can this be explained?

ANSWER:

The reply to this question is exactly the same as to the previous question. In the growth pattern of a human being, the relation between the first year and the 21st year is 600 to one. It is a thousand times greater when we speak of the separation of the continents.

Here again nothing is invariable neither in time nor space. Actually, the continents separate only a few centimeters each year perhaps, but in the beginning, they separated by many hundreds of kilometers each year.

Recently there occurred an earthquake near the Arabian peninsula, and people were surprised to note that a fault was created, separating two regions by a metre in only one night.

And yet we are in a relatively calm period of the Earth's history, the side effects of "the storm" of the creation of the original continent by our Fathers have had time to calm down in 25 millennia. In the infinity of time and space, nothing is invariable, not in matter, not in energy.

Transmission of the
Cellular Plan and the Forehead Bone.

QUESTION:

It is asked of all those who recognize Rael as having been sent by our creators, the Elohim, and being the last of the prophets, to have their cellular plan transmitted by him, or by a Guide qualified to officiate by him, all this so that the genetic code of each Raelian may be preserved, so as to permit an eventual re-creation on the planet of the Eternals. On the other hand, each Raelian is also asked to take the necessary precautions in his or her will, so that the forehead bone be sent to the Guide of Guides after his or her death; to what will that avail, since the transmission of the cellular plan has already taken place?

ANSWER:

The transmission of the cellular plan is a recognition of the Elohim as being our creators, performed by each Raelian while still alive. The conservation of the forehead bone is a recognition of the Elohim as being our creators, even after death. Together they constitute a recognition "in life as in death". The cellular plan or genetic code of each individual is registered in an enormous computer which records all our actions during our life, from the time of our conception, from the meeting of the ovule and the spermatozoon, the moment when a new genetic code is registered, hence a new individual. This individual will be followed throughout his lifetime, and at the end of his life, the computer will know if he has the right to eternal life on the planet where the Elohim accept only the most conscious of men and women.

QUESTION:

What happens to a Raelian who dies in an accident and whose body is completely destroyed?

ANSWER:

If the Raelian in question has taken precautions in his will, asking that his forehead bone be sent to the Guide of Guides, there is no problem, since it will be registered by the computer which surveys every one of us during the whole of our existence. In the same way, there is no problem for the Raelians who die without the authorities respecting their last will and testament, by refusing the removal of the said forehead bone. What is important is that each Raelian make his or her will known in the manner asked.

When there will be millions of Raelians, the government will be forced to see that their last will and testament are respected by law. The last will and testament of the first Christians were not respected either, so long as they were in a minority. Raelism will be the dominant religion in the world of the third millennium, and then the last will and testament of all Raelians will be respected.

QUESTION:

The majority of people die old. Are they re-created old, and will they live eternally old?

ANSWER:

Obviously not! A person who is fortunate in being re-created to live eternally on the planet of the Eternals is re-created young with a body in full possession of its force and its resources. At each re-creation, they will be re-created the same way eternally.

QUESTION:

It is written that only those who follow you will be saved. If a person has had a life turned towards happiness and the blossoming of humanity, but has never heard of the messages of the Elohim, has that person no chance of being saved?

ANSWER:

This person is among the just and will be saved. That part of the messages concerns those who have read the messages. Among them, only those who have decided to follow the rules given by our creators will be saved. But if there are people on Earth who live in seeking above all to help the progress of humanity, or to help their fellow men to the most of their ability, and who die without having known the messages of our Fathers, they will be among the just and will be saved. It will be more pardonable for those who do not know about the messages and who act positively than for those who know of them, because the latter have no excuse not to have changed their conduct or to have paid even more attention to their actions.

Is the Earth an Atom of the Finger of God?

QUESTION:

The message explains that our planet is but an atom of an atom of the gigantic being of which we are just a part, just as there is intelligent life in the atoms of the atoms of which we are composed. But the great being of which we are only a part, could it not be considered as "God"?

ANSWER:

It all depends on what we mean by the word *God*. If we are thinking of Infinity, then yes, but only in part; because this gigantic being of which we are only a part, also lives on a planet which is an atom of another gigantic being and so on to infinity.

If we mean by "God" a being having power over us, not at all, because there is no such "God".

The infinitely great being of which the Earth is but an atom, has no power over us, because one must not forget that for that being, time passes much more slowly. The time it takes for that being to think of something, for us a few millennia have passed. The time taken for beings who live on one of the atoms of our atoms to think of something, is for us, a billionth of a billionth of a second. This infinitely small being could think that we are "God", and would be just as wrong as us if we considered the being that we are a part of to be something divine. The universe being infinite, there can be no centre, which eliminates the possibility of the existence of an all-powerful and omnipresent God!

The Infinite is omnipresent, and we are a part of it as it is a part of us. But it has no power over us, and it is "infinitely" indifferent to our decisions or our behavior. After all, there is nothing to prove that the great being of whose particles we are the parasites, is human. It is perhaps a dog or a worm (the only thing that could be proven by the Elohim is that it is something alive).

Noah's Ark – A Space Craft?

QUESTION:

The messages state that Noah's Ark was a spaceship. However, there was a discovery a few years ago in a glacier on Mount Ararat of the remains of a boat, which some claimed to be the debris from Noah's Ark which, it would appear, was a boat. How do you explain that?

ANSWER:

The pieces of wood which were found have recently been analyzed, and it was estimated they were not older than seven hundred years, which would put Noah's Ark at around AD1200. Even if we admit that the dating system makes enormous errors, and that one multiplies the dating by three, one would obtain two thousand years, which would place the flood at the beginning of the Christian era, which makes no sense. Even if one day the remains of a wooden boat were found dating back about five thousand years, which would correspond with the period of the flood, that would not prove that Noah's Ark was a wooden boat. One would certainly find near Mount Ararat pieces of a wooden boat dating back to the epoch of the true flood, because at the time when Noah built his spaceship destined to save certain humans from destruction, there were in the ports of his country some wooden boats, which had been carried by the enormous tidal waves at the time of the huge explosions responsible for the destruction of all life on Earth. Just as today we can find in Florida, not far from the modern American rocket-site which carried the astronauts to the Moon, some magnificent sailing boats constructed with wood, and superb yachts belonging to American millionaires.

In the case of an atomic war, certain explosions could activate enormous tidal waves, which would carry away the boats to the tops of the closest mountains, like pieces of straw. The eventual survivors could, on finding the debris of those boats some centuries later, deduce that there must have been an enormous flood to carry them there; and, since certain writings report that some humans had been saved from this flood, having been protected on board a vessel, they would be certain that these would be the vessels in question.

There is a very important point which helps us to understand clearly that the flood was not the result of a continual rainfall as is generally thought, but the result of a colossal cataclysm, having completely, and in a very brutal manner, overturned the surface of the Earth. If it had been caused by continual rain, all the boats would have been saved, and of course all the sailors and navigators of that epoch would have survived without the least problem. Now it is clearly written that only those who were in Noah's Ark survived, which makes sense, it being the only spaceship!

Life After Life – or Dream and Reality?

QUESTION:

A book was published recently which related the testimonies of people who were brought back to life after having been in a coma, and nearly all of them told the same story of the visions they had as death approached – a vision of harmonious people wearing white robes and singing, a vision of people who had disappeared, etc. You claim that after death there is nothing if the Elohim do not intervene to re-create those who die. How do you explain this consistency in testimony, and does it not prove the existence of a soul?

ANSWER:

All that happens in the human brain is but the result of electro-chemical reactions. Be it of love, of hate, of pleasure, of suffering, of imagination, or all other states of mind, sentiment or sickness; the process depends in every case on the chemical reactions produced in the interior of the brain, and the resulting electrical impulses or messages, be they visual, auditory, based on memory, or an interpretation of new events based on elements that one has in the memory.

When we breathe very deeply and rapidly, we feel elated very soon, and if we make one hundred people do the same thing, their experience will all be consistent. If we make one hundred people run one kilometer, they will all be out of breath. Every given phenomenon corresponds to a given physical reaction, which will be the same for everyone. When an individual falls into a coma, the brain is irrigated by the blood in a certain manner, and the brain cells are thus oxygenated in a certain way, and these chemical facts produce certain reactions which are about the same for all of us.

If we place acid on limestone, it will always make a foam. If we hit the heads of one hundred people strong enough for them to fall into a coma, they will all have the impression of having seen the same thing. Indeed, they would describe only that which was stored in their memory of the chemical reactions to which they were subjected. It is a bit like when we dream. Nobody would think of saying that because he met 10 other people who all dreamt that they were being chased by a bull that was 10 meters high and spitting flames, that since many people reported the same thing, these sorts of bulls must exist. We have all dreamt, at one time or another, that we could fly, just by giving a little push with our feet; but no one seriously believes that this proves that they can fly around with the swallows, or that such a thing would be possible, because thousands of people have had the same dream. One must not interpret these dreams as reality, even if science endeavors to realize them technically, by building an apparatus one day which really allows us to fly. Something which all of those who were in a coma remember well, is that they were not anxious to return to their body, and this is really not surprising. It would be more accurate to say that they had no desire to be conscious of their body again, just as when we come out of a very sweet dream in the company of the opposite sex, for example, and we try to go back to sleep to recapture the happiness which we experienced.

The fact that all ex-comatose people describe almost the same experience proves that identical chemical reactions were produced in the human brain, hence their reactions to electrical phenomena are also identical. If we implant electrodes in 1,000 human brains, in exactly the same locations, and we send them an identical electrical charge, they will all feel the same thing and have the same visions. This is exactly what happens at the time of death. If certain privileged people deserve re-creation on the planet of the Eternals after their death, this will happen only when total death has occurred, and nothing will happen so long as the person is in a coma, therefore alive.

The Elohim's Scientific Level of Development

QUESTION:

There does not seem to be as great a time-lag as one would expect between our creators and us, even though they are 25,000 years ahead of us. Their slow progression gives us the impression that we will be able to accomplish the same things in much less time. How is that?

ANSWER:

In order to report what I have seen, I used words that people of today can understand, while placing myself psychologically at the level of the most numerous of those who live in technologically developed countries. In fact, we cannot even begin to imagine the capacity and the technological level of the Elohim. What we are doing at the end of the 20th century of the Christian era would seem miraculous to Europeans who lived only 100 years ago, as well as to the Amazon Indians now living in their forests, but what our creators can do would seem equally miraculous to our most advanced scientists, if they were showing it to them. Normally, the Elohim will not do it because they don't want to place us in a state of incomprehension that would inevitably lead to giving value back to beliefs that generate primitive religions. In this way, the Elohim hope that we will continue, above all, to seek to understand matter and the forces which surround us, by ourselves.

In the same manner in which they appeared to me with flashing lights and a sort of space suit so as not to disorientate me too much at the beginning, while they are able to appear instantly at ground level as they did at the meeting at Roc Plat, they could also show humanity technological prowess that even the most imaginative scientists could not understand by themselves.

They are capable of doing certain things with infinitely large particles such as planets and even entire solar systems, which we still find hard to do with infinitely small particles such as neutrons or electrons. What I mean is that they are able to modify the movements of planets within solar systems, and even displace some entire solar systems. They are able to do all this by using waves which we are not even aware of yet.

Let's go back to what was written in the first two messages. We must admit that between our present level of science on Earth and the mastery of scientific re-creation allowing eternal life, for example, there is a giant step that our scientists will take a long time to make, even if it is not entirely inconceivable for the most open-minded of them.

Neither God nor Soul, but the Elohim and the Genetic Code

QUESTION:

It is written in the messages that there is no God since the universe, being infinite in space, could have no centre, and there is no soul for much the same reasons. But could it not be said that the Elohim replace "God" in the minds of many Raelians, and that the possibility of being re-created on the planet of the Eternals, replaces the idea of a "soul", allowing access to "paradise"?

ANSWER:

Yes, there is no "God". The universe is infinite and therefore cannot have a centre by definition because of it being infinite. However, it is necessary to differentiate between those for whom "God" is a concept meaning infinity, something eternal, omnipresent, impalpable, and having no power over man and those for whom "God" is a being with a white beard sitting on a cloud who created humans in his image.

Since the beginning, there has been a conglomeration between two concepts, between two totally different things, that were unjustly put together under the same label. The Elohim explained to the first humans that on the one hand, there is Infinity, which is omnipresent and eternal and of which we are a part and which is part of us, and on the other hand, themselves, the Elohim, who created us in their image.

Little by little the properties of the Infinite were affiliated to the Elohim, and this is partly true because they are eternal; and to the Infinite, the power of manifestation through Celestial Messengers, is partly true again, because in a certain way, the Elohim could be considered as the instrument of the Infinite in their creation of intelligent beings in their image.

But the Infinite does not constantly watch over us directly and in itself is not conscious of our individual behavior. Whether mankind reaches the Golden Age or self-destructs is of no importance to the Infinite, no more than us paying attention to the molecule of our fingers which we leave on a fabric when we touch it. In relation to the Infinite, it is quite normal that there would be a natural selection at all levels, the same as for the man or the dog of which the Earth is but an atom of its skull or finger nail, and the same for the sun which illuminates it, or for the billions of inhabited planets that can be found in our thumb-nail.

Those who think of "God" as Infinity, as most oriental religions teach, are right, in as much as it represents a concept without identity, and without consciousness of our own existence, or any other for that matter.

Those for whom "God" is our creators, the Elohim, are not entirely wrong either, so long as they do not think of them as beings who must be worshiped on hands and knees or lying down with one's face in the dirt, but of elder brothers in the Infinite, whom we should love as we wish to be loved by the beings that we will create one day.

The spirit is a concept, whose etymology we will trace so as to better understand its meaning. The word *spirit* comes from the Latin *spirare* which means "to breathe" and the word *soul* comes from the same root as the French word *souffle*, also meaning "breath". We can analyze the exact composition of the human body, then mix together all the chemical constituents, but we will not obtain a living being for all that. Something will be missing, something which is needed to assemble, to articulate, to organize it in a well defined plan. Take all that is required to build the house of your dreams, such as 10 tons of stones, a ton of cement, 100 kilos of paint, two wash basins, a bath, etc., and put it all in a heap. Nevertheless, we would not obtain a house because the most important thing is missing: the plan. The creation of a person follows the same principle, there has to be a plan. This plan is the genetic code, which means that by assembling a minute quantity of matter to form the first cell containing a cellular plan, we would consider that person is, in fact, nearly completed. This first cell would use the matter we give it as food to multiply in two, then four, then eight cells, and so on, following a precise plan until all the information contained in the genetic specifications has been met.

Each and every living being possesses a genetic code, which differs according to the species, or depending on individuals belonging to the same species, in certain details, such as the color of the eyes, the hair, the character, etc. Even *The Bible* states clearly that each living being possesses a "soul" and not only man:

> But flesh with the soul[24] thereof, which is the blood thereof, shall ye not eat. And surely your blood of your lives will I require; at the hand of every beast will I require it, and at the hand of man; at the hand of every man's brother will I require the soul[24] of man.
> *Genesis 9: 4-5.*

For the soul of the flesh is in the blood.[21] *Leviticus 17: 11*

Therefore, there is no ethereal soul flying gracefully from the body after death, but there is the genetic code, which is the personality of each individual. It is through this genetic code that the Elohim proceed to re-create those people whose life on Earth is worthy of eternal life on their planet.

There is no "God", but there are the Elohim, our creators who we wish to welcome as they deserve to be welcomed, and in whom we have faith, or rather trust. Also, there is no autonomous soul flying from the body after death, but there is the genetic code which allows access to eternal life.

The Religion of the Infinite

QUESTION:

The Raelian Movement is an atheist religion whose goals are the diffusion of the messages of demystification, given by the Elohim, to the Earth's population, and to build an embassy where they will make official contact with the governments of the Earth. Supposing that humanity showed proof of wisdom and succeeded in avoiding self-destruction, that the messages would be diffused in every language, that the embassy is built and that the Elohim arrive; what will be the function of the Raelian religion then, and what will its mission be?

ANSWER:

If all that comes about, and I am of the opinion that it will, even if there is only one chance in a hundred that man will choose the path of wisdom, humanity's religion will become that of the Elohim – the Infinite. The mission of the Raelian Guides will then be the teaching of the techniques allowing man to live in harmony with the Infinite. These techniques are summarily explained in *The Keys* in the second message and in *Sensual Meditation*. In other words, all of that which enables man to raise his level of consciousness, to refine his perception of the electro-chemical reactions and interchanges produced in his brain.

The religion of the Infinite is the religion of the absolute, and it is inevitably eternal. The mere fact that people, 25,000 years ahead of us scientifically, are still faithful to this religion, is the proof that this is the absolute religion, the eternal religion for all the living species who have reached a universal level of consciousness, that is to say Infinite.

The awakening sessions that we organize regularly constitute an approach to this religion of the Infinite through sensual meditation.

The Future of Traditional Religions

QUESTION:

If the Elohim come to the embassy accompanied by Moses, Jesus, Buddha, and Mohammed, and all the great prophets who live on the planet of the Eternals, what will become of the existing religions?

ANSWER:

The majority would rally to the Raelian Movement, at least those churchgoers who are faithful to the writings of these religions, and who are sufficiently intelligent and open-minded enough to understand. Unfortunately, a great number of narrow minded fanatics, guided by the clergy of these religions afraid of losing their source of revenue, will oppose the general rally. They will allege that the Elohim are usurpers, or that they have been sent by "the devil", and facing their own Christ, they would joyfully crucify him again, just as the clergy of the Inquisition would have burned Jesus as a sorcerer in his own name if he had had the misfortune to fall into their hands in that epoch.

I recently had the opportunity to have breakfast with one of the representatives of the Jewish community in Montreal, Quebec. During the meal, I asked him what he would do if Moses himself told him to do otherwise than that which is written in *The Old Testament*. He replied: 'I would continue to apply that which is written in *The Bible.*'

Many people are like him, and this is one of the problems with which the Elohim are confronted as they seek recognition from humanity. They will have to be stronger than the beliefs that they have engendered.

If tomorrow the Elohim landed somewhere in the world and explained to the governors who came to meet them, and to the media, that "God" does not exist, nor the soul, and presented Jesus in the flesh, saying who he is, do you believe that the Vatican would place its fortune at his disposal? Certainly not, because the system has taken the upper hand over the fundamental goals of the Catholic Church.

All nuns are the wives of Jesus. Would they place themselves at his service if he returned? To be the wives of someone who does not exist materially, believing that he is alive somewhere, and being worried if he really returned: that is the problem of the nuns.

As a great thinker once said: we cannot change the minds of people, they simply die and are replaced by others more evolved who have a different opinion. Time is on our side.

Certainly there will always be a small nucleus of narrow-minded fanatics, but they will die out, the same as the pre-Christian religions who martyred the first Christians, and whose beliefs have nevertheless totally disappeared.

The problem only will arise if the Elohim arrive before the present primitive beliefs have totally disappeared.

Raelism and Geniocracy

QUESTION:

You published a book entitled: *Geniocracy*, from which a political movement was formed called: The Movement for Worldwide Geniocracy. Are you not trying to use a religious movement to impose a political doctrine?

ANSWER:

Many Raelians were particularly interested by the chapter in the first message, which explained what the political organization was like on the planet of the Elohim, and asked me to develop this idea in a manifesto which would help them to create a political movement following this ideology. The fact that the Elohim wanted us to favor the implantation of geniocracy on Earth, and at the same time, leave men free to understand something better if they could, prompted me to agree to write this manifesto. Later, the few Raelians more particularly interested in geniocracy, created the party in question, and even presented a candidate at an election only a few months after its creation.

My position is very clear in all the countries where geniocracy is progressing. I am on Earth primarily to accomplish my mission, which consists of spreading the messages of our creators and building the embassy that they have requested. Those who are involved with geniocracy know that I devote all my time to my mission, and that even though I wish them the best of results, I do not feel concerned with their problems. I have even asked all the Guides who have started these political movements to find, as quickly as possible, other non-Raelians capable of replacing them, so that the Guides in question can devote themselves to that which, in my opinion, is more important: their work as Guides.

If geniocratic candidates do seek to be elected, I will always advise the Raelians to vote for them. It becomes quite evident that a person can be a Raelian and a "Geniocrat", just as one can be a Democrat and a Christian; one can have a religion and a political opinion. Raelians do not have to get involved with the Geniocratic party, in fact, quite the contrary. I am convinced that people can do only one thing at a time, at least very well, so I advise Raelians not to become active in the Geniocratic party, but to leave that to non-Raelians. When one works eight hours a day and spends all one's free time diffusing the messages, each free moment becomes precious. Not a single minute should be wasted on a political movement when it could be spent diffusing the messages. One must make a choice, and a political ideology does not weigh very much when compared with the messages of the Elohim. I have set the ball rolling with geniocracy, and I am now counting on non-Raelians to run it. Perhaps it will develop into something enormous which will save humanity, or perhaps humanity will save itself without geniocracy, even if they come to it later. The only important thing is that the embassy will soon be built; this is my only concern, my only preoccupation, and it should be the only concern and the only preoccupation of all true Raelians. The priority of priorities is the building of the embassy for our creators, so that we can welcome them in the company of the ancient messengers: Moses, Jesus, Buddha, and Mohammed. This is my only reason for being on this Earth. This must become the only reason for living for all those people who wish to help me.

Who Created the Creator of the Creators?

QUESTION:

The Elohim created us, and other people from another planet created them. Who created the creators of the Elohim?

ANSWER:

The Infinite in space is easier for man to understand than the Infinite in time.

Once we have attained sufficient open-mindedness, we can understand that in space the Earth is but a particle of the atom of the atoms of the hand of a gigantic being, who contemplates a starlit sky which composes the hand, the stomach or the foot of a being even more gigantic, who finds himself under a sky, etc., etc., ad infinitum. The same process applies for the infinitely small. On the atom of the atoms of our hands, there exist intelligent beings for whom these particles are planets and stars, and these beings are composed of atoms of which the particles are the stars and the planets on which there are intelligent beings, etc., etc., also to infinity.

Infinity in time becomes more difficult for Man to understand because Man is born one day, he lives a certain number of years and dies, but he would like everything in the universe to be limited in time as he is. For the man who is not awakened, the idea that anything in the universe could be eternal is unbearable, even if this were the universe itself. Our present day scientists abide by the same rule and say the universe must measure so many kilometers and must be so many millions of years old. Whether in space or in time, we can only measure the part of the universe that we can sense.

Everything is eternal, be it in the form of matter or energy, and we ourselves are composed of eternal matter.

The Elohim were created by people from another planet, who had been created by other people coming from another planet, and so on to Infinity.

It is as foolish to search for the beginning of the universe in time as it is to search for the beginning of space.

Let us get back to the example where intelligent beings are living on the particle of one of the atoms of our hand and for whom this particle is a planet. In relation to space, the scientists on this microscopic planet located, for example, in the middle of the bone marrow of the first phalanx of our right index finger, these scientists will at first claim that the other particles that they can observe with the naked eye revolve around the centre of their world, their planet, the particle on which they are located. For these scientists, it is obvious that their planet is the centre of the universe. But they will progress, and one day a genius will prove that their sun does not revolve around their planet, and that the stars also do not revolve around their little world, but rather it is their planet that turns on itself in a near motionless sky, as well as turning around their sun at the same time. He will probably be burnt for his heretical theories by the inquisitorial witch-hunters of their "particle planet", but a day will come when people, having discovered more sophisticated instruments of observation, will prove that he was right.

Then the learned scientists of that period will proceed to measure the universe, in all modesty, saying that it stretches from the farthest star particle located at one end of the sky to the farthest star particle located at the other end. This measurement will represent only one billionth of a billionth of the area of our finger where they happen to be located. But, since they cannot see any further, they will assume that the universe stops where they can no longer observe.

But the observation techniques will progress even more, and they will start to perceive that there are other galaxies and clusters of galaxies. Be that as it may, it will prove only that the universe is greater than had been anticipated, and it will always measure so many thousand kilometers or light-years, a little more than before, 10 or 100 times more eventually, nevertheless, it will always measure something. We have reached this point in our progression on Earth. But let us get back to the planet located on our finger.

Science is always progressing, and the inhabitants of our phalanx are now at the level to launch always more audacious space explorations. They finally reach a new frontier, the bone of which their planet is but an atom of an atom. This way they can be sure that the universe measures so much by so much. The proof is that, after that point, there is nothing more to be observed.

A little later they succeed in crossing the immensity which separates the bone from the muscle, and their universe gains new dimensions again.

They improve their space-ships and finally reach the layer of skin which covers our finger. They have reached the end of their universe, which measures one-and-a-half centimeters by our scale, but was many light-years for them.

They will still be able, however, to pursue their space explorations inside the rest of our body. They will follow certain currents where the stars are moving mysteriously at very high speeds - gigantic corridors, which they will chart to permit them to come and go freely from their planet, but little will they know that they are travelling in our blood vessels. Their universe will be measured, demarcated. It will have a particular height, width and depth. An incredible number of light-years on their scale but only 1.75 meters for us. They will not yet have discovered that our feet, for example, are standing on a planet which for them is itself made up of a great number of galaxies, which their narrow minds, always wanting to place frontiers everywhere, cannot even begin to imagine and grasp. For the quantity of atoms contained within the Earth is immeasurable compared with the number within our body.

They would also have to become conscious that there are other "universe-men" like us, who are walking on this planet, and that in our sky there are other stars and other galaxies, and so on to Infinity.

Only some of the wisest of them, having reached a superior level of consciousness allowing them to be in tune with the universe, will thus be able to teach all this to their disciples at a time where, for the official scientists, their universe measured only a millionth of a millionth of a millimeter of the bone of our finger, which they could observe, only from the inside...

The concept of Infinity in time is the very same thing. The scientists of that mini-world could measure the age of their universe by measuring the age of the molecule of which their planet is but an atom of an atom, and the universe would have that age. Then they would realize that the age of the cell of which the molecule that they thought to be the "total universe", while it was, in fact, only a part, is much greater. Then they would discover that the limb, of which this cell is but a part, is much older still, and that the age of the being of which this member is but a part, is even greater, and so on to infinity.

What is the Purpose of Life?

QUESTION:

What is the purpose of life?

ANSWER:

As stated in the messages, everything must be estimated in relation to four levels. Our life means nothing when compared with the Infinite. If we die, if all of humanity disappears, it will not change anything in the Infinity of time or space. The gigantic being of whom we are a parasite of a particle of an atom, will continue to exist without noticing anything, and the whole of the history of mankind since its creation will have only lasted a billionth of a second for him.

The living beings on the atoms of the atoms of our hand will continue to exist as if nothing had happened, even if the atom on which their universe is located, is buried deep in the Earth in the flow of blood coming from our finger torn away by an explosion, for example. Even if this drop of blood is swallowed by a worm that retains the atom in which their universe is located, to constitute new cells for its growth, this will not affect the living beings on this little world, any more than it would affect the beings living on the atoms which make up the cells of their own fingers...

In relation to the Elohim, our life is very important, because we are their children, and we must show them that we are proud of having been privileged enough to have been created in their image. That is to say, able to become conscious of the Infinite, and also one day able to create people in our own image in return.

In relation to human society, our life is equally very important, because we are the result of a long list of survivors who have escaped the epidemics and wars which have made us the offspring of a long natural selection. We owe it to ourselves to participate actively in the plan that will allow humanity to reach the Golden Age, which it greatly deserves and which it is about to enter. We are the cells of this huge being that is Humanity, and at the time of the birth of this humanity, each cell, each one of us is very important, in that he or she has a role to play.

Finally, in relation to our own self, our life has only the importance that we give it. If we recognize the Elohim as our creators, and if we wish to contribute to the diffusion of the messages, so that they will be known all over the Earth so that mankind enters the Golden Age, and if we enjoy our participation in this gigantic endeavor, then we are enjoying life for that reason.

The question was, 'what is the purpose of life?' Life was made to be enjoyed, whether you find pleasure in the diffusion of the messages of our creators, or pleasure in contributing to the entry of Humanity into the Golden Age, or pleasure in pleasing yourself by putting yourself in tune with the Infinite, or by any other means.

What is Pleasure?

QUESTION:

What is pleasure?

ANSWER:

Pleasure is the reaction of an organism which has accomplished an act producing pleasant chemical reactions.

A baby experiences pleasure while suckling its mother's breast because its hunger is appeased, and because the chemical reaction produced by the milk on the papilla of the tongue produces a pleasant sensation. All our senses are there to give us pleasure, and *Sensual Meditation* is based on an improvement of the perception of pleasure provoked by the chemical reactions transmitted by our senses.

Everything we do during our life, we do because it gives us pleasure. There is not one action performed during our entire life which is not done for pleasure. The person who pays his income tax does it because it pleases him not to have to go to jail for not having paid it. The woman who throws herself under the wheels of a car to save her child, does it because it pleases her to see her child survive, even if it means being wounded in the process. And the soldier who throws himself under enemy fire in order to save his battalion, does so because it pleases him to die for his comrades. The suicide pilots of Japan are the ultimate example of this type of heroism – pleasure.

There is a difference between direct pleasures, such as immediate sensual satisfaction, and indirect pleasures, such as the choice of behavior, which we spoke of earlier, and which are a reaction to exterior interventions without resulting in a conscious development of our means of perception of the environment.

It is only when conscious pleasure is obtained in solitude in an attempt to improve the quality of one's perception, that true blossoming can take place. We are linked to the Infinite through our senses. Someone who cannot see, hear, smell, touch, or taste, would actually be dead, even if his heart was still beating. He would not be conscious of his environment and would therefore possess no intelligence.

It is important to note that those who are deprived of one sense develop the remaining senses to a much greater extent than people with all their senses. Blind people, for example, develop an acute sense of hearing that we cannot grasp, or can read with their finger-tips.

Scientific experiments have demonstrated that the pleasure centre is located within the brain. This was discovered by placing electrodes in that part of the brain and sending small electrical discharges. The people who were experimented on felt something which was close to an orgasm, the satisfaction of having made a new discovery and the feeling of being honorably quoted in public all in one go. It was then proven by complementary measures that it was this same pleasure centre which was activated, when one was reaching sexual orgasm, or when discovering something, or when an artist had finished a masterpiece, or when a soldier received a medal.

Better still, another experiment demonstrated that artists who were sexually aroused while creating noticed an increase in their potential of creativity.

Nothing could be more logical. Pleasure increases the potential of creativity, because it stimulates all our senses, and a creator must be linked to Infinity in order to have a harmonious masterpiece born.

We must then strive towards improving the quality of our perception of pleasure by increasing the sensitivity of all our senses.

As a direct result, other than the increased enjoyment, this increase in sensitivity will develop our total potential of creativity so that the rest of humanity may benefit from our creations, thus improving the general level of consciousness.

This is what is being taught at the courses of awakening that we organize for the Raelians.

By improving the level of individual consciousness, we improve the level of consciousness of Humanity, and so increase the chances of entering the Golden Age.

In order to change society, we must first change the individuals of which it is composed. Violence is always produced by those who are unhappy.

By improving the individual's happiness, we help to lessen the potential for violence. Moreover and quite often, violence is produced by individuals who believe that they are unhappy, and the art of politicians is to strengthen this belief so as to overthrow those in power, to take their place. Then the former use the same tactics to reach the same goals, thus maintaining a feeling of dissatisfaction, which could one day, through the amplification of successive overthrows, result in the general feeling that the cause of the dissatisfaction is in another country. This is how wars are started.

If each individual becomes conscious of the Infinite, by developing his own sensuality, then the whole of society will be transformed. This will start by the awakening of the consciousness of people more developed than others, who once they have attained a certain level, will become Guides for the people around them, and will allow others to become fully awakened, who will in turn awaken others, and so on. Thus gradually, the level of consciousness of Humanity will be raised to such a point that a fatal world conflict would become impossible.

The process has already started, and thousands of small, non-violent manifestations have taken place around the world, organized by students or intellectuals in favor of peace, of unilateral disarmament of such-or-such a country, and it is amplified by television, the central nervous system of Humanity.

Each individual contributes at each moment of his life to the awakening or the stifling of planetary consciousness. You must not be afraid to influence others, as we are here for that purpose. But we should direct all our efforts and every word that we say, at every moment, so that all we say and every action we do has a positive influence on the course of human history.

One must never seek to convince others, because people who perceive that we are trying to convince them, have a tendency to strengthen their position. Whereas, if one discovers a point in common with the other's philosophy, then one can concentrate on this common point, and from there, unveil a new path for our listener, so that he will have the impression of having found it out by himself.

It is foolish to say that we will not influence anyone else by stubbornly following our own way and letting others follow theirs. The mere fact of not trying to influence others influences them even more than if one takes a fanatical stand on something. People fear fanaticism more and more, whatever the subject, and they are right to do so. This is in fact the beginning of wisdom.

On Earth, there are people who seek the truth and show it, and others who seek the truth and hide it, but there is not one single person who does not seek it. Then there are people who pretend that they have found the truth and show it, too often concerned with maintaining traditions, and last there are people who have found the real truth and show it: the Raelians.

We are very interested in those people who seek the truth and show it, because it shows that they are sincere and open-minded, generally very intelligent and relatively harmonious. In any case, for the most part, they are ready to accept a new vision of the world without fearing that this change will traumatize them to the point of unbalancing them. These people represent a great majority of present-day Raelians; they are the pioneers.

Those people who seek the truth and hide it, are also very important to us, but they will be more than likely to join us when they have overcome their self-consciousness, and no longer worry what other people think of them.

Those people who pretend that they have found the truth, and show it, will come to us when it becomes evident that nothing is constant in the universe, and therefore it is nonsense to try to preserve traditions that no longer mean anything. They just love their traditions but could not care less about what "God" really is.

All of these people do this for pleasure. The latter get pleasure in thinking that their children will pray in exactly the same way as they have, and that their children will teach their own children the very same ways of praying, even though school will teach them that man is descended from the monkey. So what if it is wrong? What is important to them is for the teaching at school to be respected, yet also for what the priest says to be respected. The fact that they are both contradictory is neither here nor there, what is important is that they are both traditions, and according to these lovers of tradition, it is not up to us to question which one is right.

Christians would surely crucify Jesus a second time if he himself were to ask them not to go to church on Sunday, or not to baptize their children before they had reached adulthood. This is the position adopted by the worshippers of tradition.

Those people who seek the truth and hide it, feel pleasure in thinking that what people think they are is more important than what they truly are. Those people would not crucify Jesus, they would even be against it, but they would still not intervene or even say anything. They do not want to get involved in anything, not even if it means defending what they believe to be the truth.

When all of Humanity enjoys its sensuality to the full, the risk of a world conflict will have disappeared. At the root of all violence, there are always sensually dissatisfied people. This is why we must learn to enjoy all of our senses, and help everyone around us to discover their total sensuality, starting with children. It is not sufficient to show them "how it works", like sexual education tends to do, but we must teach them "how to use it" so as to obtain and give more pleasure.

Sexual education should be replaced by sensual education.

Pleasure is always fulfilling, direct pleasure that is, and not the pleasure of the soldier who dies for his comrades. Direct pleasure develops in each individual the means to become in tune with the Infinite, and really feel a part of the Infinite.

Our body is nothing more than an accumulation of atoms organized according to a master plan, the genetic code, which interacts with the environment through an infinity of chemical reactions of which we are not always aware. Raising our level of consciousness corresponds to feeling an even greater number of these chemical reactions, so as to better situate ourselves in the Infinite, and so as to become more harmonious. When we feel linked to the universe, eternal and Infinite, we can never be unhappy, because we have then discovered the pleasure of being.

What is Death?

QUESTION:

What is death?

ANSWER:

Death in relation to the Infinite means nothing. The matter of which we are composed is eternal. Therefore, we are made of eternity. The infinitely small particles which compose our nose existed before they became part of us. Some of these particles were contained in the steak that our mother ate while we were in the womb, and those particles passed through her body and became part of our face. Other particles were in the fruit that we ate yesterday, they came into our abdomen and then travelled through our bloodstream to land on our nose. This is true for every part of our body. After death, the reaction will be exactly the same. The particles will return to the Earth to be recycled, and some particles will land in animals, others in plants, but most of them will remain in the Earth 'for you are dust and you will return to dust.'

Death, however, is the final cataclysm for the mass formed by this accumulation of organized matter, which makes up what we are.

Death is the beginning of the process of dispersion of the matter of which we are composed.

But to understand death, one must truly understand what life is all about. Life is nothing other than the organization of the unorganized. The Elohim came on Earth at a time when life did not exist. There existed only unorganized matter at our level - what we call the biological level.

They took this matter, they "kneaded" it, as stated in *The Bible,* and they "shaped" it to create living beings. This was all done at the molecular level, but for primitive man, this was impossible to understand, so they related it to pottery. They believed that the creators took a little piece of clay and created Man like you would do a flower pot. It is true that the creators did take chemical components from the Earth, but they combined them scientifically in such a way that the inanimate became animated.

Every living thing on Earth has been created by the Elohim, starting from a basic "brick", a molecular structure composed of atoms judiciously assembled. Our scientists are starting to discover that all living things, animal or vegetable, man or beast, have similar basic components. It's like a sort of alphabet, where every letter is an atom which makes up the genetic code of each living species. The order in which the letters are placed may differ with each species, but the letters of the alphabet would always remain the same. So with one relatively simple "brick", our creators were able to make an enormous quantity of "houses" that differed in their appearance, but which were all identical in their basic components. When the species reproduce, they are doing no more than "reproducing" the genetic code of the first model of their species.

So then, life is the organization of the unorganized, and death is disorganization of the organized.

Life is like a house that would build itself, by itself, starting from its own plan, and furthermore, it would maintain itself automatically. Death is the end of this automatic maintenance and the beginning of the dispersion of the basic materials of which the house is made, finally ending in the destruction of the plan which it had contained.

The Great Architects of our universe who have designed the plans of these "houses" designed a type which would be capable one day of matching its creators and becoming architects themselves, by creating other plans able to build "houses" which build themselves, by themselves. This type of superior "house" is Man, who will soon be able to create new synthetic genetic codes, new plans, starting from inanimate matter.

The living being was created with the ability of situating himself in his own environment through his "perception feelers", his senses.

Humans are nothing more than self-programming, self-reproducing biological computers.

There is no difference between humans and highly sophisticated biological computers, such as those we are now able to produce, only our computers are far more perfected and can perform far more accurately than a human.

The computers can be equipped with means enabling them to situate themselves in their own environment. Recently, a computer was equipped with wheels enabling it to move by itself around obstacles, thanks to TV cameras wired to its "brain". It can "see" exactly as we can with our eyes, and it can move in its environment.

A computer only does what it has been programmed for, and so does Man; but let us continue our comparison between Man and the computer.

As far as hearing is concerned, it is easy to endow a computer with a microphone that will pick up noise as we do with our ears.

It is also possible to give it an analyzer, which will identify the perfumes that surround it, just as we do with our nose.

Then it is also possible to give it a taste analyzer that would indicate the taste of various substances as we do with our mouth.

Finally, it is possible to equip the computer with feelers capable of functions that we perform with our hands, such as measuring temperature, hardness and weight.

Better still, the computer can be equipped with "organs" infinitely superior to our human organs. Let us take sight, for example. The cameras used on the computer can be equipped with multiple lenses, including a zoom lens, which will enable it to see clearly what is going on many kilometers away, or a microscopic object; things that the human eye is unable to see unless equipped with artificial prostheses such as binoculars or microscopes.

The same thing applies to the sense of hearing. While we can only perceive the sounds that exist around us in a very narrow range, certain animals, like dogs, can perceive a wider range. So our computer can be equipped with receptors sensitive to ultra-sounds or infra-sounds and directional microphones allowing it to hear sounds that are many kilometers away at a precise location.

Getting back to sight, the cameras could be equipped to pick up ultraviolet or infrared rays enabling it to see at night, something we are not capable of doing with our limited vision.

And as for the sense of smell, the odor analyzer could identify odors and instantly transmit the chemical composition of the perfumes or surrounding gases, something which our nose could never do.

For the sense of taste, we could also equip it with flavor analyzers capable of making a detailed chemical analysis of any given substance.

Finally, for the sense of touch, we could give it feelers, a touch mechanism able to analyze with precision the temperature, the weight and the hardness of objects or substances, other than saying it's hot or it's heavy. It would also be able to manipulate things at temperatures that our skin could not endure, things weighing a thousand times more than our poor human muscles could lift.

We could go even further and equip our computer with senses that man does not possess or that he is unable to make use of. We could, for example, give it radar, permitting it to move in complete darkness, a sonar, an x-ray detector, a compass, a gravity detector, a radio communication system, so many senses that our body is not provided with, and that we cannot even perceive, except with the use of electronic prosthesis that we can rarely have altogether in the same place and at any given time.

Let us compare the energy requirements of the human computer and the machine. When a man needs energy, he says, 'I am hungry', looks for food and eats it. Scientists have recently completed a computer equipped with electrical batteries. It works, and its cameras enable it to move and to store and move about heavy boxes just like a fork-lift truck. Suddenly, the battery charge becomes too weak, and it loses its efficiency. Its energy indicator shows that the time has come to charge the batteries. Then, by itself, it will move to an electrical outlet, plug itself in, and wait patiently until the charge is sufficient, then disconnect itself and return to work. This is no different from the man who says 'I am hungry' and proceeds to the cafeteria to get food at mealtimes and then returns to work.

What happens when a man is injured? He stops working, he gets medical attention, then returns to work. A computer can be programmed for self-maintenance, just as it was programmed to feed itself. If one of its parts becomes defective, it will go to a workshop, remove the part and replace it with a new one, and this is done without human help. This computer will then become eternal and will never be faced, as man is, with the issue of death.

Man is able to reproduce himself, and so is the computer. It only needs to be programmed accordingly. If a computer is programmed to make replicas of itself, which have the ability to do the very same thing, then in a very short time, we will have an overgrowing population of computers. This is why they must not be programmed to reproduce; for humans, this is called the species conservation instinct, the unconscious desire to reproduce. Humans find pleasure in copulating, unaware that they are in fact responding to an impulse, the species conservation instinct. If there was no pleasure in copulating, then there would be no reproduction. The human genetic code was programmed so that pleasure is obtained through copulation, in order for reproduction to take place. The humans who use a contraceptive method, such as the pill, the cap or the condom, etc., make a fantastic "nose-thumbing" to their genetic code. They consciously take pleasure without it leading to reproduction. Pleasure always brings an expansion of the mind, but overpopulation is certainly a serious danger for Humanity; contraception is a magnificent way that humans have of showing that they are conscious of themselves and conscious of the importance of their actions in regard to the whole of humanity.

Let us get back to our computer; it could also be programmed to feel pleasure in doing certain things. Every computer which performs as it has been programmed to perform, experiences pleasure from its performance. When the computer "feels" that its energy level is low, it says, 'this is wrong', then runs over to recharge. When it feels the new energy running through its circuits, it can say 'this is good' and in doing so 'feels pleasure'.

What goes into the program of a computer? Information contained in a memory bank that will rule the behavior of the computer. If it is programmed to calculate, it will calculate; if it is programmed to draw, it will draw; if is programmed to play music, it will play music. But it will not play music if it has been programmed to calculate and vice versa, unless of course it has been programmed for both functions.

How is a human programmed? On the one hand, there is the genetic code, which is filled with information related to his behavior, to his sensual means, which enable him to communicate with his environment, to his physical means so that he can move, feed himself, reproduce, etc. This is what each human receives at birth (more or less in relation to his heredity), and which constitutes the innate. On the other hand, his education will provide him with a language so that he can communicate with his fellow humans, laws which will regulate his behavior, a set of "moral values", a teaching, a concept of the world, a religion, etc. All these things will determine the individual's behavior. The individual will be under the impression that he is performing on his own, of living in a world where his values are those which he has chosen, but they will be only those which his education has imposed upon him, those ideas received from people who have played the role of educator or programmer. This is called experience.

Ordinary people, unconscious people, are incapable of doing anything other than that which they have been programmed for by their genetics or by their experience, by their heredity and by their educators. The "total man", the man who raises his level of consciousness so as to situate himself in the infinity of space and time, becomes a self-programmable computer. He can question the program which has been imposed on him by his education without asking advice, and replace his total or partial education with a new and more appropriate set of values that will seem better, in relation to higher standards, than those antiquated ones which had motivated his family and his environment. Those standards were aimed generally at conditioning him to keep alive the traditions of the past, of times when men were totally primitive, with a low level of consciousness in their conception of the world, and the role that humans had been created to play in it.

An ordinary man who wishes to become a "total man", a man with a higher level of consciousness which would enable him to exploit a little more than 10 per cent of his brain – percentage used by ordinary men and partial men – must be able to do his own in-depth "brain-washing". This operation will enable him to look at everything in his brain, to put back what seems to be good and to disregard what seems to be bad. He will keep his own ideas and get rid of the ones he received either from other people, his family, or his environment, ideas which he has received from those people who wanted to model him after their own conventions and for their own convenience. This applies to his behavior, his reactions to world events, the way he awakens, gets up, gets dressed, works, speaks to others and listens to them, the blossoming of his sexual life, etc. - everything, each gesture, no matter how small or insignificant it may seem. A total man is conscious of each movement of his eyebrows and the effect it could have on the people surrounding him.

Quite obviously, this great "spring cleaning" in order to be efficient, must be done in the company of someone who has already crossed the line which separates "ordinary men" from the infinite universe of "total man", someone who knows all the different paths, and who is able to lead this new traveller in the proper direction, and to guide without forcing him, letting him choose his own path freely.

A man's consciousness is a house which has been built usually by other people, based on standards which have never been questioned, since the same thing had been done to them and to their parents before them. The total man will destroy this house and build a new one, adapted to his taste, and to his imagination. He will recover from the old ruins certain things which seem reusable, and combining them with the new components, he will build a new house, perfectly suitable to his new personality. Men have houses built in conformity to their level of consciousness. Houses have always been square or rectangular, with slanted roof tops, and nothing could change that. They keep building the same type of house over and over again. Every house is like a Greek temple with vertical walls, like pillars, and a slanted rooftop, like a pyramid sitting on top of the Greek pillars. Modern construction techniques allow for more personalization when building a house. For instance, it could be completely round, it could have the shape of a ball, or an egg, or an Egyptian pyramid, or a bird, or a tree, etc. Houses which are built in series all looking exactly the same and forming morbid looking uniform villages, are the exact reflection of the level of consciousness of their inhabitants. And yet paradoxically, the house is a typical example of Man's capacity for self-programming. The blackbird has always built his nest in the same way, and it cannot change that because this is programmed into its genetic code. Man, however, is capable of adapting his shelter to his environment. He can build Greek temples, pyramids, huts, igloos, wooden cottages, skyscrapers made of iron and cement, cathedrals made of stone, and towers made of metal or glass.

The mere fact that Man is a self-programming computer does not make him different from the machine. All computers can be programmed to do the same as we do, and like us, they could be programmed to reproduce themselves. It could be also possible to program a computer so that it could be self-programming. It would be able to live, to work, to reproduce itself from a basic program, based on its experiences, and to give this information to its descendants, to the computers that it would reproduce.

We could even imagine a "mind expanding" computer which would have the ability to awaken the programs of already existing computers which had been created as non self-programming, so that this feature would be transmitted to them...

Man is therefore starting to discover, through the machine, that there is nothing mysterious about himself nor his origins, nor his behavior. Everything that a man can do, a computer can do, and what is more, it can do it much better. This applies to everything that can be done by a human, and it includes artistic creativity. There are computers capable of composing music, of drawing and so on.

We could never find a human ability that cannot be programmed in a computer, even getting in tune with the Infinite could be programmed. All of this is simply fantastic, and Man is able to look upon himself as a wonderful machine and concentrate whole-heartedly on seeking happiness and total blossoming through the fulfillment of his own needs and that of his fellow men, in order to build a world in which all men will be happy to feel that they are infinite and eternal.

Sexual Freedom and No Obligation

QUESTION:

The message mentioned total sexual freedom. But for a couple who read the books and wish to become Raelians, does it become mandatory to practice the exchange of partners?

ANSWER:

Freedom to do something and obligation are two different things, which must not be confused. A Raelian couple who love each other deeply, where both partners do not wish to share a sexual experience with other couples, should stay together. If they feel happy being with each other without the need to experience anything else, that is just fine. Everyone must do as he or she pleases. Sexual freedom of choosing a single partner, once you have discovered who you really are, and once you have discovered a partner who fills your every need and whose every need you seem to fill, becomes a question of choice to live together. However, quite often an experience with another person will render you more appreciative of your partner's company, as you become more conscious of his or her qualities. In so far as sexual contacts are concerned, everything is possible, everything is permitted. I must insist on the word permitted for it does not mean mandatory.

Since the creation of the Raelian Movement, I have had the opportunity to see many couples start new relationships. Some of these seem to be so successful that I can very well see what they hope to gain in seeing other partners. Perhaps these experiences would only confirm that they are truly made for each other. Some people are sufficiently awakened to understand that the experience in itself is not really necessary. When a man is totally conscious, he does not need to do something to find out what the result is going to be, he knows it, he can feel it, unless the experience is aimed at the awakening of a disciple, or it is felt essential to his own personal progression. Each person is free to follow his own chosen path so long as the following three fundamental rules are observed:

Respect the tastes and decisions of others in the free choice of their partners; be permanently conscious that others do not belong to us and that nobody can be the owner of anybody; and always seek above anything else, the happiness of those we claim to love.

On this basis, everything is possible, couples, threesomes, foursomes and "more-somes" of Raelians living a perfect happiness, whether they be homosexuals, heterosexuals, or bisexuals.

Raelism and Homosexuality

QUESTION:

What is the position of the Raelian Movement on homosexuality?

ANSWER:

It is quite simple: each individual has the right to do with his or her body as he or she sees fit. Homosexuality is not a normal or abnormal mode of behavior. Each person must live an harmonious sexual life corresponding to tastes and natural tendencies. In the mother's womb the sexual differentiation is felt at a very late stage of development. There are very masculine men, and men who are more feminine, just as there are women who are virile and others who are very feminine, with all the possible and imaginable shades in between.

It is foolish to condemn a homosexual because he is a homosexual, just as it would be foolish to condemn a man because he is a man, or a cat because it is a cat, as all of this is genetic. Many types of animals are homosexual, and in the country one can see frequently, dogs, cattle, and chickens indulging in homosexual behavior. Homosexuality is as natural as a dog or a hen is natural.

What is not natural is the wish to obligate others to have the same sexuality as oneself. It is generally what those who torture people who do not resemble them are doing. They are generally the same as those who are racist, traditionalist and militarist.

The aggression aimed at homosexual people is a form of racism. It usually comes from people who lead a miserable sex life, and cannot tolerate that others could blossom while living something else.

These same people who condemn homosexuality will forgive very easily a man charged with raping a woman, even though it is an abominable crime. Among the Raelian Guides there are male and female homosexuals, there are heterosexuals and bisexuals. All of them are blossoming because they are conscious of being loved as they are with the opportunity to fulfill themselves living in their body as they please, in a fraternal communion of thought that no other religion is able to give them. How can one still be a Roman Catholic follower when one hears the "Vatican Usurper" condemn homosexuality while depriving women of their rights of becoming priests. These are two proofs of racism and sexism that can help those who have eyes to see the truth.

Deists and Evolutionists: The False Prophets

QUESTION:

It is written, 'When the age of the Apocalypse will arrive, there will be many false prophets.' Who are they?

ANSWER:

There are many false prophets in our day and age. Do not forget the meaning of the word *prophet*, its etymology. It means "the one who reveals", as we have stated earlier. The false prophets of our time, that is to say, those who reveal or teach false information, are all those people who try to bring humanity back to primitive beliefs in an immaterial and impalpable, yet almighty "God" who watches over each human being to either punish or reward him, as the case may be. It is a concept which mixes the infinite, which is indeed impalpable in its totality because of it being infinite in space and eternal in time - yet without any consciousness of its own and thus with no power over humanity as a whole, nor over any single person, for that matter – and the Elohim who are our creators, who are real and almighty in this sector of the infinite, but who love us, their children, and who allow us to evolve freely in our scientific and spiritual progression.

The second category of contemporary false prophets are all those people, scientists or not, who claim that life on Earth, and therefore Humanity, is the result of successive random chance events, which all happened during what they call "evolution". As Einstein said, there cannot be a watch without a watchmaker. All those people who believe that we came from the monkey through a slow evolutionary process, believe that the beautiful watch which we are, has built itself by accident. It is a bit like saying that if we put all the components of a watch together in a bag and shook it around for a while, we would eventually get a perfect working watch. Try a billion times if you so desire...

The evolutionists are also false prophets, false informers, people who lead the majority of the population away from the truth about our creators, the Elohim. This population, which easily swallows and dumbly believes in everything said by these narrow-minded high priests in white coats - who compose the majority of the scientific community - is purposely kept ignorant and so inevitably believes that which officialdom says is true. Can you begin to imagine what the Elohim feel when they see that humans attribute their masterpiece to random chance?

Suicide

QUESTION:

It is said in the second message that one who suffers too much pain has the right to commit suicide. Does it mean that suicide is a good thing?

ANSWER:

We will all be judged according to our actions while living on this Earth. The person with more positive than negative actions will be entitled to eternal life on the planet of the Elohim. If a person suffers too much physically, and if human science is unable to relieve his pain, then he has a right to put an end to his life. If most of his actions in his life were positive, he will be re-created to live eternally. If they were mainly negative, he will not be re-created, and for him there will be nothing. However, if most of his actions were negative, he could be re-created to be judged later by those same people whom he made to suffer.

Someone who is not physically suffering, or who has no handicap, must not commit suicide, as we all have a mission to accomplish on this Earth, especially Raelians. They must dedicate their lives to the diffusion of the messages given by the Elohim, of whom they are the spokes-people. To end one's life is like an act of treason, it's like running from one's post during combat. I am referring to the combat which will awaken humanity and allow it to survive in order to reach the Golden Age. The Elohim are counting on each one of us, and each Raelian is very precious to our creators.

Allow me to repeat myself: the only time when suicide is acceptable is when a person is in extreme physical pain, which cannot be relieved by science, or when his faculties have diminished to the point where he can no longer act effectively.

All other people are messengers of our Fathers who are in the sky, and we must all dedicate our lives to the spreading of the good news.

2

THE NEW REVELATIONS

This chapter contains revelations that the Elohim had asked Rael to keep secret until three years after his journey when the second message was revealed to him. Now that we are in the year 34 (1979), these things can be known to all.

The Devil Does Not Exist, I Met Him

Do not tremble when wondering if a creature with horns, with cloven feet, well hidden, waits for the right moment to come and prick your backside with a trident. Since there is no "God" sitting on a white cloud, holding a flash of lightning in his right hand, the devil does not exist either.

For the average person, *Devil, Satan, Lucifer* or *Demon* are different names attributed to a single person who is one and the same, and personifies the forces of evil, just as they would think of "Apocalypse" as meaning "the end of the world".

Let us trace the true meaning of these words. *Satan* is chronologically the most ancient. When the Elohim created the first completely synthetic living beings in the laboratories on their original planet, a certain group of people from their world protested against these genetic manipulations, which they thought were dangerous for their civilization. They were afraid that one day the scientists would create monsters that would escape from the laboratories and would commit murders within the population. Unfortunately, we know that this is what happened, and the movement that was trying to have this genetic engineering work forbidden, triumphed. So the government of the planet of the Elohim ordered the scientists to halt their experiments and forced them to destroy all their works.

The group which led the battle against these genetic manipulations was presided by an Eloha called Satan.

The scientists were finally permitted to go to another planet and pursue their experiments. A description of this event is described in *Matthew 13:3-4*. It is a parable which describes the works of the creation of life on other planets by the Elohim:

> A sower went forth to sow; and when he sowed, some seeds fell
> by the way side, and the fowls came and devoured them up.

The birds are the messengers sent by Satan, who thought that the planet chosen for their creation of life experiments was far too close to their own, and that if by chance the beings created in a laboratory were in fact more intelligent than their creators, and became violent, they could prove to be dangerous for the population of the Elohim's planet. The government gave them permission to once again destroy the works of the scientists.

They had to search for another planet which lent itself to the creation of life, but they failed twice. The first time, the chosen planet was too close to a star, and the creation was burnt by the harmful rays coming from that star, and on the second one, they were invaded by the vegetation. Finally, they reached a planet which offered all the necessary elements so that their creation could survive, and it was located far enough away so as not to show any signs of danger in the eyes of the association presided over by Satan.

> Some fell upon stony places, where they had not much earth: and
> forthwith they sprung up, because they had no deepness of earth:
> And when the sun was up, they were scorched; and because they
> had no root, they withered away. And some fell among thorns;

and the thorns sprung up, and choked them: but other fell into good ground, and brought forth fruit, some an hundredfold, some sixtyfold, some thirtyfold. Who hath ears to hear, let him hear. *Matthew 13: 5-9.*

We know the Elohim also created life on two other planets at that time, hence the allusion to "three harvests".

We also know that the permission which allowed the scientists to come to Earth to create life was granted to them on the sole condition that they did not create people in their image. The first message explains how they overruled this order and also shows the reaction of their government, which strictly forbade them to reveal to the first terrestrial men, whom they had fabricated, how they had been created and who they were, and demanded that these first men be obligated to fear their creators, by asking the creators to show themselves as supernatural beings, divine beings in some way.

Satan thought that one could not expect anything good from these scientifically created creatures, and that out of Man only evil could come.

So we understand perfectly that Satan was just one of the Elohim, leading, in some way, a political party on the planet, that was opposed to the creation of artificial beings in their image by other Elohim who themselves thought that they could create positive and non-violent beings.

Then came Lucifer, which means "light bearer". Lucifer is one of the Elohim who created life on Earth, thus created Man.

Lucifer was heading a small group of scientists working in one of the genetic engineering laboratories which studied the behavior of the first synthetic men. Noticing the extraordinary aptitudes exhibited by their creation, Lucifer decided to overrule the order and reveal to these first humans that those whom they had mistaken for "Gods" where in fact men like themselves, made of flesh and blood, and who came from another planet in flying machines made of palpable material. Lucifer, and the Elohim who followed him, felt love and affection for their synthetically created humans. They started to love these beings as their own children - these beings that they studied all day long, who were obliged to look upon them as "Gods".

They could not bear to see their creatures, who seemed to be a physical and psychological success, and who were beautiful and intelligent, on their hands and knees adoring them as if they were idols, all of this just because the government of their planet of origin, of which Yahweh was the president, strictly forbade them from telling their creations the truth and forced the Elohim to play the role of supernatural beings permanently.

Lucifer, "the bearer of light", enlightened the first men when he revealed that the creators were not "Gods" but men like themselves. This attitude is directly opposed to that of Satan who thinks that only evil can be expected from men, and also to Yahweh, the president of the council of the Eternals governing the Elohim's planet.

So far, no creature with horns.

Yahweh condemns the scientists who had disobeyed his orders to spend the rest of their lives in exile on Earth. He condemns the "serpent" to crawl on Earth, as it is so poetically written, and evicts Man from the laboratory, the "Garden of Eden" where they were fed and lodged without having to make the slightest effort.

But Satan doesn't give up over this, as what he wishes is that all the beings that have been created, be totally destroyed, because he judges them to be dangerous, due to their violence. As time passes, Satan accumulates proof of Man's aggression by observing the way in which humans kill each other with the weapons that are given to them by the sons of Lucifer's exiled group of Elohim. The latter is involved in "tender" relations with the daughters of men who manage to receive weapons in exchange for their charms, under the false pretense of giving them to their fathers or brothers so that they can hunt for food. In fact, men choose to fight abominable battles among themselves with this arsenal.

Seeing the proofs of such a slaughter, brought by Satan before the Council of the Eternals, Yahweh decides to do what Satan asks, that is to say, totally destroy the life that has been created on Earth, and by the same token allow Lucifer's group to return to their own planet and be forgiven, thus putting an end to their exile.

But when Lucifer's group learns that their fabulous creation is soon to be destroyed, they decide that they cannot allow that. They still feel very strongly that among men there are some who are positive and non-violent, full of love and fraternity. Among these was Noah whom they helped build a space craft which would protect him from destruction, by staying in orbit around the earth. This craft contained a few men and women and the genetic codes of some animal species, which would be used to re-create them after the cataclysm.

It was only then that the Elohim discovered that they too had been created in the same manner that they had created man, scientifically, in a laboratory, by other people coming from another world. They then decided never again to destroy humanity, and helped Lucifer's group to re-implant the life forms preserved in the "ark". Satan is still convinced of the evil in Man, but he bows before the majority of those who, behind Yahweh, think the contrary within the council of the Eternals. Yahweh understood, through the message contained in the unmanned spaceship coming from another planet which landed on their planet, that if men are violent they will "self-destroy" when they discover energies enabling them to enter an interplanetary level of civilization.

The Elohim decided to let men progress by themselves, but chose certain people, or had them born on Earth, who would be responsible for the creation of the religions, which were designed to keep traces of their work on Earth, so that the creators of Man would be recognized as such when the time came when mankind had sufficiently evolved, scientifically, to be able to understand rationally.

Messages of such importance could be given only to trustworthy people, and first of all, the Elohim had to assure themselves that their chosen ones were faithful to their creators, so that they would not betray what was revealed to them. So Satan was given the responsibility of testing the prophets.

How are they going to test the faithfulness of these people? Once a person has been contacted by the messengers of the Elohim, telling him of his mission, Satan or one of his men would contact the prophet-to-be and by slander would destroy the Elohim in his mind, trying to get the human to abjure his fathers, or to accept to betray his mission on the promise of material advantages, for example. What is the word for slanderer in Greek? Simply *diablos*. Here is our famous devil, but he still has no horns, no hooves...

Jesus, for example, was taken into the desert for forty days for his initiation period, and was at certain times confronted with, "the devil" to see if he would deny his father:

> Then was Jesus led up of the Spirit into the wilderness to be tempted of the devil.[17] *Matthew 4: 1.*

Or, to be clearer: 'Jesus was taken to the desert to be tested by a slanderer.'

The many tests imposed by "the devil" are also described. First of all, he asks Jesus to turn the stones into bread to prove he is the son of God:

> 'If thou art the Son of God, command that these stones become bread.' But he answered and said, It is written, Man shall not live by bread alone, but by every word that proceedeth out of the mouth of God.'[17] *Matthew 4: 3-4.*

Jesus tells Satan that it is more important to be faithful to the Elohim than to eat. The devil is tempting him with food since Jesus has fasted for quite some time. Then Jesus is carried to the pinnacle of the temple and told to jump so that the "angels of God" will cushion his fall to prevent him from being injured:

> 'If thou art the Son of God, cast thyself down: for it is written, He shall give his angels charge concerning thee: and, On their hands they shall bear thee up, lest haply thou dash thy foot against a

stone.' Jesus said unto him, 'Again it is written, Thou shalt not make trial of the Lord thy God.'[17] *Matthew 4: 6-7.*

Jesus replies to the devil that he has not been placed on Earth for the useless exercise of testing his creators, thus proving that he does not ask for their help at every moment.

Then Satan leads Jesus to the top of a high mountain and proposes to make him a great and very rich king on the Earth.

> Again, the devil taketh him unto an exceeding high mountain, and showeth him all the kingdoms of the world, and the glory of them; and he said unto him, 'All these things will I give thee, if thou wilt fall down and worship me.' Then saith Jesus unto him, 'Get thee hence, Satan: for it is written, Thou shalt worship the Lord thy God, and him only shalt thou serve.' Then the devil leaveth him; and behold, angels came and ministered unto him.[17]
>
> *Matthew 4: 8-11.*

Jesus shows his loyalty to the Elohim whom he prefers to serve rather than become a powerful and rich man. It must be noted in these verses that Jesus refers to the slanderer by his name, since he calls him Satan. Since the test was successful, the "angels", the Elohim's messengers, came down to Jesus to complete the initiation.

Jesus was not the only one to be tested by "the devil"; Job was also tested by Satan. The beginning of *The Book of Job* is quite eloquent, as it shows clearly what good relations, or even fraternal relations there were between Yahweh and Satan:

> Now there was a day when the sons of Elohim came to present themselves before Yahweh, and Satan came also among them. And Yahweh said unto Satan, 'Whence comest thou?' Then Satan answered Yahweh, and said, 'From going to and fro in the earth, and from walking up and down in it.' And Yahweh said unto Satan, 'Hast thou considered my servant Job, that there is none

like him in the earth, a perfect and an upright man, one that feareth Elohim, and escheweth evil?' Then Satan answered Yahweh, and said, 'Doth Job fear Elohim for nought? Hast not thou made an hedge about him, and about his house, and about all that he hath on every side? thou hast blessed the work of his hands, and his substance is increased in the land. But put forth thine hand now, and touch all that he hath, and he will curse thee to thy face.' And Yahweh said unto Satan, 'Behold, all that he hath is in thy power; only upon himself put not forth thine hand.' So Satan went forth from the presence of Yahweh. *Job 1: 6-12.*

We can see clearly that Yahweh is above Satan in the Elohim hierarchy. But still he authorizes Satan, in his capacity of "opposition party leader", to do as he pleases, by giving him Job, so to speak, so that he can prove that he can take a man who loves the Elohim profoundly, and bring him to hate them if he is afflicted by misfortunes, ruin or sickness.

In fact, Satan ruins Job totally, but the latter continues to love and show respect for the Elohim:

Then Job arose, and rent his mantle, and shaved his head, and fell down upon the ground, and worshipped, and said, 'Naked came I out of my mother's womb, and naked shall I return thither: Yahweh gave, and Yahweh hath taken away; blessed be the name of Yahweh.' In all this Job sinned not, nor charged Elohim foolishly. *Job 1: 20-22.*

But Satan doesn't give up; he reports to the president of the Council of the Eternals:

Again there was a day when the sons of Elohim came to present themselves before Yahweh, and Satan came also among them to present himself before Yahweh. And Yahweh said unto Satan, 'From whence comest thou?' And Satan answered Yahweh, and said, 'From going to and fro in the earth, and from walking up and down in it.' And Yahweh said unto Satan, 'Hast thou considered my servant Job, that there is none like him in the earth, a perfect and an upright man, one that feareth Elohim, and escheweth evil? and still he holdeth fast his integrity, although thou movedst me against him, to destroy him without cause.' And Satan answered Yahweh, and said, 'Skin for skin, yea, all that a man hath will he give for his life. But put forth thine hand now, and touch his bone and his flesh, and he will curse thee to thy face.' And Yahweh said unto Satan, 'Behold, he is in thine hand; but save his life..' *Job 2: 1-6.*

Yahweh therefore allows Satan to ruin Job's health so as to see if he will always love his creators. And Job continues to respect the Elohim. Only then he began to ask Yahweh why he had been brought into the world, if it was only to be afflicted with all kinds of misfortunes. Finally, Yahweh intervenes and briefly explains to Job what has happened. Yahweh tells Job that he is wrong to judge his creators who ran the test, and to regret having been born. Yahweh restores Job's health, and even more possessions than he had before he was ruined.

At the end of the meeting I had with Yahweh on the relay vessel, he stepped out for a few moments, telling me that he would meet with me later. Then one of the other two Elohim asked me to follow him.

He took me to a small room, marvelously decorated. The walls were like the interior of a round pyramid, and those walls were covered with luminous sound waves which gave the impression of multicolored water waves. Everything was moving to a marvelously relaxing rhythm of musical vibrations. After having me seated in a comfortable chair which was covered with black fur, giving it the impression of being alive, he said:

'I must warn you that among the Elohim there is not only one opinion as to the future of Humanity on Earth. Yahweh thinks that men are good, and he feels that we should let them progress by themselves, convinced that if they are negative, they will self-destroy.

All my many followers and I, think that men are evil and that we should help mankind hasten its self-destruction. We propose that you help us accelerate the final cataclysm, which would only purify the universe of beings who are only the result of an unsuccessful experiment.

If you try to accomplish the mission given to you by Yahweh, you will always remain a poor man, and you will have to put up with the sarcasm of everyone. You will suffer, perhaps even be put in jail, or even worse, put to death by your own blood brothers. If you accept my offer, and carry out my plan based on increasing the various racist tendencies existing in human beings so that a racial world conflict erupts, I will make you very powerful and rich. Your role will consist of publishing the books which I will dictate to you, and which will enable you to create various political and spiritual movements preaching the destruction of the Arab race, the yellow race and the black race, who have taken over all the riches and the raw materials that the white race needs and deserves to have, since it was the efforts of white men which permitted them to develop techniques to search for them and to utilize them in the first place. As soon as this planetary conflict breaks out, you and all those people who have helped you to bring it about, will be saved. We will take you to safety on board one of our crafts, and eventually you will be allowed to return to Earth when everything has been destroyed, so that you can start a new humanity. You will govern this new civilization as you may desire, and with our help of course.

In the meantime, as soon as you return to Earth, there will be a sum of 1 billion, 5 billion, 10 billion, or more if you wish, deposited in the name of a foundation in a Swiss bank account, to help you get started. Tell us what that sum should be, and if it is not sufficient, other deposits will be made immediately.

Furthermore, if you accept to help us, you and all of those people who will have helped you, will have the right to eternal life.

The only thing we ask is that you do so, so that Humanity destroys the horrible civilization that is theirs today. For this, you will also have to tell them that you have met with an extra-terrestrial, and he has warned you of an invasion of the Earth by them. We will give you the necessary proofs of our existence, and no one will doubt your words anymore. In this way, Humanity will increase its armaments to prepare itself against possible attack from the sky. This will prevent Yahweh from another approach attempting to stop men from killing each other, from building up an even greater stock of nuclear weapons and aggression on Earth.

Consider on the one hand, some people are asking you to work for an already lost cause, since sooner or later, men will blow themselves off the face of the Earth. These same people will not even give you proofs of their existence to help you to convince your brothers, nor any financial aid. They will leave you to face the sarcasm, the police and judicial pressures that might lead you to prison, without counting the possibility that some fanatic might kill you because you claim that there is no "God". On the other hand, my proposition makes you a rich and very powerful man immediately, a man who will only have accelerated a course in which humans are already destined.

So, what is your decision? Do you want to think about it for a few days before giving me your answer?'

And I answered: 'I am not at all convinced that Humanity will self-destroy, even though there is a nine out of ten chance that it will. Even if there was only one chance in a thousand that Humanity suppressed its aggression and escaped destruction, I think that it would be worthwhile taking this one chance. I would like to think that men will understand before it is too late. And even if the final cataclysm occurred, Yahweh told me that all the people who will have fought for peace and non-violence will be saved, in order to re-populate the Earth and try to build a loving world. Your proposition does not offer anything more, except perhaps that in your plan, only those people who will have contributed to the explosion of violence will be saved. The new civilization which they would then structure could not avoid being violent, because of the dominant characteristics of its founders, directly, socially and hereditarily.

The mere fact of telling Humanity of the invasion of Earth by extra-terrestrials would be sufficient to trigger more fear and then increase aggression on our planet. So even if there is only one chance in a thousand that the Earth could be saved at the present time, this chance would be cut in half upon hearing the news of a possible intervention on your part. One of the most important factors which can contribute to lessening violence between men is the awakening of the mind to the universe and to the infinite. If all men looked to the sky with hope and fraternity, then they would feel much closer to each other and would think less about killing each other.

I am not interested in becoming rich and powerful. I have almost nothing, but the little I have is all that I need to live very happily. My mission which I am accomplishing fills my life with happiness. All I need is food for my children and a roof over their heads. All of this has been given to me by faithful disciples who wish to help me bring the truth to all the people of Earth. I cannot live in two houses at the same time, nor can I drive two cars simultaneously, and even if I owned my house, that does not mean that I could sleep any better, nor would the fire be warmer. As for the mission entrusted to me by Yahweh, I would much rather that it be carried out through the collective efforts of those who wish to welcome the Elohim, as this would certainly be the most beautiful proof of love that we can give to our creators.'

'So you are refusing my proposition?' asked the Eloha.

'Yes, and for all the reasons which I have just mentioned, since I am fundamentally opposed to violence.'

'Are you sure you will never regret this?' he asked. 'Would you not rather wait and think about it?'

'I will never change my mind, no matter what happens to me. Even if my life was in danger, I would much rather direct my efforts so that love and fraternity unite all men, so that they welcome their creators, as the Elohim deserve to be welcomed.'

At that moment, the door opened, and Yahweh entered with the other Eloha. He told me, 'I am very pleased with the reaction that you have had to the proposals which were made to you. I was convinced of your reactions, but Satan, our brother, who has just tested you, will not be convinced that something good can be expected of men until they are united, and money and all weapons are destroyed. My second companion who is so happy with your behavior is Lucifer, who was the first to put faith in mankind even before I had understood the need to let Humanity progress, and let Man go alone through the final test of resolving violence without an intervention on our part.'

Satan then told me that he thought there were not more than a dozen men like me on Earth. Love and fraternity shone from his face, and he was of the opinion that it was not because some rare exceptions existed, that Humanity deserved the right to exist.

Then we returned to the more spacious of the two ships, the one that would bring me to the planet of the Eternals, where my initiation was to be completed. All of this is related in the book which contains the second message, *Extra-Terrestrials Took Me To Their Planet*.

My Father Who Art in Heaven

On my first encounter with this extra-terrestrial, whom I did not then know to be Yahweh, the president of the Council of the Eternals, I was wondering why they had chosen me to become their messenger on Earth. He told me that they had decided to "choose" someone after the first atomic explosion at Hiroshima, which took place on August 6th 1945. Then he added: 'We have been following you since your birth, and even before.' (Refer to pg. 8 of *The Book Which Tells The Truth*).

In the beginning, I found this answer to be very intriguing, and during the two years between the first and second message, I often pondered on this subject.

I had to wait until I met Yahweh again to clarify this matter in full.

He revealed the truth of my origins at the end of his remarks addressed to the people of Israel, as reported in the second message when we were then on the planet of the Eternals.

Once again I was told to put on one of these belts with a large buckle, which enables one to travel in the air by following certain wave currents. I found myself flying about 20 meters above luxuriant vegetation after a smooth exit from the laboratory, where my mind had been modified in the strange shell-shaped chair.

In ten seconds or so, we had reached a paradisiacal clearing where a few prophets, with whom I had a meal earlier, were sitting. A few hundred meters below, I could see immense and magnificent sandy beaches, bordering on a sea of deep blue waters of such depth and beauty that none of the coves of the Mediterranean sea could match it, or even come close. The blue of the water was like that of a Californian swimming pool, but it spread out to the horizon, with great pink and green areas within the blue sea. When I looked more attentively, I could see traces of every color, each more beautiful than the next, as if the bottom of the sea had been painted for some 10 kilometers. I asked where these extraordinary colors had come from, and was told that the seaweed gave the water its coloration. The seaweed had been created and implanted artistically to produce the special effect that I had noticed.

The belt allowed me to descend gently in the small clearing near the group of ten or so prophets. The one who had been introduced to me as Jesus, came to meet us.

Following Yahweh, we all went and sat on seats carved out of the rock. All the seats were covered with this marvellous black fur which seemed to be alive. We were located on a cliff overlooking the sea.

Yahweh asked me if during the last two years since our first meeting, there had been some question which has preoccupied me more particularly. Without hesitation, I told him that I had often wondered what he had meant when he had explained, 'we have been following you since your birth and even before.'

I had twisted the question many times in my mind wondering if it had meant that my parents had been chosen before my conception, and if they had been guided telepathically to each other to bear me, or if they already knew each other when they were chosen, or if I had been conceived when they were chosen, or rather when the embryo which they had created was chosen.

Yahweh answered this question that was very important to me. His answer was even more extraordinary than I had anticipated.

At that moment, he stopped addressing me in French by the polite form of *vous* and started addressing me by the personal form of *tu*. He then said:

'The person whom you looked upon as your father was not your real father. After the explosion at Hiroshima, we decided that the time had come for us to send a new messenger on Earth. He would be the last prophet, but the first one to address Mankind asking them to understand and not to believe. We then selected a woman, as we had done in the time of Jesus. This woman was taken aboard one of our ships and inseminated as we had done with the mother of Jesus. Then she was freed after we had totally erased from her memory all traces of what had happened.

But before all of this had happened, we had arranged so that she would meet a man, who could support the child financially and would raise him decently. This man had to be from a different religion than that of the woman so that the child could be raised without strong religious conditioning. This is why the man whom you took for your father and believed that he truly was, was a Jew.

Your real father is also the father of Jesus, and that makes you brothers. You are presently looking at your father. Your foster-father was like Joseph, he was to take care of you and your mother until such time as you could provide for yourself. From this moment on, you can talk to me using *tu*, because you are my son and I am your father.'

Of the entire journey, this was the most touching moment. And I could see in Yahweh's eyes an equally great emotion and feeling of love. Jesus too seemed to be moved by the same feelings. Then I kissed my father and my brother for the very first time.

Then Yahweh asked me not to reveal this parental tie until three years had passed. This is the reason why I have never talked about it until now.

In any case, it is of no importance, we must not make the same mistake as those men who recognized Jesus as a messenger who came from the heavens. It is not the messenger who is important, but the message itself.

'Jesus came on Earth to show the way but men kept looking at his finger.', said a great thinker, and it is unfortunately true.

I, Rael, am also showing you the path to follow, in revealing the messages given to me by my father "who is in heaven". It is more important to recognize the Elohim as our fathers and to prepare their embassy on Earth as they requested, than to pay attention to the messenger. Only the messages are important and through them the recognition of those who sent them, but not the messenger.

Do not look at my finger, but rather in the direction in which it's pointed.

Message from Yahweh to the Men of the Earth: The Apocalypse of the Final Nuclear Cataclysm

I, Yahweh, through the words of my prophet Rael, address all the people of Earth:

There is, unfortunately, but one chance in one hundred that your Humanity will not self-destroy, and every Raelian must act as if Mankind would be wise enough to understand and grab this tiny chance of escaping the final cataclysm, so as to enter the Golden Age. Better still, each Raelian, by his work of awakening minds, contributes to strengthening this unique and minute chance of survival to prevent it from becoming even weaker.

It is impossible to predict the future, for it is impossible to travel in time, but it is always possible to predict the future of a biological entity, and the whole of Humanity can be considered as a biological entity. If a primitive woman was inseminated by a scientist, the latter could predict this woman's future. He could predict that in nine months she would give birth to a child, and could even go so far as determining the sex of the child.

In the same way, we who are used to creating life on an infinity of planets, know what happens to a Humanity which has reached your level of technology, without having reached an equivalent level of wisdom.

This is why, although we cannot predict the future of individuals, we can predict, however, what should normally happen to a living organism during the gestation period or to a Humanity in the course of its development.

When the first cell is created in the mother's womb by the meeting of the spermatozoon and the ovule, this first cell contains all the necessary information to create a complete being, able to accomplish a multitude of functions. And the more numerous the cells, the more numerous are the functions developed. The number of functions is proportional to the number of cells obtained by successive divisions, until the child is ready to be born, because only then does he become a complete organism, with all the organs which he will require to accomplish all the functions which will fill his every need.

It is exactly the same thing for humanity, considering each human to be like a cell of the great being in gestation, that is, Humanity.

The number of functions, of discoveries, and the technological level of Mankind is proportional to the number of humans. In this way, we can easily predict that the age of the Apocalypse will be achieved when Men are able to make the blind recover their sight with electronic prostheses, when Man's voice will be carried beyond the oceans through satellite telecommunication, and when Man will be equal to those he had mistaken for "God", by creating synthetic beings in a laboratory, etc.

All these predictions rely on an in-depth knowledge of the biology of the species. We know that a foetus will develop his eyes at a certain month of his growth, and his sexual organs at another month, and that the same rule applies to all living species which are developing. We know that it will make discoveries permitting the accomplishment of such and such a scientific prowess after so many hundreds or thousands of years. It's exactly the same thing.

We have dictated our messages to the prophets of old, so as to be recognized by men when the time would come for us to show ourselves openly, without this creating new deistic religions, i.e. when all men would be capable of understanding.

Among these texts is the *Apocalypse,* which we dictated to John. We showed him, through a visualizer similar to your television sets, the events which would happen to men when they would reach the Age of the Apocalypse.

The text of the Apocalypse of John was unfortunately overloaded and distorted by primitive transcribers who could not be anything other than God-believing people.

John starts his story by telling of his encounter with us:

> I was in the Spirit on the Lord's day, and I heard behind me a
> great voice, as of a trumpet.[17] *Revelation 1: 10.*

Here he explains that he is trying to communicate with us telepathically, this is what he calls being "in the spirit" on the Sunday, referred to as the "Lord's day", and that he heard a metallic voice "as of a trumpet"; this is something you all know: The sounds produced by an electrical loudspeaker.

Then John turned around to see what was behind him:

> Then I turned to see the voice that spoke with me. And having
> turned I saw seven golden lampstands, and in the midst of the
> seven lampstands One like the Son of Man, clothed with a
> garment down to the feet and girded about the chest with a

golden band.

His head and hair were white like wool, as white as snow, and His eyes like a flame of fire; His feet were like fine brass, as if refined in a furnace, and His voice as the sound of many waters;

He had in His right hand seven stars, out of His mouth went a sharp two-edged sword, and His countenance was like the sun shining in its strength.[12] *Revelation 1: 12-16.*

John saw seven flying machines made of a golden metal, "seven golden lampstands", in the middle of which stood a little being, "one like the Son of Man", dressed in a flying suit which was molded to his body, even his feet, and he is wearing a large belt. His skin and his hair are white; his helmet is equipped with two small projectors which John mistook for his eyes. His feet are standing on thick, insulated soles of yellow metal, and he speaks with a powerful voice, "and his voice as the sound of many waters".

In his hand, the little person holds an apparatus made of seven luminous signals, which are bridged to the seven vessels placed near him. The two-edged sword, on the other hand, is only a detail added later on by the transcribers to reinforce the menace of apparition, to increase the power of "God" and the fear of "God" of the first Christians. The being who appeared in front of John was indeed one of us.

John, panic-stricken, fell with his face to the ground:

And when I saw him, I fell at his feet as one dead. And he laid his right hand upon me, saying, 'Fear not; I am the first and the last, and the Living one; and I was dead, and behold, I am alive for evermore, and I have the keys of death and of Hades. Write therefore the things which thou sawest, and the things which are, and the things which shall come to pass hereafter.'[17]

Revelation 1: 17-20

We asked John to get up, and we told him that he must write everything that he had seen, and everything that would be dictated to him, so that men could find those writings when the time would come. We told him that we were "the first and the last", that is to say, the first on Earth and the last if men self-destroy when they discover energies to permit them to do so. We explained to him that the one who was speaking had known death, but had been re-created, thanks to the process explained in the first message, which permits us to live eternally through many bodies.

> And behold, a door opened in heaven, and the first voice that I heard, a voice as of a trumpet speaking with me, one saying, Come up hither, and I will show thee the things which must come to pass hereafter.

> Straightway I was in the Spirit: and behold, there was a throne set in heaven, and one sitting upon the throne.[17] *Revelation 4: 1-2.*

John sees "a door opened in heaven"; the door of one of our machines is opened, and he is taken inside on a carrying ray. This is totally incomprehensible for him, and this is why he says, "in the spirit".

There he sees someone sitting in a chair and around him a total of 24 other people also sitting on "thrones".

I, Yahweh, was this person sitting on the throne, and around me were sitting 24 other Eternals representing the Council of the Eternals, the governing body of our planet.

Then I turned on the apparatus designed to visualize thoughts, and he saw what would normally happen to Humanity, and also what would happen when the time would come:

> And I saw, and behold a white horse: and he that sat on him had a bow; and a crown was given unto him: and he went forth conquering, and to conquer. *Revelation 6: 2.*

This is in relation to the first of the seven seals, or if you prefer, the seven chapters of the history of Humanity. This is, in fact, the triumph of Christianity on Earth, and it allows The Old Testament to be revealed to everyone. Then the second seal is opened:

> And there went out another horse that was red: and power was given to him that sat thereon to take peace from the earth, and that they should kill one another: and there was given unto him a great sword. *Revelation 6: 4.*

This red horse represents the religious wars and wars in general, which will be one of the principal causes in the tardiness of humans to increase their number. Then comes the third seal:

> And I beheld, and lo a black horse; and he that sat on him had a pair of balances in his hand.
>
> And I heard a voice in the midst of the four beasts say, 'A measure of wheat for a penny, and three measures of barley for a penny; and see thou hurt not the oil and the wine'.
> *Revelation 6: 5-6.*

The black horse is the famine, which will claim a considerable number of lives before Mankind solves the problem on Earth completely. And then comes the fourth seal:

> And I looked, and behold a pale horse: and his name that sat on him was Death, and Hell followed with him. *Revelation 6: 8.*

This pale horse represents the great epidemics and plagues, and many others which have decimated Humanity. Then the fifth seal is broken:

When He opened the fifth seal, I saw under the altar the souls of those who had been slain for the word of God and for the testimony which they held.

And they cried with a loud voice, saying, 'How long, O Lord, holy and true, until You judge and avenge our blood on those who dwell on the earth?'

Then a white robe was given to each of them; and it was said to them that they should rest a little while longer, until both the number of their fellow servants and their brethren, who would be killed as they were, was completed.[12] *Revelation 6: 9-11.*

This scene represents what happened when the great prophets, living eternally in our company on our planet, asked us to allow men who had lived a positive life to be re-created before the final judgment. We gave permission so that a few thousand people from Earth, who we re-created, could live among us immediately, whereas first we had decided to keep their genetic code in order to re-create them only when Humanity had completed its evolution. Then the sixth seal was opened:

I looked when He opened the sixth seal, and behold, there was a great earthquake; and the sun became black as sackcloth of hair, and the moon became like blood. And the stars of heaven fell to the earth, as a fig tree drops its late figs when it is shaken by a mighty wind.

Then the sky receded as a scroll when it is rolled up, and every mountain and island was moved out of its place.

And the kings of the earth, the great men, the rich men, the commanders, the mighty men, every slave and every free man, hid themselves in the caves and in the rocks of the mountains.[12]
Revelation 6: 12-15.

The sixth seal represents the final danger for Humanity, the greatest danger, the one which could destroy it completely: the atomic war. The "great earthquake" is the explosion itself, the "black sun" is the darkening of the sky by the mushroom cloud, and the fall-out dust that you all know so well will darken the moon. "The sky receded as a scroll" is when the clouds are chased abruptly by the sudden surge of hot air coming from the explosion. The men who hide in the rocks of the mountains are the people who rush into anti-nuclear shelters. It is from this final cataclysm, if it happens, that people who will have followed our prophet, will be saved - those people who will have had their cellular plan transmitted after having read or heard of the messages.

Those people will have been selected by our huge computer, which follows all people from conception to death.

> Then I saw another angel ascending from the east, having the seal of the living God. And he cried with a loud voice to the four angels to whom it was granted to harm the earth and the sea, saying, 'Do not harm the earth, the sea, or the trees till we have sealed the servants of our God on their foreheads.'[12]
>
> *Revelation 7: 2-3.*

The people who will be sealed in the forehead will be those who will have their cellular plan transmitted by manual contact between our prophet and their forehead bone, which contains the purest and the most authentic genetic code. The total of those who will be "sealed in the forehead" will be around 144,000, which will include those people already re-created on our planet, those people who will have led a life dedicated to the blossoming of Humanity without ever hearing of the messages, and also those people who will recognize Rael as our messenger after having read the messages.

For as long as the total of these human beings does not reach 144,000, we will help to delay the final cataclysm, so as to have a sufficient number to start a new generation on Earth, when it has become a suitable place again for humans to live.

If the sixth seal represents the discovery and the first utilization of the atomic weapon, the seventh seal represents the final cataclysm, a worldwide atomic war, which ends with the destruction of all life on Earth.

When the first trumpet of the seventh seal sounded:

> ...and there followed hail and fire mingled with blood, and they were cast upon the earth: and the third part of trees was burnt up, and all green grass was burnt up. *Revelation 8: 7.*

One third of the Earth is burnt by radioactivity; the trees and the green grass no longer grow.

> And the second angel sounded, and as it were a great mountain burning with fire was cast into the sea: and the third part of the sea became blood; and the third part of the creatures which were in the sea, and had life, died; and the third part of the ships were destroyed. *Revelation 8: 8-9.*

The explosion produced an enormous eruption of lava which ran into the ocean, destroying one third of the marine life and one third of the ships.

> And the third angel sounded, and there fell a great star from heaven, burning as it were a lamp, and it fell upon the third part of the rivers, and upon the fountains of waters; and the name of the star is called Wormwood: and the third part of the waters became wormwood; and many men died of the waters, because they were made bitter. *Revelation 8: 10-11.*

Atomic explosions follow in retort to the first attack; the missiles, "great burning stars from Heaven", fall everywhere. Most of the drinking water becomes polluted, and many people die from it.

> And the fourth angel sounded, and the third part of the sun was smitten, and the third part of the moon, and the third part of the stars; so as the third part of them was darkened, and the day shone not for a third part of it, and the night likewise. *Revelation 8: 12.*

The dust and the ashes raised by successive nuclear explosions are so thick that the sky is darkened, obscuring the Sun, the Moon and the stars, which gives the impression that the day and the night are shorter.

> And the fifth angel sounded, and I saw a star fall from heaven unto the earth: and to him was given the key of the bottomless pit.
>
> And he opened the bottomless pit; and there arose a smoke out of the pit, as the smoke of a great furnace; and the sun and the air were darkened by reason of the smoke of the pit.
>
> *Revelation 9: 1-2.*

This is the description of a missile falling and the mushroom cloud it creates.

> Then out of the smoke locusts came upon the earth. And to them was given power, as the scorpions of the earth have power.
>
> They were commanded not to harm the grass of the earth, or any green thing, or any tree, but only those men who do not have the seal of God on their foreheads.
>
> And they were not given authority to kill them, but to torment

them for five months. Their torment was like the torment of a scorpion when it strikes a man.

In those days men will seek death and will not find it; they will desire to die, and death will flee from them.[12] *Revelation 9: 3-6.*

The locusts are airplanes loaded with atomic bombs which will fall on the great cities, and through exposure to radioactivity, will inflict terrible suffering on those people who will have survived the explosions. They will be poisoned by radiation, in much the same way as one can be poisoned by the sting of a scorpion.

And the shapes of the locusts were like unto horses prepared unto battle; and on their heads were as it were crowns like gold, and their faces were as the faces of men.

And they had hair as the hair of women, and their teeth were as the teeth of lions.

And they had breastplates, as it were breastplates of iron; and the sound of their wings was as the sound of chariots of many horses running to battle.

And they had tails like unto scorpions, and there were stings in their tails: and their power was to hurt men five months.
Revelation 9: 7-10.

Those metallic locusts covered with metal, looked like horses going to war, in the eyes of a primitive man. They had a cockpit inside of which a man's face could be seen "as the faces of men", and in flying very high, they left behind a trail of white smoke that John calls hair, and their "teeth" are the missiles tucked under their wings. The "breastplates of iron" are the fuselage, and the noise comes from the jet engines, as is familiar to you. The power in the "tails like unto scorpions" is the radiation produced by the missiles which were dropped on the population of the countries that were attacked.

> And the sixth angel sounded, and I heard a voice from the four horns of the golden altar which is before Yahweh...
>
> *Revelation 9: 13.*

John describes the four loud-speakers located in front of me while I was making him see all this.

> And thus I saw the horses in the vision, and them that sat on them, having breastplates of fire, and of jacinth, and brimstone: and the heads of the horses were as the heads of lions; and out of their mouths issued fire and smoke and brimstone.
>
> By these three was the third part of men killed, by the fire, and by the smoke, and by the brimstone, which issued out of their mouths.
>
> For their power is in their mouth, and in their tails: for their tails were like unto serpents, and had heads, and with them they do hurt. *Revelation 9: 17-19.*

Again this is the description of more planes; the "heads of the horses" are the jet-engines from which flames and smoke come out. The tail with "heads, with them they do hurt" are the nuclear missiles, and you can understand that the "heads" refers to the head of the missile, whether it's self-directed or not. We gave John the most detailed description possible, and this story reflects what he had seen with his primitive eyes. Take this same story and tell it to an Amazonian Indian, then ask him to write it down in his own words, and you will get approximately the same type of recollection, more so, if you ask 10 of his fellow tribe members to transcribe the story, while the first man is not present.

And when the seven thunders had uttered their voices, I was about to write: and I heard a voice from heaven saying unto me, 'Seal up those things which the seven thunders uttered, and write them not.' *Revelation 10: 4.*

At this point we clearly told John that there was no "God" and that we were men like him, and also we explained that he should keep this as a secret and not write it, so as not to create a greater confusion among the people who still needed a crutch to lean on, until the day when Humanity had reached a sufficient level of technology when everyone could understand what we had spoken of.

But in the days of the sounding of the seventh angel, when he is about to sound, the mystery of God would be finished, as He declared to His servants the prophets.[12] *Revelation 10: 7.*

We clearly explained to him that when the time would come, men would understand that there is no "God" and by the same token would also understand that we were their creators.

...for the devil is come down unto you, having great wrath, because he knoweth that he hath but a short time.
Revelation 12: 12.

This final test of Humanity, that is, the choice between self-destruction or the passage into the Golden Age, is the last opportunity for Satan to prove that he was right in saying that humanity was bad.

If Humanity brilliantly overcomes this last ordeal and succeeds in obtaining total disarmament on the planet, then men will have proven themselves worthy of receiving our inheritance, since they will have shown they are truly non-violent. The "beast", as described further on in the text, is simply the use of nuclear energy for murderous means:

> Here is wisdom. Let him that hath understanding count the
> number of the beast: for it is the number of a man; and his
> number is Six hundred threescore and six. *Revelation 13: 18.*

In fact, 666 is the number of human generations which will have
existed on Earth since the creation of the first men in the original
laboratories. The very first humans were created some 13,000 years
ago, and a human generation is estimated at an average of 20 years,
so if one multiplies 666 by 20, it equals 13,320 years.

The generation born at the beginning of the Age of Apocalypse in
1945 of the Christian era, was in fact the 666th since the creation of
the first man in a laboratory by the Elohim. This generation coincides
precisely with the first use of nuclear energy for destructive purposes
at Hiroshima, on August 6th, 1945.

Once again, interpretation was not required in order to
understand. One had only to read what had been written. 666 was
effectively the "number of Man", the number of men who descended
from the creation, that is to say, the number of generations.

> And there were voices, and thunders, and lightnings; and there
> was a great earthquake, such as was not since men were upon the
> earth, so mighty an earthquake, and so great. *Revelation 16: 18.*

The after-shocks from the atomic explosions are tremendous, and
they are increased if they start a chain reaction.

> And every island fled away, and the mountains were not found.
> *Revelation 16: 20.*

This monstrous explosion due to a chain reaction will brutally
divide the continents, engulfing the islands and sweeping the
mountains like a wisp of straw.

And there fell upon men a great hail out of heaven, every stone about the weight of a talent. *Revelation 16: 21.*

In those parts of the Earth untouched by the bombs, rocks are falling from the sky, thousands of kilometers away from where the bombs had fallen.

And I saw a new heaven and a new earth: for the first heaven and the first earth were passed away; and there was no more sea.
Revelation 21: 1.

John was able to see what one could see from a rocket moving away from the Earth. It seemed as if it was the Earth that was retreating, rather than the craft itself moving away. Then the spacecraft travels through a starlit sky unfamiliar to a man of the Earth, "a new Heaven". Then the spaceship reaches another planet, "a new Earth".

And I John saw the holy city, new Jerusalem, coming down from Yahweh out of heaven, prepared as a bride adorned for her husband. *Revelation 21: 2.*

Looking from the spacecraft, the primitive has the feeling that the city towards which the spacecraft is going, is "coming down out of Heaven", while it is evidently the spacecraft that is approaching.

And I heard a great voice out of heaven saying, 'Behold, the tabernacle of Yahweh is with men, and he will dwell with them, and they shall be his people, and Yahweh himself shall be with them, and be their Elohim.

And Yahweh shall wipe away all tears from their eyes; and there shall be no more death, neither sorrow, nor crying, neither shall there be any more pain: for the former things are passed away.'
Revelation 21: 3-4.

This is the description of the planet of the Eternals, where all the people that we will save from the final cataclysm will live with us while waiting to be re-implanted on Earth when it will be habitable again, in order to re-create a peaceful civilization.

This is the outcome with which Humanity is faced, if it does not reach a level of wisdom as high as its level of technology.

All this was seen by a primitive, because John was a primitive compared to us, as was Moses, as was Jesus as well, as were all the prophets compared to our level, before we gave them a sufficient initiation so that they could foresee what was a certain mastery of matter. Your most advanced scientists are also primitive compared to what we can achieve today, the same as the Indians of the Amazon are, compared to the scientists at Cape Canaveral.

This is, unfortunately, what awaits Humanity, with a 99 per cent probability of occurring.

So that all of you who recognize us as your creators and who recognize Rael as our last messenger on Earth, all of you must wrestle to ensure that Humanity reaches out to this one little chance of survival, by revealing our messages to the whole of Mankind. If this is what you are doing, you can live in peace, and all the while try to expand and fulfill yourselves even more, for if you are among the just, who are doing everything within their power so that the truth and non-violence may finally triumph, you can rest assured that we will save you from the final cataclysm, if it should ever happen. Strive for love, strive for fraternity, strive for intelligence, but do not despair if you see that the great majority of men remain violent, aggressive and stupid. Whichever way you look at it, your efforts will be rewarded. Either Humanity will develop an interplanetary consciousness, and the whole of Mankind will enter the Golden Age, or everything will explode, and you will be those who we will save to rebuild everything.

I, Yahweh, the alpha and the omega, he who was the first one on Earth and also he who will be the last, I am sending this message to all humans of the Earth through the words of my prophet, Rael, to all those humans whom we have created, and whom we have tried to lead towards the Golden Age, and who we love as if they were our own children.

Peace on Earth to all men of good-will and to all those who have the will to be happy.

Our inheritance is ready, let us hope that the child will not die at birth.

It's your move!

3

AN ATHEIST RELIGION

Angels Without Wings

An angel from Heaven contacted me. He said that I was the Messiah of the Apocalypse and told me to go and evangelize the earth, and to create the church of which I would be the pope and pontiff, I, the prophet of this Catholic religion.

Those people who know me, would probably say in reading these words: 'That's it, now he has become irrational, the immensity of his task has caused a serious psychological disorder, and he is betraying the cause.'

This introduction could be interpreted at first as:

A being with wings, coming from the sky, contacted me. He told me that I was a divine being, sent to announce the end of the world, and that I should set out to preach the Gospel all over the earth, and to build a church with stones and cement, of which I would be the pope with a tiara and the pontiff sitting on a throne and I, the prophet of this Catholic religion affiliated to Rome, I was going to announce what is going to happen in the centuries to come.

Now let us try to find the true hidden meaning of the words contained in this sentence.

As we have done for the words *Elohim* and *Apocalypse*, we must first of all search the etymology, or true meaning of each important word.

While we are at it, let us start with the etymology of the word *Etymology*, that is to say, its original meaning from the Greek *eutemos* which means "true", and *logos* which means "science". The "science of that word which is true" or the "science of the truth". What could be more natural for people who are gathered around *The Book Which Tells The Truth* than to be etymologists, "seekers of the truth"?

Elohim was wrongly translated by the word *God*, since it really meant "those who came from the sky" in Hebrew, and *Apocalypse* was translated by "the end of the world" and all the while it meant *Revelation*, as we are all now aware. So let us take the words one by one in this apparently mystical introduction.

An angel from the sky contacted me.

Let us look it up in the dictionary: *angel* from the Greek *angelos* means "messenger". That alone changes the whole meaning. We can now read:

A messenger from the sky contacted me.

The supernatural becomes understandable. Let's continue:

He told me that I was the Messiah of the Apocalypse.

Messiah from the Aramean *meschika* means "anointed by the Lord" or "sacred, chosen by the Lord". Let's first look at the word *Lord* to better understand the word *messiah*. One discovers that the word *Lord - seigneur* in French - comes from the Latin *senior*, meaning "the oldest". According to the vocabulary of the middle-ages, the "Lord" was a person who ruled over a province. The "God" in whom *The Bible* would make us believe is eternal, is obviously "the oldest", thus the "Lord" ruling the Earth. Through time, the word was transformed, and the Catholic religion adopted "my Lord" – "Monseigneur" in French, equivalent to the English word *sire*.

When the revolution came – in France – removing all the Lords, unfortunately it spared those within the religion, which is why within it, we still address bishops etc., as "My Lord" or "Monseigneur".

So then, *messiah* means "chosen by God", and as we know *God* is a bad translation of the word *Elohim* which means "those who came from the sky", so we can therefore say that, in fact, *messiah* means "the one chosen by those who came from the sky". As we have already seen, *apocalypse*, from the Greek, means "revelation", and so we can write clearly:

> He told me that I had been chosen by those who came from the sky for the Revelation.

It's all clear. But let's continue:

> ...to go and evangelize the earth.

Evangelize, is from the Greek word *euagelion* which means "good news". Then we can read:

> ...to go and spread the good news on Earth,

then:

> ...to create a church.

Church – *eglise* in French – *ekklesia* in Greek, which means "assembly". Then it becomes:

to create an assembly.

Then it is written:

> ...of which I would be the pope and pontiff

Pope from the Greek *pappas* means "father", and *pontiff* from the Latin *pontiflex* means "to link", like a bridge links two shores, or two places on the Earth, or one planet to another planet.
We can thus clearly read:

> ...of which I will be the father and the liaison person between the planet of our creators and the earth.

And lastly:

> I, the prophet of this Catholic religion.

Prophet from the Greek *prophetes* means "the one who reveals".
Religion from the Latin *religio* means "that which links" or "the tie", which unites the creators to their creation. *Catholic* from the Greek *katholikos* which means "universal".
Therefore, the end of the sentence means:

> I, the one whose mission is to reveal the universal tie which unites Man and his creators.

Let's put all the pieces together, and we read:

> A messenger from the sky contacted me. He told me that I had been chosen by those who came from the sky, for the revelation, to go and spread the good news on Earth, to create an assembly,

of which I would be the father and the liaison-person between the planet of our creators and Earth, I, the one whose mission is to reveal the universal tie which unites men and their creators.

If you take the mysticism out of the words, then the sentence becomes rationally understandable for everyone. And yet the sentence at the beginning of this chapter had exactly the same meaning. In the mind of a mystical, narrow-minded primitive as shown, our example demonstrates clearly how easy it is to change the true sense of a sentence if the precise meaning of the words is not respected.

Thus it becomes clear that the Raelian Movement is a religion; it ties the creators of Humanity with their creation, even if it is in fact an atheist religion, in the sense that it does not believe in the existence of a God - *atheist* from the Greek *atheos* which means "denying the existence of any form of divinity".

Many people say that the practice of a cult defines the character of a religion. What is a cult? Derived from the Latin *cultus* meaning "tribute rendered to a God", but we would then say "tribute rendered to the creators", since *Elohim* is a plural. The telepathic contact on Sunday mornings at 11 o'clock, the obligation of thinking at least once a day about the Elohim (Book 2, pg. 175), the obligation of inviting the regional Guide at least once a year to one's table so that he can talk about the messages, the monthly meeting with the regional Guide, the annual meeting on the 6th of August to celebrate the entry into the Age of Apocalypse - all of those ceremonies could be qualified as a cult, for each one of them is designed to pay tribute to our creators, at regular intervals, alone or in groups.

Even if the Raelians do not believe in a "God", they still recognize Jesus as a messenger sent by our creators, just as they do Moses, Buddha, Mohammed, Joseph Smith, and all the other great prophets who have lived on this Earth, and await their return in the company of the Elohim as the scriptures have predicted. The Raelian believes in the deeper meaning of the scriptures, more particularly the biblical

Genesis, but also in the *Koran* and many other religious books, all their writings being stripped of their mystical meaning by the messages of the Elohim.

Therefore the Raelian ignores the human laws which have been grafted to the religious writings, these laws having been made by Men, so as to enforce respect for governments and laws which were purely human.

The tribute which we render to the Elohim could be called a "cult", why not? The cult in itself is not wrong, so long as it is not performed by people who think of the Elohim as being divinities, but rather by people who love them sincerely for the extraordinary act of love which they have accomplished in giving us life, and in leaving us free to progress by ourselves until such a time as we would be equal to them.

There is no need to kneel down or to lie down with your face in the dirt, under the stars, but rather look up at the sky, standing tall, proud of being conscious of the privilege of living in this day and age when we are able to understand and show love for our creators, to love them for the fantastic potential they gave us to create life by mastering and transforming minute particles of matter at our level, to raise towards the galaxies, a forehead full of love and hope, the hope to one day meet those to whom we owe our existence and the fact to be able to understand why we are here and what our mission is in the infinite of space and time.

Until recently, Humanity was worshipping the creators who had created each man with the ability to understand the creators, so now Man must understand the creators, so as to be able to love them even more.

If Mankind uses science negatively, and a fatal nuclear cataclysm occurs, all those people who will have worked to prevent this catastrophe by trying to make Mankind aware of its errors in the name of the Elohim, those people shall be saved by our creators. Those people who have faith in our fathers will be rewarded by the Elohim who have already provided access to eternal life on their planet, where all the great prophets sent to Earth to awaken

Humanity are presently living. The word *faith* comes from the Latin *fides* and means "commitment, link". So, it is therefore possible to not "believe without understanding", while, at the same time, giving your trust to the Elohim, having faith in them, because those who have the intelligence to have faith in them will be rewarded regardless. While trying to prevent Humanity from committing the irrevocable error, a Raelian has faith in the Elohim, because he knows that they will not forget him in the event of a fatal cataclysm.

'Deresponsibilisation'

If there had been a newspaper in Jerusalem 2,000 years ago, it would have reported on the unemployment, the energy crisis due to a shortage of slaves, and also of the ever increasing cost of living due to the exorbitant Roman taxes. These headlines would have fed the front-page of all the newspapers, if they existed, and would have fed all the conversations. Then there would have been a few lines written by the official "scientists" of the day, or an editor seeking recognition, on this false prophet claiming to be "the king of the Jews", and it would be suggested to the authorities that this man be arrested immediately because he is dragging a hoard of credulous people, his "followers", around with him. One should not abuse the public's credulity in this way...

So this "illuminated person" is then arrested, tried and sentenced to death. This man who had dedicated his life to spreading the messages of our creators will be found crucified between two bandits. What crime had he committed? Unlawful practice of the truth reserved only for the representatives of the officially registered religions: those which had been in existence for at least two or three hundred years? You could call it a sort of "controlled appellation".

> But the chief priests and elders persuaded the multitudes that
> they should ask for Barabbas and destroy Jesus.[12] *Matthew 27: 20.*

The "high priests" of the official religions and the news media convince the masses that a religion has to be a few thousand years old in order to be "acceptable", and so all the others are nothing more than dangerous sects.

All of those people stand between Man and the truth, by allowing Man to believe in the religion of the "high priests" of the State – those scientists who claim that Man comes from the monkey, but who, on the other hand, baptize their children and place a cross on the grave of their parents. They also obstruct the truth by allowing Man to believe in the religion of traditions, which permit the great fundamentals of our rotting society to survive a few years longer, which promote and protect the family as a tax-payer, as a stagnant closed system, and a strangler of personalities, which uphold the nation which feeds the political men, who are capable of doing anything to continue to get their pay. The military also do exactly the same thing, as do, finally, all the low paid government employees who have been taught not to feel responsible for their own actions and who think they are protecting society when they condemn, torture or even kill someone.

These are the religions that governments endorse, but by the same token, they try to eliminate the ones that could make the young generation vibrate with joy when it discovers the truth, which could get them to think of destroying the outdated primitive structures and replacing them by newer ones, much more adaptable to the futuristic technological world in which we live.

The top priority of all those people who wish to manipulate the population is to take away human responsibility, it is called maximum "deresponsibilisation". They are well aware as to why it should be so. They know that a soldier will not kill someone else unless he is totally convinced that he is doing it for a cause, that same way that this soldier will not torture a prisoner unless he has been convinced that this will help a great cause. They also know that a citizen will oppose paying higher taxes unless he is told that it is to help the farmers or victims of drought.

People will do anything for a great cause. The art of governing is to convince people of the greatness of their country.

American scientists have recently conducted a conclusive experiment in the field of responsibility. They hired actors who would pretend to be subjects in an experiment on the potential of human violence. Then through classified ads, they recruited people willing to participate in an experiment to explore the possibilities of the human brain. The people were placed one at a time at a desk equipped with different levers which were supposed to send electrical charges to a cubicle in which actors pretend to receive the charge. There were thirty levers in all, which could supposedly each send out a charge of 15 volts and so altogether could send charges of 15 to 450 volts. They were placed from left to right, and indicated whether the electric charge would be light, moderately strong or very strong. On the other hand, the actor could see the lights light up on the panel in front of him showing the intensity of the shock he was supposed to have received from the electric chair to which he was tied, and he could therefore act accordingly. If the shock was light, he would simulate a light reaction, if it was moderate, he would jump a little more and give out a little cry, then he would protest by saying that he did not wish to continue the experiment; if the intensity was increased, he would scream and beg to be released, and finally when the maximum voltage of 450 volts was reached, he would pretend to collapse. The shocks were sent to the actors by those people who had been recruited in classified ads. However, the recruits did not realize that they were actors, and thought that they were sending real shocks to real people. The actor was asked a simple question by a scientist, and when he answered incorrectly, the classified ads recruits were to let them know by giving them an electrical shock. This same scientist was urging the sender to increase the voltage consistently, without listening to the supplications of the receiver, saying to the sender that this experiment would help science to progress immensely, and therefore all of humanity.

This experiment, in which the observer was really the one being observed, was repeated many times, so that statistics could be established to know how many people would go as far as killing other people in the name of scientific progress. It was also conducted in many countries, so that the results could be compared and analyzed.

Contrary to the expectations of the scientists who had put together this experiment, and the psychologists whom they had consulted, it was not just a minority of people who were unbalanced enough to go as far as pushing the 450 volt lever. In the US, 60 per cent of the people obeyed the scientist, who told them not to listen to the cries of those whom they were electrocuting, and continued to administer shocks, even when those being shocked could no longer say anything, which itself counted as an incorrect answer; and this three times in a row, after which a new electrocutor was selected. This experiment was also conducted in many European countries, where over 70 per cent of the people went as far as the maximum voltage. The record high was reached in Germany where 85 per cent of the people would have been responsible for homicide by electrocution...

The conclusion of Professor Stanley Milgram of the Department of Psychology at Yale University is as follows:

> When the individuals are placed in a position of hierarchical control, the mechanisms which ordinarily assure the regulation of the individual's actions cease functioning, and his actions become controlled by the people occupying the senior position...The disappearance of the sense of responsibility is the greatest consequence of submission to authority...

> Most of the subjects place their behavior in a large context of undertakings, useful to society: the research of scientific truth. A laboratory of psychology could clearly claim to this legitimacy, and so inspire confidence in those who were invited to work.

An act such as the electrocution of a victim, which seems bad when considered on its own, takes on a completely different meaning when placed in this environment.

Morality does not disappear, but it is focused in a radically different way: the subordinate person experiences shame and pride depending on his good or bad execution of the act commanded by the authority. Language offers a great number of terms to designate this type of moral: loyalty, sense of duty, discipline...

Such is without doubt the fundamental lesson of our study: the ordinary people, by simply doing their job, and without any particular hostility on their part, could become agents in a terribly destructive process.

Moreover, even when the destructive effects of their work become absolutely evident, and one asks them to execute actions incompatible with the fundamental norms of morality, relatively few people have the interior resources needed to resist authority.

It is a mortal fault which seems to be natural in most people, and which, in the long run, leaves our species with only a mediocre chance of survival.[25]

It's quite clear. Now we can understand why Jesus was crucified, why millions of people died at the hands of the Inquisition, during religious or civil wars, and in the Nazi massacres. It becomes easier to understand how an honest greengrocer or banker could have been a crucifier, or burn witches or become an SS soldier, sending women and children to the death chambers. They all thought they were doing something for the good of Humanity. The first ones were getting rid of an "illuminated" man who wanted to overthrow their traditions, and others felt that people who lived differently were surely responsible for the bad crops or the plague or even the economic crisis. The fact that ideas so stupid could germinate in the brains of retarded people is forgivable. What is not, is that governments could use the masses by utilizing such monstrous ideas to motivate them and give them reasons to act.

The French leaders in Algeria acted along this same principle. They forced their officers into torturing North-Africans under the pretense of obtaining information useful to their country. Those officers who did the torturing even considered that they were "sacrificing themselves", by acting this way, "bravely", in the best interests of their country.

Men of the Earth, be very vigilant and do not accomplish the slightest action without asking yourself whether it is in contradiction to your deep sense of respect for the human being. Refuse any hierarchy implying a suppression of your responsibility for the actions you carry out.

Every Nazi war criminal, while on trial, defended himself in good faith, by claiming that he was only following orders. The man who launched the bomb on Hiroshima was only following orders. In every powerful country, there are people who are ready to launch nuclear missiles in good faith and with a clear conscience, knowing that they are only "doing their duty in executing the orders received". They are responsible for their actions! In every part of Nazi Germany, men, women and children were tortured because people were following orders, and according to them the only man responsible for all of this would be Hitler. It would be much too easy if it were so! For example, there are hundreds of nuclear missiles ready to be launched from France and destined for other countries where thousands of women and children are living, and if the massacre happened, would the only man held to be responsible for it be the President of the Republic? Of course not! Each man holding the power to kill others is personally responsible for the utilization of this power. The man who lights the crematorium furnace where children lie moaning, is more responsible than the one who has given the order in the first place, just as the man who delivers a bomb on a city is more responsible than the one who made the decision.

Each person is totally responsible for his actions and can never hide behind the excuse that he was only following the orders which had been given to him by his superiors.

If tomorrow I were to ask anyone of you to kill someone so that our movement may progress faster, you must not do it. Better still, if an Eloha were to ask you to kill another man, you should refuse to do it, for it would probably be Satan who would be trying to prove to the Eternals that all men are fundamentally bad.

All your actions should be based on a deep feeling of respect for the life of others, their ideas, and their tastes. We fight ideologies without ever using violent physical actions towards those who do not agree with us.

Awaken the people around you, show them how to become respectful of other people and how to refuse "deresponsibilisation", whose most dangerous propagator is the armed forces. Remember, 85 per cent in Germany and 60 per cent in the USA. You must use all your energy so that tomorrow there is only 10 per cent of weak-headed people who would agree to perform violent actions ordered by a political and military hierarchy.

Those who killed Jesus did it in all serenity. They were not responsible; they were only following orders. Pontius Pilate himself refused to endorse the responsibility for this crime, and he "washed his hands" of the whole mess. He allowed the fanatics conditioned by the rabbis, just like the SS, to crucify Jesus. If we were to ask all those people if they feel responsible, none of them probably would. They would all "wash their hands" like the Romans did. The rabbis would claim that they followed the law and a chief, the fanatics as well, and so perhaps we could hold one person responsible, even though the whole of the population were the ones who committed the crime, the crime of not intervening to prevent the assassination of an innocent man.

Those who sent the first Christians to the lion's den were also only following orders. Those who burnt the witches, those who martyred the protestants, as well as the Nazis at Auschwitz were also only following orders, as was the pilot of the plane carrying the bomb over

Hiroshima, or the helicopter pilots who burnt the villages in Vietnam.

We all have a choice at every moment of our lives: remain responsible for our actions or become an irresponsible person. But the irresponsible are still responsible for their actions, and will one day have to account for them, for they are all committing crimes against Humanity.

Learn this by heart if you must, but refuse to obey a hierarchy which seeks to make you perform an action to which you would not like to be held responsible. The armed forces are the most dangerous example. It would be much better to die for having refused to kill, than to kill under the pretext of obeying orders. He who executes these monstrous orders is in fact more responsible than he who has given them.

No cause would justify the imposition of pain on others. If the survival of Humanity depended upon the pain inflicted on one man, a single non-violent man, then it would be better to let Humanity perish. Even more so if it means the survival of one's country, or rather a frontier arbitrarily traced on a globe which belongs to all men.

Absolute respect for this principle is the only way to prevent the imperceptible slipping of Humanity towards deresponsibilisation of individuals.

The following sentence should be ever-present in our minds:

'I am totally responsible for everything I do to others even if I am ordered to do so.'

'No cause could ever justify inflicting pain or death on a non-violent person, and even if the survival of Humanity depended on it, this would not justify an exception.' This is the second sentence which must be ever-present in our minds.

It is evident of course, that this rule does not apply in the case of legitimate self-defense, which is explained in the messages and which permits the possible overpowering, even by force, of one who tries to use violence against your person or your loved ones. If a military man was threatening the destruction of Humanity with nuclear missiles, it would then be justifiable to overpower him by force, and even to execute him if there were no other means available. Violence could only be applied to those who threaten Humanity with violence, while attempting to disarm them and render them powerless.

There is, however, a very good way to control those people who have the power when obeying orders to launch nuclear missiles capable of destroying cities in a few seconds. Their identity should be made known on a precise list, and they should be made aware, that in the case of the utilization of any such missiles, they would be judged along with those who gave the orders. This is what we are trying to do with Nazi criminals today; but if such a list had existed, with similar dispositions before 1939, many people would have thought twice before torturing their innocent victims.

Non-violent civilians should have the right to place neutral observers among the military forces, to note down the identities of those who carry out cruel acts using the excuse that they were obeying orders, so that inhuman missions are not carried out solely on the pretext that the order has been given. There is policing of the police, but there is no policing of the armies. They are free to command, knowing full well that while at war, a soldier could be shot to death for refusing to obey an order.

Until the Earth gets rid of the armies and the wars, the neutral observers would oppose the execution of soldiers who have refused orders that could qualify as crimes against Humanity. The UN could impose these observers on all the armies of the world, and then a military man could not be sentenced until his disobedience is judged by a council of these observers, to investigate if the order which he refused to obey could have constituted a crime against Humanity. Because it is in this way that people are forced to execute orders of which they disapprove; they are afraid of being punished if they don't obey. They prefer to kill innocent people or to torture them, rather than be imprisoned or killed themselves. Refuse to bend to authority! Be the real heroes of humanity by preferring to be imprisoned or killed yourselves rather than laying into innocent people. When you have motivated millions of people so that they act in this way, those giving the orders will see an army of people refusing to carry out the crimes which they ordered, and then it will be time to punish those who dare give such orders, hoping they will be listened to.

Men have had enough energy to refuse non-unionized work, like before 1936, where the all-powerful bosses exploited humans like cattle, even if it meant death for many of them at the hands of a policeman, so-called "protector of the law". It is possible to find the same energy to fight the last form of tyranny imposed on the inhabitants of this world: militarism.

Many people with powers and honors are disturbed by what I have to say. Unfortunately for them, they are too late in noticing my presence. If I was worried in the first two years of my mission, I am now no longer worried. In the beginning, if I had been sent to jail, I could not have carried out my mission on Earth. Fortunately, the powers at hand smiled when they saw this long-haired young man who spoke of flying-saucers and Martians with pink antennae... Now they understand that the contents of the messages from our creators are revolutionary, questioning and uprooting everything which they have used to gain power: religion, politics, the armed forces, work, the family, the country, etc. So now they are trying to stop me by using their "justice" as they used it against my brother Jesus.

There is always a justice to justify the worst injustices. The first Christians were sentenced by official tribunals, the same for the burning of witches, or the sending of Jewish people to extermination camps, or the Soviet dissidents to psychiatric hospitals or labor camps; all those people were "non-conformists", they were upsetting because they refused to be "normal" and conform. Unfortunately, they have woken up too late. Even if I were put in one of their prisons, there would still be thousands of messengers like you in many countries of the world, to carry the messages of our creators. I am no longer alone, I am 3,000 of you. I would then enter their cell with a smile, thinking of you, who, around the world, will be other Raels working together so that the embassy can be built, so that Humanity enters the Golden Age.

In my dungeon, I would feel the happiness of someone who has fulfilled his mission, that for which he has been created, and even though he has been put out of action, everything he has started continues to advance without him. Also hoping that my father who art in heaven will realize that I am no longer needed on this Earth, and that he will allow me to join my brothers, the prophets, on the planet of the Eternals.

This thought alone is sufficient to make me want to sing the glory of our fathers, to say again the words that men have been repeating without being able to understand: "Alleluia! Alleluia!" which means: "praised be Yahweh" in Hebrew. Yes, praised be Yahweh who has given me the strength to carry out my mission until the end.

My Raelian brothers, I am now relaying to you the torch so that you can accomplish your mission. Even if the time when the truth will be triumphant is not here yet, you can rest assured that it is not very far, and you will have the opportunity to live it. It is written in *The Bible*: 'This generation will not pass that everything shall be revealed.'

These words are addressed to those who will have the opportunity to live this Age of Apocalypse, which we entered in 1945. You are this generation! Either you will know the Golden Age on Earth because of your efforts which have contributed to world peace and the awakening of Mankind, or Humanity will destroy itself and you will know the Golden Age amongst the great prophets who are already on the planet of the Eternals.

The Elohim are counting on each and every one of you to shed the light. My last word will again be an etymological demystification: "Amen", which means in Hebrew: "So be it!"

And to those of you who are reading this book without having complete knowledge of the messages from our creators, be sure to read the other books as soon as possible, and then join us in making Humanity aware of them and in building the residence in which the Elohim will officially contact the governments of the Earth, where they will come in the company of the great prophets, Moses, Jesus, Buddha, Mohammed and others as the scriptures have announced.

Then write to me. I will personally answer your letter and indicate when and where you can have your cellular plan transmitted, your first action which recognizes the Elohim as our creators, the name and address of your regional Guide, and the dates when the next Raelian courses of awakening will be held, which could make you a Guide, an efficient messenger of our atheistic religion of the Infinite, of blossoming, and of love for Humanity.

Take your pen. Don't be the spectator of your life anymore! Become actors on the stage of this sad, grey, and resigned everyday life that is yours, to enlighten it with a thousand shimmering colors of absolute consciousness.

Take a pen and paper and write to me very simply, and modestly with your everyday words, tell me if the discovery of the truth has been a shock for you. Follow the impulse which came up inside of you and which said: 'Ah! It's not bad, but what will I be able to change, I am only one person, and then, what will the neighbors say?'

Don't hide your head in the sand, come out of the fragile shell that society has given you so freely! Your head is already sticking out, and it feels marvellous, but you are afraid that this will only be another illusion, a very short-lived pleasure, which would only bring you problems afterwards. Untrue! Live out completely the fantastic exaltation which you have felt. You will enter a new world, in which you will meet hundreds of people like you, who have read the messages in only one night, and who like you, have hesitated in getting involved in the diffusion of the messages. These people will help you by explaining how they have progressed, and you will find yourself filled with happiness, while seeing yourself through them, and while talking freely about your anxieties without the worry of being made a fool, since you are assured that the people around you share your conception of the universe: the conception that you had within you, although you never expressed your thoughts, for fear of being ridiculed.

Peter, one of our Guides, once said: 'One does not become a Raelian: one discovers that one always has been, when one discovers the messages.'

If you have discovered that you are a Raelian, then I am waiting for your letter, and the Elohim are waiting for you to drop it in the mailbox! My address is:

Rael,
International Raelian Movement,
Case Postale 225, CH–1211,
Geneva 8, Switzerland.

or email me at: headquarters@rael.org.

4

COMMENTARIES AND TESTIMONIALS OF RAELIANS

Raelism Through the Eyes of Science

MARCEL TERUSSE – *Chemical Engineer & Raelian Guide*

1: EVOLUTION, OBSCURANTISM AND THE NEO-DARWINIAN MYTH

Many of us were taught the theory of evolution at school and even suffered its influence which permeated from our history lessons to philosophy and even religion. To quote Jean Rostand: 'We have been impregnated, saturated and conditioned with this idea... we learned this on school benches by repeating parrot fashion that life evolved and that organisms transformed themselves into others.' Unfortunately, even those who didn't go to school and undergo this spoon-fed learning process or those that did but didn't understand the theory, still believe in it more fanatically than those who did. In the end, this continual indoctrination, generation after generation, must inevitably bias our minds, especially since the enormous quantities of evidence against it is never presented to the pupils.

How many people would have the courage to be seen as heretics if they dared question evolution when so many well known scientists, professors and clergy state it as fact?

This is a big problem especially for those who envisage following a scientific career, but luckily for them, some clear sighted minds do exist within the scientific community, such as the above mentioned eminent biologist Jean Rostand. In his book, *Evolution*, written in 1960, he wrote:

> ...are we really as sure as would certainly be the wish of the neo-Darwinians, that the problem of evolution is really solved? The mutations that we are familiar with and which they wish to consider responsible for the coming to being of the whole of life on Earth are not more than organic deprivations, deficiencies and losses of pigments or appendices, or doubling of pre-existing organs. In any case, they never bring anything really new and original to the organic layout, and nothing that we believe might be the beginning of a new organ or the start of a new function. No, decidedly, I cannot admit that these mistakes of heredity could build the whole of the living world in all its richness, its structural delicacies and astonishing adaptations, even with the competitive factor of natural selection and the help of immense durations.

Many experiments have been designed in the last decade to understand the mechanisms of mutations, and again the same conclusions are reached.

One of the pioneers in this field of study was 1946 Nobel prize winner H.J. Muller, who concentrated particularly on the common fruit fly, Drosophila Melanogatser. He concluded that 'it is so rare that a mutation allows survival that we can consider them as disadvantageous.'

Almost all mutations, including both those occurring in the wild and those provoked in the laboratory, result in hereditary illnesses, deteriorations of survival value and genetic monstrosities. The chromosome plan of living organisms is extremely complex, and any modification will inevitably result in its disorganization.

In the laboratory, we have been able to cause hens' necks and even whole bodies to have no feathers or to change the color of insects' eyes, wings, posteriors, etc. We have even slightly altered other organs, but in the natural environment, not one mutation was advantageous to ensure its survival. An accident of this sort can never increase organization but will result only in damage, in the same way as throwing a watch on the ground can never increase its precision, nor can hitting a computer with a spanner endow it with extra calculating properties. And the time factor will not change anything since what was impossible yesterday will also be impossible today.

The mutation itself always stays within the confines of the species. For example, among the innumerable mutations provoked in Drosophila, not one produced a different species or anything different from its ancestors. The flies' size, color and morphology may vary but not even a series of mutations has ever produced a new organism with attributes that never existed before. Living cells are composed of extremely complex molecules, themselves made up of many combinations of atoms; so how is it possible that these delicate structures spontaneously form their constituent parts, randomly scattered around? Inanimate matter doesn't seek to complicate itself, but on the contrary tends towards disorganization and stability. It is no use saying that it will happen someday, since with time comes decomposition and disintegration.

The tendency that every organic structure has to revert to disorganization is spelt out in the thermodynamic law which defines the function of entropy. There is never a gain in order without the intervention of an outside force. Therefore, inanimate matter containing no energy or movement will always stay inert in the absence of any guiding hand to organize and direct it. Thus the theory of evolution lies in direct contradiction with the law of entropy.

The methods that have been used for building the theory of evolution are totally unscientific, and will continue to be so for as long as the transformists don't consider objectively the evidence and continue to force the facts.

True advances will happen only when glory seeking, petty arguing, fear of reputation and egocentrism disappear to allow honest conclusions to be made, based on solid facts instead of preconceived ideas.

Life on Earth is not the result of random chance, but is the fruit of outside intervention, of the Elohim, our creators.

2: A NEW HYPOTHESIS FOR THE HISTORY OF HUMANITY

When the CIA, the Central Intelligence Agency of America, gave the Hudson Institute the task of studying the world distribution of natural resources such as petrol, gas and coal, Professor Nebring, who was put in charge, discovered a rather strange phenomenon.

He put together the continents as they would have been at the end of the geological tertiary period before they split up, and found that all the main oil springs such as those in the Arctic and Alaska, the asphalt sands of Alberta, the bitumen schists of Colorado, Mexico, and Venezuela, the heavy oils of Orenoc, Nigeria, South Sahara, Lybia, Arabia, Iran and Siberia all formed a circle.

Present studies on petrol reveal that it is the result of what used to be living organisms, such as plants, animals, etc., which have decomposed in anaerobic conditions, that is to say, in the absence of air, where special bacteria reduce and transform their proteins and fats. Dead trees are the main source of these proteins and fats, but what usually happens when one of them dies is that normal air-breathing bacteria decompose it and recycle it into the forest food chain without producing petrol, so for the above to occur the trees must be buried straight away to prevent access of air.

But when oil fields are examined, one finds that they are extremely deep (2,000 meters deep in northern France) and cover considerable areas (18,000 kms in the Appalachians, USA), so the actual volume of material which must have been brutally buried all in one go was enormous.

No theory up to now can account for these facts satisfactorily, but we Raelians hold the key to this enigma.

When the Elohim decided to destroy their bases, their laboratories and all that they had created on Earth, they must have used extremely powerful methods of destruction, which, as well as breaking up this original continent and sending each respective fragment drifting outwards from the centre of the shock, must also have swept the whole land surface. Since the impact must have spread outwards from the bombs' point of impact, all the living matter including immense forests, animals and even Man would have been buried deep, immediately and all together under tons of earth in a ring shape, circling the central explosion.

This would explain how extremely large volumes of living matter were buried quickly enough to provide anaerobic conditions in the large circular formation which intrigued Nebring so much when he pieced back together again all the fragments of what was once our unique single continent.

During the time when the Elohim built the first continent until they broke it up, erosion would have accumulated sediment rich in animal matter such as corals and shells into the oceans, especially around the edge of the continent. As what later became the North and South American continental plates scraped along the ocean bed, all the sediment built up to form the Andes and the Rocky mountain ranges.

The same for the Indian sub-continent which broke off from Africa, and sliding northeast, trapped in its path enormous amounts of material which we now know as the Himalayas. The Antarctic continent drifting south became covered with a huge coating of ice, preserving until today traces of tropical vegetation. Meanwhile Australia, part of Africa and India, went southeast, accumulating along its edge sediment which was to form the Australian Great Dividing Range.

The destruction was cataclysmic and provoked not only large geological changes, but also climatic ones, obliterating innumerable life forms, burying them under layers of sand, lime, earth and a sort of muddy ice which preserved them until this day and from which they periodically emerged, released from their frozen coffin of the greater north Siberia.

Only a small handful of humans were protected in the ark during the "flood". Upon their return they found the continent completely unrecognizable and ravaged by the destruction, the geological upheavals having resulted in parts of the surface being decapitated and the appearance of cracks in the crust layer causing volcanic activity.

It is easy to see how the story of the unique continent breaking up into many fragments 'where there was once land but now is water' and vice versa became distorted into the legends of Atlantis or Mu, where a continent is reputed to have disappeared into the sea. In fact, it did not sink, it merely moved aside.

Not all the living organisms were re-created after the flood, some considered to be monstrous and detrimental to the ecological balance, such as the large reptiles and dinosaurs, were left out, which explains the sudden and simultaneous disappearance of these antediluvian beasts.

After the "flood", the Elohim cohabited with the humans of Earth, and the traces of their presence which we can still find scattered all over the world are post diluvian.

Let us learn to open our eyes, we have everything around us to enable us to understand. We are in the age of the Apocalypse, the age when we can once again hope to meet our creators, the Elohim.

3: TRANSMISSION OF THE CELLULAR PLAN IN THE LIGHT OF SCIENCE

So far today, spectral studies investigating the relationship between matter and energy have allowed us to achieve a certain understanding of the structure and make-up of molecules. Although matter may appear to our human eyes to be homogeneous, be it in gaseous, liquid or solid state, it is in fact made up of many building blocks called molecules, which themselves are composed of atoms.

An atom can be compared to a miniature solar system with a positive nucleus in the middle, around which electrons rotate, each capable of spinning on themselves, just as the Earth does on its journey around the sun. The electrons' movement is described by four quantum numbers (principle, secondary, magnetic and spin). Wave mechanics associated a particular vibration to all moving particles, the motion of which can be predicted by Shrodinger's equation.

An atom can only emit or absorb energy of particular frequencies. This is accompanied by a spectrum of separate and distinct radiations which are related directly to the energy state of the atom. Therefore, every type of atom has its own specific type of atomic spectrum.

The nuclear magnetic resonance can also provide detailed information on the nature of the bond holding the atoms together forming the molecule.

Within the molecule the atoms will also vibrate relative to each other. If there are only two, there is only one fundamental frequency following the joining at the two centers of gravity of the two nuclei, and it is, therefore, linear. Molecules composed of more atoms will have a larger number of fundamentals.

Atoms can also rotate around their own axes. Their vibrational and rotational energies can vary only in a discontinuous way. The jump from one energy level to another is done either by absorbing or emitting energy. Every chemical reaction is based on such energy changes, and the emission resulting from these matter transformations can be measured and recorded as "rotational and electro-vibrational molecular spectrums". Every molecule of our body is vibrating in such a way and is, therefore, emitting a whole host of vibrations which at first sight might appear to be a huge cacophony. Thus the human body is an electric and electromagnetic wave emitter.

Today, our technology does not yet allow us to record such phenomena on an organism as complex as the human being. Neither are our methods of analysis fine enough to distinguish the emission coming from a particular molecule and that of the background noise, but with time...

Remember that Hertz discovered the waves which are named after him only in the 1920s, and nuclear magnetic resonance has been known only since 1946, so where will we be in 50, 100 or in 1,000 years? Let us not forget that the Elohim are 25,000 years in advance of us.

The principle of baptism, the transmission of one's cellular plan, is today understandable to us, and this ceremony is scientifically explained as follows: every individual has a cellular chromosomic plan, specific to him, which vibrates with its own electromagnetic spectral emission.

A Guide, whose own frequency has been noted by the Elohim during his or her initiation, can act as a relay between the new Raelian and the Elohim's satellite which records every human's thought.

Water is used between the new Raelian's forehead and the Guide's hands so as to establish a good electrical contact, and the Raelian baptism indicates to the Elohim that the Raelian has both understood the messages and lives by them. It is an act of recognition.

Impressions of a 'Priest'

VICTOR LEGENDRE – *ex-Roman Catholic Priest*

I was in Europe on holiday when I learned of the messages given by the extra-terrestrials (Elohim) to Claude Vorilhon, "Rael". I had already visited France, Spain and Italy, since June 10th, 1976, when I laid hands on the first message, *The Book Which Tells The Truth* on June 30th and a few days later on July 2nd, I picked up *The Extra-Terrestrials Took Me To Their Planet*. I found the first book in Geneva and the second one in Clermont Ferrand in France.

Words could hardly describe what I felt while reading these two messages: surprise mixed with admiration and fear, a shock of joy! This is a very poor description. I was transported with joy into a state of well-being or an indescribable euphoria and a profound sense of peace, with a new outlook. No! A renewed outlook on everything. If the word *resentment* (from the French word "ressentiment" also meaning to feel again) did not have this pejorative sense, I would use it to explain the various feelings which I was living so intensely.

Two days before my departure from Europe, I had visited a musician friend of mine who had asked me to bring back *The Book Which Tells The Truth*, as he could not find it in Canada, since he did not know who the editor was. He made me listen to a recorded interview which the CBC International had released in Europe, and which had been transmitted several times during the 1975-76 season. I had only a vague idea of the messages then; and to please my friend, I had promised to bring him back this book.

Before his waiting period was rewarded on my return on the following July 10th, it was I who had been rewarded and beyond all my expectations! It was as if I had discovered a precious pearl, without having really looked for it! I am speaking of course of what the messages contained. It was only upon my return that I had started to investigate this message intelligently, if I may say so; a little "at random", I tried to understand the essence of the messages. I looked at the biblical writings which I had studied in theology on my way to priesthood; then in the Kabala wich was unfamiliar to me, except for a few Hebrew words which I had learned in theology; also in the history of religions, particularly in the history of Christianity; and finally in the scientific field. I formed my opinion based on this research. What was it that struck me most in these messages? What impressed me the most?

Without too many comments, I will outline the strong points, in a synthesis of my impressions, although these points should be discussed at greater length:

The original *Bible*, written in Hebrew, speaks of Elohim, which means literally "those who came from the sky". Elohim is a word which has been unjustly translated by the word *God* in current bibles. So there is no immaterial, supernatural or almighty God; but there are Elohim, constantly present in *The Bible*, and who, among other things, have created life in a laboratory, including human life, through inert chemicals associated with DNA. Therefore, the Elohim, or Extra-terrestrials, are clearly present at different epochs for different civilizations. Thus we are far from this narrow-minded conception which says 'the extra-terrestrials and *The Bible* should not be mixed.'

There is no soul which leaves the body after death, but there is the genetic code which is the principle of life.

The title of the first message was announced in *Ezekiel 2:9-10,* in *Revelation 5:1* and in *Daniel 10:21,* 'But I will reveal to you that which is written in the book of truth'.

And *Daniel 12:4,* 'And thou Daniel keep secret these words and seal the book until the time of the end. Many will look here and there, and knowledge will increase.'

The notion of the infinitely great and the infinitely small, the awakening of the mind to the infinite, is where truth resides. Evolution by chance, or successive random events is a myth. On the contrary, evolution resides first in the minds of our creators.

No one can belong to someone else; you cannot be owned by someone, whatever the relationship, be it in work, marriage, or any other situation.

The affirmation and development of basic human objectives which each one of us is called upon to follow in his or her life is: think, create and expand!

The solutions proposed to solve the great problems of humanity: among other things, selective democracy or geniocracy which would apply to humanitarianism; the genius being the raw material of humanity; the procedure to follow to create a geniocratic world government; the creation of robots to abolish manual labor; a unique world currency until money is suppressed totally; a universal second language, each region conserving its mother-tongue; the abolition of military service and the placing of career soldiers at the service of world peace: we cannot continue to search for "peace and security" at the same time, as Paul of Tarsus said in Chapter 5 of his first Epistle to the Thessalonians.

The perfect meeting of science and religion in our epoch, the age of Apocalypse (or revelation), where the two blend so perfectly: all the religious writings, notably *The Bible*, have announced the return of the great prophets – nearly 40 in all – in the company of our creators, the Elohim.

When I had finished reading these first two messages, I felt vividly inside me the hypocrisy of Christians who pray only from their lips, while the precept of loving their neighbors is almost always forgotten. I felt this temporal and spiritual domination of the Church by the money and the riches which it has accumulated.

This domination is maintained and encouraged by the political powers which see only advantages in it; I felt this mystification which only makes people dormant; we are far from the vigilance recommended by Jesus, to read the signs of the time, and recognize them when they happen; but it is the cult of the traditions which has made people blind. I remember those words from the book of *Ecclesiastes, 7:10*, 'Do not say: how is it that the past is better than the present, for it is not wise to pose such a question.' To me it felt that this guilt of conscience was accentuated by the idea that Man is a sinner, that Man is imperfect, explained by this rejection of intelligence, i.e. Man is told to believe without understanding, and maintained by the idea that sexual pleasure or even sensuality is contemptible.

I have linked the signs of the time announced in the religious writings with our epoch where we see them happen. This epoch is ours, the *Age of the Apocalypse* or the *Age of the Revelation*, when everything can be understood. The signs of the time reveal the original mystery in the light of scientific progress. Anyone who searches in *The Bible* in particular, and compares the predictions with the achievements of our scientific age, unveils, ascertains and understands only that which is "the foundation of the Earth", and that which has been kept hidden since the "foundation of the world".

Allow me to enumerate some of these signs with their accomplishments: Man will be equal to the Elohim (creators of life); the deaf will hear; the blind will see; the crippled will regain the use of their limbs (electronic prosthesis); Man will have his voice carried to the four corners of the Earth (telecommunications and radiotelephony); the healing of poisoned people (antidotes, anti-venum serums); the healing of sick people by the imposition of the hands (development of surgery); the prolongation of life; the people of David find their country again (the creation of the State of Israel); numerous signs in the sky (UFOs); thousands of false prophets trying to plunge Mankind into fanaticism, obscurantism and mysticism (religions and sects).

Even if the Roman Catholic Church does not recognize me as a priest, since I have adhered to the Raelian Movement, I nevertheless remain a priest. I was entrusted with a fantastic mission, the spreading of the messages to the greatest number of people possible; I am still a "priest" since, like Rael, I am the messenger of those in whom I have always believed (the Elohim) while only now understanding truly their work, the creation of Man and the mission of Jesus. I am still a "priest", but I am vigilant; since I have opened my mind, I have also become a "mind opener", and no longer the one who puts human consciences to sleep; I am and I will remain a "priest", that is to say a guide for Humanity on the path of peace and universal love.

Yes... I am Raelian

MARCEL TERRUSSE – *Chemical Engineer and Raelian Guide*

Yes, I am Raelian, a disciple of the religion of the infinity of time and space, a child of the Earth who has rediscovered traces of our fathers of the stars, and who is trying to make known to the rest of Humanity this fabulous story of ours.

Unfortunately, I believe that one does not become Raelian, one day one discovers the messages and one finds an echo of one's own thoughts, of one's own preoccupations.

Some day or another, dizzy before the unfathomable whirlpool of time and space, we have all tried to dissipate the mystery of our origin and the uncertainty of our future. The messages have provided me with the answer to this preoccupation.

Of course, for someone who had received a technical and scientific education, certain passages in the messages do not appear very "orthodox" and not very consistent with traditional teachings. But let us apply the advice of Montaigne 'and make all pass through the sieve and lodge nothing in our mind by mere authority and confidence.'

If we try to sift all the elements of the messages by critical analysis, we are soon conscious that we are dealing with an extremely solid monument.

I have always had the intuition that there existed a link between all the more or less fabulous stories that come to us from ancient times, and that there exists in each of them some gold nuggets in a jumble of nonsense...

I started to research Arian's clew, and I had the confirmation that the contacts with the Elohim had always existed. We have found traces in the myths and souvenirs of ancient civilizations:

- Greek mythology, which relates a whole series of gods, demigods, and giants of ancient times; Mahabarata, mythical epic poem of India, with its two parts: Vedas and Ramayana
- *The Epic of Gilgamesh*, Sumarian-Babylonian

- *Kojiki of Japan,* which reported that which happened at the beginning
- *The Popol Vuh* and *The Chronical of Akakor* in Latin America
- And nearer to us, *The Book of Enoch, The Kabala,* and *The Bible*
- Some physical traces can be seen on the plain of Nazca (engravings), at Baalbeck, and certainly at Tiahuanaco, Easter Island (Ile de Paques), and in many other places throughout the world.

We have at our disposal all the pieces of the puzzle to reconstruct the story of our origin.

In the reading of the messages, I have certainly had occasion to pose some questions on the apparent contradictions which could have existed between certain cited facts and common knowledge. It appears that we make what we consider to be scientific achievements based on frail and contestable hypotheses, and I find insurmountable contradictions in today's scientific teachings.

I have always thought that all the phenomena of nature susceptible of being understood in the universe are coherent, and that they all depend on one another in a more or less complex fashion.

The development of a more and more abstract mathematical tool has orientated physics on a path which is strangely logical, but outside of material realities.

It is thus that Einstein postulated that the speed of light was an insurmountable limit of all speeds in the universe, committing the monumental error of taking as principle that space is uniformly empty and identical to itself in every part of the cosmos, apart from the stars and the planets.

Beyond the clouds which encircle our planet, the density of the gaseous molecules diminish progressively with altitude, until they attain a level which we call "emptiness".

But the interstellar "emptiness" is pervaded by waves of every kind: x-rays, infrared, radio waves, etc. So all undulation implies the existence of an environment which undulates, the interstellar space is not empty as appearances would have us believe, but full of a substance capable of undulating: a sub-quantum composed of infinitesimal particles compared with the size of the atoms we know.

Undulation implies movement, and movement, energy. In a century where we believe that the equivalent of mass and energy is absolutely true, it is not logical to deny the existence of a mass of interstellar and intergalactic space.

Space is heterogeneous and the local characteristic of this space depends on the energetic gradient in the part under consideration. The Earth and the solar system bathe in a diffuse energetic environment of "sub-quantal" particles whose pressure is responsible for what we call the forces of attraction.

The gravitational space is comparable with a gaseous atmosphere, similar to the aerial atmosphere.

The speed of propagation of waves is a function of the local density and not a constant, as the relativists believe, so all the cosmic distances must be recalculated.

All the distances in light years calculated by the traditional methods are overestimated. The stars that surround us are much nearer than we believe. Moreover, the development of theories which confuse the dimensions of space and time are ridiculous.

The factor of time, which is parasitic to all the formulations and equations of physics, is an arbitrary element.

Time has no existence in itself; the notion that we have is subjective, and it is derived from our own biological and mental organization. We project it in the exterior world, draw an irresistible illusion of an "absolute universal time".

'Scientific time is conventional; it is based on physical standards susceptible of being coordinated under different forms, in an arbitrary way.'

Our conception of the cosmos is fundamentally false, together with our philosophic concepts.

I find everywhere around me confirmation of the messages. It suffices to open our eyes to understand this fabulous story of the coming of the Elohim to Earth, and scientific creation of life in laboratories, which we ourselves will soon repeat.

No doubt my background as a chemist has made me familiar with the affinity existing between chemical elements and biological structures participating in the mechanisms of life. But even for an ordinary person with a curious mind, the rapid reading of popular scientific reviews allows us to foresee the direction towards which the biochemical and medical research is going.

Become conscious that we have synthesized certain genes by combining nucleotides; that segments of molecules of DNA had been implanted in the interior of bacteria chromosomes; that the transfer of genetic material from one organism to another is becoming increasingly familiar to us...

Look at the direction taken by the researchers of the last Nobel prize winners...

The understanding of the molecular structure and the mechanisms which they control open up the possibility of regeneration of tissues, and the replacement of organs, and of the creation of new animal species, and with time, of the synthesis of humans in our image, and the cycle starts again.

The study of the mechanisms of the coding of information in the molecules of DNA will lead us to understand and to utilize the memory substances in our brain - substances that could be transferred from one individual to another. Become aware of the biological revolution in progress, and how the consequences of which will create a fundamental change in the whole of our social and political structures.

Wake up, this is not science-fiction.

To be Raelian does not mean to be secluded in a "self-centered" group always staring at their belly buttons, persuaded they have found the truth, feeling superior in I don't know what; the Raelian Movement is for me just the opposite to a sect.

Our proceedings have an ambitious goal, but they progress with humility, being conscious that Humanity is penalized by aggression, pride, vanity and egotism.

I love the philosophy of our existence developed by the Movement, because it seeks the complete expansion of individuals. It teaches us to listen to that which we have in the depths of ourselves and to reveal the best in us.

Life is everywhere in the universe, but our life is unique, and it is important to make a success of it: 'Life is a lost blessing if one has not lived as one wished to' (*Eminescu*).

I have found a blossoming through the in-depth study of the messages, a better understanding of others and of myself, and they have allowed me to become more conscious of our degree of solidarity.

The philosophy of the Movement is a philosophy of the love of life and of its creators, a tolerant and pacific philosophy, which tends to remove guilt from sensuality and to disengage from all the taboos, prohibitions and inhibitions connected with sexuality.

The adhesion of the Movement is not a brigading, towards which I have always had a great distrust, but a voluntary and enriching act which has brought me great pleasure, by the personal blossoming that I obtained, and the joy in the diffusion of the messages around me.

I believe that we must not commit the error – that which happened with Christ – of attributing more importance to the messenger than to the message. The essential thing is becoming conscious that the extra-terrestrials have always played a role in our history, and wish nothing better than to renew that contact today.

The past history of Humanity shows us that each stage of its development necessitated an uprooting and renewing of fundamental beliefs in our scientific, social, philosophic and religious conceptions. Unfortunately, 'a new scientific truth does not usually impose itself by convincing its adversaries; its triumph results by progressive extinction of its adversaries, and the appearance of a new generation for whom this truth had always been familiar' (*M. Planck*).

I believe that we should help people to stand on their own two feet and to get rid of the crutches that are the beliefs and religions; we should seek to dissipate obscurantism by raising the level of consciousness. For, if over the centuries, religion has asked and sometimes imposed on the faithful to "believe" the mysteries and the most delirious fables, today our history is understandable, and it is up to us to open our eyes and minds to prepare our future.

In the present is contained the beginnings of our future. Humanity is at the eve of its birth and perhaps of its death, and those who have not understood the meaning of the word *apocalypse* will nevertheless perhaps be right.

We, Raelians, participate in the awakening of Humanity and in the development of the cosmic consciousness.

That is the direction of my involvement in this ambitious work, which is the preparation of Humanity for the welcoming of our creators, the Elohim.

The Consecration of My Priesthood

YVAN GIROUX – *ex-Roman Catholic Priest and Professor of Catechism.*

I would like it to be known that I became interested in everything related to Man and God at the very early age of 12 years old. I saw them as two similarities, Man and "God", constituted from infinity, and constituting infinity. I then became really interested in "God" and my relation to Him. I was soon led to contemplation, to mysticism, as if I had been trying to escape this Earth to reach the heavens.

So I read, asked questions, researched and meditated. I undertook long years of study to go even deeper into the subject. I studied the humanities, philosophy, theology, and finally, "religiology", because I had faith in Man (I still have faith) and his intelligence.

Since I am a complete and total person, I searched for a family where I could dedicate my whole life to this "God" whom I was forever questioning, whom I looked for, whom I materialized in meditation and contemplation, this "God" with whom I had lengthy conversations, as if he were an old friend. But I kept this part a secret because I could have been thought of as crazy.

I found a religious community of fathers to which I devoted six years of my life, as a student and pastor (seminarist), and I spent marvellous moments of discovery and formation within this community. But I soon became conscious of something which I found superficial. There was something which did not seem to satisfy my most profound aspirations.

I enjoyed praying (I still enjoy praying) as the contact with my creators, my source of infinity. I was thought to be mystical by many people, but I saw the father of Jesus as being human just like Jesus when he said 'my father who art in Heaven...' My thought of there being more than one creator was then true. Furthermore, I had researched *The Bible* and had come to the conclusion that Jesus was not God, and I was impassioned by an aspect of theology, "the theologians of the death of God" or "theology of the death of God". In some way I was an atheist, but I was afraid of admitting this truth.

I detected in these schools of theological thinking another form of mystification.

I could not find complete satisfaction to my numerous questions, interrogations on Man and his faith, on man in his religious and social involvement, in this Church that I found to be out of phase, even false, at times.

Nevertheless, I worked in the midst of the "Church" said to be of Christ, in the numerous movements which it includes, all the while specializing in religious science (religiology) to search even deeper.

My studies impelled me to work within my environment, to question it as well as shake it. I still felt misunderstood.

This research, which took me three more years, led me to a sort of emptiness, a sort of sadness. I could not tolerate so much mysticism, so much blindness. I liked to study, but I had reached the point where I could no longer feel a solid base. I felt that the slow process of reasoning used to justify some pastoral and ecclesiastical structures, mysticism and obscurantism, was irrelevant, out of phase, and I was rejecting it more and more. Those people who did not share my views thought of me as being critical and superficial. They accommodated themselves with banal ideas in their faith and in their religion, and still do the same today.

It was then that I decided to take a step backward for a year and search for the truth within my "soul". I was still teaching, but I did not get involved in any movements. I questioned Jesus, and I felt that I was starting to see the light.

On November 9th 1976, I attended a conference at the Plateau Auditorium, in Montreal, given by Claude Vorilhon, "Rael". On that night, I really felt that my years of study had not been in vain. I understood many things, among others that I had always been an "atheist" deep down inside of me, and that I was profoundly religious as well. I was interested in the matter; I loved Man; prayer had kept me in constant communication with this group of extra-terrestrials, our creators, the Elohim, who I de-mystified more and more each day. I understood everything in a flash. I was happy; I recognized in Rael, Jesus speaking in his own era. Something happened to me, awakened me, enlightened me, I felt drawn to him; in 90 minutes, everything inside of me was reconstructed again; everything was being connected; everything was becoming harmonious again, and it has never ceased since. I was enraptured, and it showed.

After all, from his mouth I had heard a truth, so simply, so clearly, and with such evidence, this truth that I had searched for so many years the hard way. It was as if a mental block had been removed in an instant.

I had gone to the lecture with some friends, but as was confirmed later, it had not triggered such a reaction in them. Just the same, they had noticed a change in me that night, and they noticed it even more afterwards. It was as if the messages had provoked a "click" inside me, but they would not admit to what they were seeing. I became silent, happy and luminous. I could hear them trying to reject, to destroy by mystical reasoning, this beautiful, simple and liberating truth, which had become soft music to my ears, this good news in all its plenitude, in its entirety, in its clearness. They rejected Rael and his messages from the Elohim in the same way that people had tried to reject Jesus and his message.

Those few moments with Rael had revealed the synthesis of more than 12 years of research, analysis, commitment, sufferings and the gift of myself.

Now I would be able to dedicate my whole being to the diffusion of this great news, of this great liberation, and this would happen through intelligence, comprehension, harmony and balancing of my shaken mind. It was not easy to cope with the reactions of my family, my wife, my friends, my professional environment, the Church and my friends who were still priests. But I received a lot of help from so many awakened friends and by the guidance which I received while attending the mind and body awakening sessions. I look at all my years of studying as having been spent in a laboratory, a direct preparation for life which I am presently leading as a Guide in this magnificent movement, in this "strange" but beautiful "new" religion, this young atheist religion. I don't feel that there has been a breaking off with things of the past, because I am continuing what I had started as a child: the understanding of the beginning of Man, the genesis, to be able to walk in the light and build the present, always to de-mystify and always to decant and cream off the truth from some 2,000 years of crust by deepening my understanding of the numerous theological, philosophical and religious aspects of the messages given to Rael by the creators of Humanity, the Elohim, so as to live out the present and to look forward to a splendid future.

That night I had been shaken by the messages, so much so because I had felt them for so many years, almost unconsciously. Since then I have felt the messages in every part of my life, even in the most hidden corners, in my professional work as an educator, in my family, social and political life. They have turned all my beliefs upside-down, but I had been ready for a long time. I had been waiting, and I had even taught about this prophet of the Elohim. But I could not very well understand. Then... suddenly, everything became clear: the messages awakened me, they stared me in the face. All at once I could understand *The Bible*, Jesus and Yahweh.

I was so happy that such an event had happened that I trembled with joy. It was like an ice-cold shower on a hot, humid, summer's day.

I met Rael a few days after the conference for the first time. In one weekend I had read the two messages twice over. Rael said to me: 'You have everything within yourself to find the answers to your problems. Once they will have been solved, you will be 80 per cent more efficient. Your family problems are crushing you; they are stopping you and paralyzing you.' Now I know what he meant. I am so happy at having chosen the path of awareness and consciousness.

Since then, I have read the messages many times over, and becoming a Guide was the consecration of my priesthood for which I had always been searching. I understood that I had not waited in vain, and that I was continuing the true church, the original church, since I was going to follow the last of the great prophets of the Age of Apocalypse, and I was going to work at the diffusion of the messages of the Elohim, our creators, going to work at this "unity" to which I had already dedicated my life, since these messages announce the "religion of the religions", the religion of the infinite, the religion of the intelligence of Man and the eternity of matter.

Thus, then, is my end and my beginning. I am happy and I love. I was relieved of my duties as a specialist on religion. I am teaching French and mathematics as my main subjects, and religion and moral behavior as my second subjects. I never speak openly of the messages in my professional environment, but people can feel them in my behavior, and I am respected for it. The time is near when my colleagues will ask me about these messages; I can just feel it; I am sure of it. Everywhere else I go, I diffuse the messages by my presence and by my words. I have "apostatized" the Roman Catholic church, even though I am still convinced that there has been no breaking, but rather a continuation of the truth. This rejuvenates and gratifies me.

My entire life is dedicated to revealing to all men of good will, this de-mystified truth, this message of love, fraternity and peace, this serenity, this unique and revolutionary message for those who seek to understand it with the eyes of intelligence, which our creators, the Elohim, have given us, the eyes of wisdom, created and infinite.

To Become Active So As Not To Become Radioactive

MICHEL BELUET – *Former National Guide for the USA*

Here is my testimony, where I will elaborate the profound and fundamental reasons which have led me to become a Guide in the Raelian Movement, after I had given serious consideration to the implications brought about by my adhesion. The message given to Claude Vorilhon, Rael, by the Elohim, implies a total reconsideration at all levels: individual, social, political, scientific, philosophical and religious. This allows universal involvement in the building of tomorrow's society. But how did I come to these conclusions?

Since the age of 12, I have been interested in a wide range of topics, and I tried to stay on top of whatever was going on, as well as whatever had happened in the past, when I reached a stage where I wondered about the evolution of Humanity. And I, like many people, was questioning everything, while dreaming of a perfect world. What did I discover, and what were my hopes? Here they are synthesized:

THE ORIGINS OF LIFE

I was not satisfied with the theory of a divine creation, although there seemed to be one constancy: throughout the world, all religions and mythologies speak of the creation of Man by one or a number of Gods who came from Heaven. I then concluded that there had to be some truth in this first thought, palpable and material, which implied that Man had come from somewhere other than Earth. The theory of evolution, which claims that Man is the result of successive mutations starting from inorganic matter which resulted in the organic beings that we are, seemed to have too many faults to be a truly valuable theory. Moreover, it is presently being seriously questioned by eminent scientists.

MAN

I had noticed that since the beginning of time, Man lacked tolerance, love, respect and fraternity, in his relationships with others. I wished that these shortcomings would be erased in human relations.

SOCIETY

Throughout history, the repeated failures of every type of government to solve the fundamental problems of Humanity, have forced me to think of a system which would allow the election of the best qualified people on Earth, who would be concerned only with improving our society.

This would imply that they would not be paid by the political, military or industrial trusts which have permitted a great number of deadly wars and an everlasting increase in weapons of destruction, in the name of values such as the mother country, work and family, and the servitude of Man by Man. I became conscious that Humanity had reached a crucial epoch, decisive in its evolution, where Man's future had become a gamble.

THE RELIGIONS

I felt that there existed, at the base of all the religions, a fundamental and accessible truth, but also that the primitive and obscurantist systems had used this truth to enslave men to absolute restriction. I also felt that this truth, as revealed by the prophets, had to come from beings who had reached a very high level of wisdom. I opposed the notion that Man had to be guilty because of his carnal nature, as I was against everyone who sought to diminish humans under the pretense that they would be greater after death, in another dimension. I was convinced that Man could reach a superior level of consciousness while remaining in complete harmony with his human nature.

SCIENCE

This original curiosity which Man has transformed into a systematic study of himself and the environment in which he lives, has permitted Humanity to push back the frontiers of the unexplained. I knew that the use of science to solve the problems with which our civilization is confronted is possible, if science is used wisely. Pollution, overpopulation, hunger, the energy crisis – all these problems could be solved by science in harmony with Nature, and it is imperative that this ideal be attained as soon as possible. I was equally conscious of the temporary aspect of our knowledge and that every theory is but a tentative interpretation of facts, which themselves are undeniable.

THE UNKNOWN

I was aware of everything which is unexplained on Earth, and which led us to believe that extra-terrestrial intelligent beings intervened in the course of our history. All of this being quite natural for me, knowing that one day we could explain everything.

I was then conscious of the present state of things, and my hopes for a better world and an evolution of Humanity towards more harmony, non-violence and more fraternity, and I could not be satisfied in any existing organization, whether it be religious, political or social. I felt powerless and alone. It was then, in 1978, that I learned of the messages that extra-terrestrials had entrusted to Claude Vorilhon, in December 1973, which were contained in *The Book Which Tells The Truth* and in a second book, written later after the 1975 encounter, *The Extra-Terrestrials Took Me To Their Planet*. I was filled with joy in reading these two books, in which were synthesized all my hopes of attaining this harmony, this peace and this fraternity which has always been missing on this Earth. The books also tell of the means used by our Fathers to overcome the same problems with which we are faced. But like good fathers, they are leaving us free to choose, because they consider us as being individuals capable of choosing.

I decided to become a Guide so as to be able to communicate this hope to the world, so that Humanity is able to reach the Golden Age where Man will be able to blossom totally. I did not want to remain a passive witness to the evolution of humanity towards a possible self-destruction, but rather an active man, so as to avoid the possibility that one day we would all become radioactive.

From Marxism to Raelism Adhesion

JEAN-BERNARD NDJOGA-AWIRONDJOGO –
Political Scientist and ex-Marxist

It was not easy, for someone accustomed to reasoning in terms of evolution, of classes and the struggle between classes, to understand and accept that something fantastic, marvellous and reassuring exists behind "tradition".

But through the messages of the Elohim, all the seeming absurdities of the biblical writings suddenly became for me, noble, practical and of infinite importance.

The knowledge that man is not the result of random chance, but the scientific and wise creation of someone who made him in His image and in His resemblance! What a sublime truth!

And to think that one day, men of the Earth will be equal to their creators, the extra-terrestrials!

Now the time announced has arrived.

Rael, the light of the Elohim close to men has started his mission.

It now rests with us as Guides, who would help him, to continue to help him by spreading the messages of our heavenly fathers more than ever, so that the Earth, in turn, will join the concert of intergalactic civilizations who exist in the infinity of the universe.

A New Art of Living

MICHEL DEYDIER – *Psychologist*

There exists in the universe an indefinite number of psychosomatic emotional entities, or if you prefer, personalities, with their respective biological, energetic and mental activities. The social relationships of these entities necessitate a very important adaptation faculty, without which Man could not form a social group. Man's mental riches are conditioned by his aptitude, which allows him at any given time, to question all which composes his life, and makes him happy or unhappy.

I have used this same faculty when trying to trace the path which would lead me to personal consciousness and progress. The knowledge of Man is a question of versatility. One must slip into the smallest openings of the conscious, then evolve in the deepest layers of the subconscious, without destroying their fauna, "the devil take the frustrations", but one must nevertheless acknowledge, "I frustrate you, you frustrate me". The story never changes, and we are always the same.

If you wish to climb inside your head, you must first learn to be scratched as you climb; there are so many things that you will not want to see. So, face them and start laughing at yourself, seeing how vain you can be; the more conscious you will become of your stupidity and your vanity, the greater person you will become, and you will never hurt again, because you will have assumed yourself totally, before loving yourself.

It was in this state of mind that I recognized the finality of the messages; first, I recognized, then I digested in a long digestive process, which had its periods of activity, I must confess.

At first it was not a simple coincidence, but a real collision, where an enormous brain-washing, more or less conscious, was released, putting back each thing in its place. A psychologist being by definition a disorganized person on the outside (but fairly well organized on the inside), I was stunned to see how the information revealed by the extra-terrestrials not only found its place in my mind, but also established an incredible synthesis between the elements of my life. What is even more incredible is the creative changes which I now use to help my patients.

Actions causing reactions, I was led to verify one by one each of the principal elements of the messages. Quite honestly, I came to a number of conclusions; some were absurd, others less so. I refuse to follow a credo, because the mental operations related to believing have nothing to do with the operations conducting logical reasoning, even with subjective verifications.

I do not blindly believe in extra-terrestrials, I truly understand their role and their presence in a true and reflected manner, in complete understanding of the decor. Thus supported by these conclusions, I took a second look at the important points of my formation. I turned upside down and then side-ways, but to my great surprise, I did not find much of anything, either on one side or the other. I was supposed to remedy the sickness of the mind, and I had just discovered how ridiculous and limited I really was. I have discovered that psychotherapy rests on a Judeo-Christian base, which is well disguised. If you look at it from this angle, this thought is not very reassuring, nor is it very clean. But on the other hand, who has never been cheated by Society? Be that as it may, one must react to those usurpations; and so here I am on this slow boat which carries the truth, beauty, sanity and which builds a liberating progress.

The messages given to Claude Vorilhon by the extra-terrestrials, are in my own mind, the most intelligent answer which I could ever find on the origins of Humanity, as well as the destiny of our civilization and enlightenment on the anatomy of a new art of living.

I adhere to this impulse without any hesitation.

I refuse to concentrate my life on an egotistical individual ideology. A profound instinct has led me to study this report, an old instinct a little forgotten, which gives a man the strength to rise again. Each man has it, each one of us can participate in the renovation of the collective life, at his own level, while using his adaptation faculty and his instinct for survival.

Here are the two things which make Man the creature which is more likely to be able to modify his terrestrial and cosmic environment, and which authorize him to make the ultimate choice in the great passion-filled moments of history.

Never has Society been so close to its goals, and it's only natural for it to be so disturbed.

Past history overflows with events, incontestable proofs of evolutional values of suffering. The present shows the logical issues of the great rules of evolution. The future offers a panorama bursting with possibilities, due to the union of moral values with the capital, technical and scientific values.

These are the motivations which have led me to understand the messages given by the extra-terrestrials. I am happy to have had the opportunity to give my testimony. I give my firm support to the messages, without any reservations, and my aspirations are in the image of the steps which brought about the creation of life on our planet.

5

Addendum

Encounter of October 7th, 1976

On October 7th 1976, about 50 Raelians were at La Negrerie, near Roc Plat, in Dordogne in the South West of France for the first anniversary of the contact of October 7th 1975, commemorating the time when Rael had been taken to the planet of the Eternals and had received the message contained in the second book: *The Extra-Terrestrials Took Me To Their Planet*. The meeting was to take place at 3pm. At 2:45pm, everyone had arrived and gathered around Rael. There was a profound feeling of harmony among the participants who were all thrilled to spend these few moments with the last of the great prophets. Suddenly, someone cried: 'What is that falling from the sky?' Great flakes were falling from the near cloudless sky. They seemed to be made of a cottony substance, which when touched, melted in a few seconds. Then someone cried: 'Look, there is something very shiny in the sky!' Two luminous objects, both very bright, were just above us. The fall of the flakes lasted about ten minutes, then the objects suddenly disappeared. Roger, a Guide from Toulouse who worked in a research laboratory, was able to obtain a sample of the cottony flakes, but upon taking them for analysis, they vaporized.

All the people who were privileged to live this extraordinary experience had not been disappointed, even if it had meant a long trip half way across France for some, and for others even further, to have their cellular plan transmitted by Rael. At the precise moment and the exact location of where the meeting was going to take place, the Elohim had offered a sign to those present, which they would never forget.

For the first time, Rael had not been the only witness to the Elohim's activities. There were 50 people with him who can testify to the phenomenon.

Philippe, the Guide from Belgium, found out later from reading a book that the same phenomenon had been observed in Brazil, Belgium and most noticeably in Italy during a football game which had to be interrupted. There were always the same brilliant vessels and the cottony flakes.

Rael insists that the gatherings are not aimed at being witnesses to the sighting of UFOs, but nevertheless, many participants still wish that the Elohim would again grant them the pleasure of appearing...

The Message of the Elohim, March 14th, 1978

Transmitted telepathically to Rael at Midnight:

'I, Yahweh, through the words of my messenger, Rael, address to the people of the Earth the following message:

Beware! It is not impossible that other extra-terrestrial civilizations will make contact very soon with the people of the Earth. They are people we have also created scientifically in another part of the universe, and with whom we maintain presently no direct communication for reasons that we cannot explain to you now without creating a serious imbalance. You must simply know that we are counting on you to reveal to those people their true origin, for they are your brothers from space and like you are looking for their creator. Tell them the truth about their creation, by revealing to them *The Book Which Tells the Truth* and the message of October 7th of year 30 of the Age of Apocalypse.'.

It is important to note that this is the one and only message which Rael has ever received telepathically in three years. All that men should know, or nearly all, has been said in the first two messages.

Modification of the New Commandments

The sixth of the new commandments found in the second message is modified: In order to avoid exaggerated ageing of the Head of the Raelian Movement, the Guide of Guides will be elected for a seven year term, by level five guides, who must number at least 12 to vote. Until there are at least 12 level fives, the levels four and five Guides will join together in a vote, and there must be a total of 12 people to decide. If there are not sufficient Guides at these two levels, the level three Guides will be admitted to vote. The Guide of Guides will be elected between the levels four and five, and will be eligible for re-election at the end of his mandate of seven years.

This modification also implies a modification of the fourth of the new commandments also contained in the second message: The annual donation, which is equal to at least one per cent of net annual revenue should be made payable to the Raelian Foundation. This will provide for the needs of the Guide of Guides, and permit him to devote himself full time to his mission: spreading the messages. This modification suggested by Rael was accepted by our creators who understand the need for these changes, so that the Movement may become more efficient and accelerate the diffusion of the messages.

Message of the Elohim, December 13th, 1997

It is now 24 years ago that, through the mouth of our prophet, RAEL, our beloved son, we gave to the Men and Women of the Earth our final message. The one which, as predicted, came to destroy the "Mystery of God".

It has been 24 years during which you Raelians, who have officially and publicly recognized us as your Creators, have worked so that we may be welcomed in the requested Embassy. Your devotion and your efforts have warmed our hearts, and the most devoted among you are among those who will be rewarded.

In all the religions, there are people who deserve our love, but Raelians are the ones closest to us. They are our new Chosen People and will one day have a new Promised Land, because their love is based on consciousness and understanding, and not on blind faith.

Those who loved us as one or several supernatural gods were precious to our eyes, and they did not have a choice in prescientific times; but those who, knowing that we are not supernatural but created in their image, continue to love us and even to love us much more, touch us to a greater extent and will be rewarded more, because they love us with their consciousness and not only with their faith. And it is consciousness that makes them similar to us.

We asked that an Embassy be built to welcome us near Jerusalem, and the authorities of the stiff necked people have refused several times to grant the necessary authorizations and extra-territorial status. Our preference for Jerusalem is merely sentimental, because for us Jerusalem is everywhere where human beings love us, respect us and wish to welcome us with due respect, and the chosen people are those who, knowing who we are, want to welcome us, meaning the Raelians. The real Jews on Earth are no longer the people of Israel but those who recognize us as their creators and wish to see us return.

The link we have with the people of Israel is about to be severed, and the new Alliance is coming to an end. They have very little time to understand their mistake before being dispersed once again.

In the meantime, we must from now on ask for the necessary permission and extra-territorial status from all nations on Earth for the erection of our Embassy, and the radius of one kilometer can be composed of water as well as firm land, with the condition that navigation be prohibited.

When a country grants this authorization, Israel will have, for the last time, a short period of reflection to grant this authorization and will keep the privilege, or the Embassy will be built elsewhere, and the people of David will lose our protection and will be dispersed.

The country which will build the Embassy on its territory or on a territory it will give or sell to this effect, with the necessary extra-territorial status, will have a guaranteed and flourishing future, will benefit from our protection and will become the spiritual and scientific centre of the whole planet for the millenniums to come.

The hour of our Great Return is near, and we will support and protect the most devoted ones among you. Your enemies will witness our might more and more, most especially the usurper from Rome, his bishops and all those who act in our name without being appointed.

Year 2000 is nothing for us and nothing for a very large majority of people who are not Christians, but many false prophets will try to use this change in the millennium to mislead humans. It was expected, and it is a selection of the most conscious ones. Follow your Guide of Guides; he will know how to avoid the dangers of this time of transition because he is the Way, the Truth, the Life.

Buddhism is more and more successful on Earth, and this is good, as it is the religion that is closest to the Truth and to the new scientific-spiritual equilibrium necessary for human beings of the new age. Buddhism without the mystical load of the past gives Raelism, and more and more Buddhists will become Raelians.

May your joy in seeing the approach of our Great Return give you wings to overcome the last obstacles of the journey. We are so close to this day, that whenever you meditate, you should be able to feel our presence. And this sensation will illuminate your days and nights and will make your life wonderful, no matter what obstacles are left to overcome. The joy of seeing us will be lesser than the pleasure of having worked for this day to come. The greatest pleasure is in the accomplishment of your mission, not in its result. In the meantime, our love and light will guide you, through the words of our Beloved Prophet, and do not forget that even if we constantly see you, each time he looks at you, we see you even more because he beautifies what he sees through the Love he has for you.

The more you love him, the more you love us, because he is a part of us on Earth. If you find it sometimes hard to show us affection, it is because you do not have the consciousness of seeing our Beloved Son walking amongst you once again.

You cannot love us and neglect him because, once again, you reach the Father through the Son, because he is among you, eats when you eat, sleeps when you sleep, laughs when you laugh and cries when you cry.

Do not pretend to love us if you do not treat him as the dearest among us.

His Love for you is so great that he constantly asks us to forgive things we judge as unforgivable. He is your best advocate in the eyes of your Creators. And on your planet where Love and Forgiveness are more and more rare in a society which is becoming more and more barbaric through a lack of these values, he is your most precious asset. You lack Love? Look at him; he is alive among you!

May his light guide you to us whether we return or not because in either case, we await you among our eternals.

Peace and Love to all Humans of goodwill.

The United Nations - Rael, September 2005

The UN Must Disappear To Be Replaced By A More Democratic Organization

This is what I have been saying for the last 30 years...The UN is not a democratic organization. It is an elite club run by a few ex-colonial and modern imperialist superpowers, all of them from white and western countries.

For the UN to be truly democratic, each nation should be entitled to a vote proportional to its population, which means that India and

China, who represent almost 50% of humanity with a joint population of almost 3 billion, would have a corresponding "voting power" of 50%. The US on the other hand, with only 300 million inhabitants, which only represents 5% of the world population, should have a voting power of only 5%, and the UK, with only 60 million inhabitants representing just 1% of the world population, should have a voting power of only 1%. But instead, the UN is ruled by a small group of rich western nations who represent less than 10% of humanity, especially those in the so called "security council"...

If Bush, Blair and other leaders of imperialist, ex-colonial countries really want what they claim they want: to promote democracy, then they must accept a truly democratic UN.

But the truth is that they don't really want it; what they really want is to continue ruling the world, both economically and spiritually. As my setting up of the ICACCI (International Committee Against Christian Calendar Imperialism - www.icacci.org) pointed out, why is the UN, which is supposed to represent the whole of humanity, using the Christian calendar for all its official documents when only 25% of humanity is Christian? Why should Muslims, Sikhs, Jews, Buddhists and Shintoists, etc. who each have their own calendar, be forced to sign UN papers using the Christian calendar?

The UN could adopt a neutral calendar, using as year zero the year of its own inception or the year Hiroshima was bombed, as a symbol of peace. But instead, it still uses the Christian calendar which forces non-Christian countries, who happen to be the majority, to recognize Jesus' supposed birth date when signing documents – without any sensitivity to the feelings of those whose forefathers were massacred, bonded into slavery or rampaged by crusades in the name of Christianity.

The UN has only two choices: completely change and become a truly democratic, non-religious organization or be destroyed and replaced by a truly neutral and democratic organization. Maybe the latter is the best solution, as it is always very difficult to change existing things. Maybe the new world body which would replace the UN will cost much less and be much more democratic: "made by the people for the people". It could even be a virtual internet-based world government, where the people can express their choices directly online. This on-line democracy would have the added advantage of dispensing with the most dangerous, least trustworthy and expensive people on Earth: politicians. My proposition of a web government (www.upworldgov.org) could be the right solution to replace the obsolete UN.

AUTHOR'S POSTSCRIPT

Some thirty years have passed since I wrote the three books that now make up this new compendium edition re-entitled *Intelligent Design - Message from the Designers*. I will discuss the reasons behind this new title further on, but in the meantime, it is important to reflect that a great deal has happened over the past thirty years. Our world has continued to change very rapidly during that period, always in the direction of the revealed information I was first given in the early to mid 1970s. That is why the books are reproduced unchanged here to demonstrate that the extraordinary truths first revealed three decades ago are being gradually and successively proven by new scientific discoveries and developments.

I originally published the first part of this book as *The Book Which Tells the Truth* in the French language in early 1974. After a sudden, unexpected and unforgettable space journey in October 1975, I followed the first book with *Extra-Terrestrials Took Me to Their Planet* in 1976. In 1979, I wrote and published *Let's Welcome the Extra-terrestrials*, making known for the first time information which I had earlier been asked by the Elohim to withhold for three years. I have written four other books, one entitled *Geniocracy* (1978), which describes an advanced form of democracy advocated by the Elohim, *Sensual Meditation* (1980), a teaching book of vital meditative practices designed by the Elohim to awaken our senses fully and help us achieve true inner harmony, *Yes to Human Cloning* (2000), which outlines the scientific advances soon to be part of our lives in the areas of cloning and nanotechnology, and *The Maitreya*, an anthology selected by leading Raelians of my more recent contemporary lectures and talks.

These books have now been translated into nearly thirty languages by volunteer Raelian supporters. In all, more than two million copies of my books have been sold worldwide. The vast majority have been printed, published and distributed under the control of various national branches of the International Raelian Movement (IRM).

In the thirty-two years of its existence, the IRM has grown steadily. Currently, the organization has a total of more than 65,000 members worldwide, and national branches are now established in nearly 90 countries, including all the world's major nations. At present, the Movement is strongest in France, Canada, Japan, South Korea and Africa. It is also expanding strongly in the United States, Australia, Britain, South East Asia, Latin America, and most of the other countries of Europe. More recently, new national branches have been founded in Bulgaria, Mongolia and Lithuania.

At regular seminars held on every continent of the world, the teachings of the Elohim as outlined in these books have been passed on to many thousands of people of all ages by myself and senior members of the IRM. In all, there are now over 200 Guides, or Raelian priests, worldwide. The Movement has two main publications in which I and other leading Raelians write of current developments: *Apocalypse*, an international glossy magazine which is published twice a year, and *Contact*, a weekly e-newsletter that is distributed online at raelianews.org. These publications help to further disseminate the philosophies and insights of the Elohim.

The birth of Dolly the sheep was a landmark event in human scientific history, and it then became clear that very soon the cloning of human beings would become fairly commonplace. Just as on the Elohim's planet, cloning on Earth will become a means for human beings to achieve eternal life.

After Dolly the sheep was cloned in 1997, I initiated a project called Clonaid to bring attention to the issue of human cloning. Soon after, Dr. Brigitte Boisselier, a brilliant scientist and Raelian Bishop, took over the project and created a company. I withdrew myself completely from any and all involvement, since my initial purpose was simply to promote the concept of human cloning, so the IRM has no direct connection to Clonaid whatsoever. I will, of course, continue to philosophically support Dr. Boisselier and her company in continuing their work, and I was especially pleased when she dramatically announced in December 2002 the front page global headline news that was perhaps the biggest breakthrough of the entire 32-year mission to date: Clonaid had successfully assisted the birth of the world's first cloned human baby, a little girl nick-named "Eve".

Although up to the time of writing, legal complexities have delayed publication of the scientific proof of this successful human cloning, there was no doubt that the name of the Raelian Movement and what it stood for had become common knowledge everywhere around the planet.

The next step required will be to make possible the transfer of mental information, memory and personality from an aging individual into a new, physically young adult clone. This transfer of memory directly into a young adult means that effectively the same individual can live indefinitely. Human laws will have to be adapted to our changing culture and increasing technological advances. These are still early days for all such issues, but new laws will have to be passed to define criteria setting out who will be allowed to benefit from these technologies. Here, as on the Elohim's planet, the number of clones may need to be limited to one per individual, and then only after death.

This year, another breakthrough of perhaps similar magnitude occurred, as is mentioned briefly in the Foreword to this book, when a peer-reviewed article appeared in a Washington scientific journal effectively announcing the academic acceptance of a new theory of *Intelligent Design*. This publication marked the first formal high-level academic challenge to Darwin's outdated and unproven evolutionary theory. As a result, over the past year or so, Intelligent Design, or ID, has attracted growing attention and inspired much debate in academic circles and beyond in America, Europe and worldwide. In particular, as I write these words, a raging debate is underway in the United States about the introduction of the Intelligent Design theory into schools as an alternative to Darwin's Theory of Evolution.

Opponents of this see the move as an attempt to reintroduce "God" officially into the nation's schools despite the Supreme

Court's refusal to allow this almost 50 years ago on the grounds that the clear separation of church and state is written in the Constitution. Indeed it is very evident at present that American religious conservatives are definitely using this camouflage to infiltrate their dogmatic religious views back into America's schools.

But our very original and unique Raelian explanation of the origin of life on Earth effectively offers a third option, and one which cannot be denied by the Supreme Court, as it doesn't promote religion in schools! It can best be described as *atheist Intelligent Design*, which is the scientific creation of life on Earth performed by an advanced human civilization from another planet. This brings into being a completely new rational theory explaining our origins which is actually reproducible in a laboratory, as evidenced by the recent announcement by scientific researcher Craig Venter, that he has started the process of creating the first totally synthetic unicellular organism. The essential prerequisite for something to be scientific is that it can be reproducible in a laboratory. Evolution has never been reproduced in any laboratory; that's why it's called a "theory", and the same goes, of course, for the theory of "God". This third way, atheist Intelligent Design, is the only one which can be reproduced in a laboratory right now and is actually about to happen.

The idea that there are billions of planets similar to Earth in the universe is also accepted by most scientists, as is the fact that our planet is *not* necessarily the most advanced in the universe. So, having a much more advanced human civilization coming to Earth a long time ago to create life in a kind of panspermia is the most rational explanation of our origins. At the very least, it is worth being taught in schools as an alternative to the theory of Evolution, and no school can deny access to an atheist Intelligent Design theory on the grounds of church and state separation. Even believers in "God" would stand to gain by using our explanation as a "Trojan horse" to enter the school system as an alternative to the monolithic, dogmatic and intolerant Darwinist theory of evolution.

Having said that, it is important to also say that preparations to build the embassy requested by the Elohim are also progressing well.

The embassy and residence need to be protected by extra-territorial rights like any normal international diplomatic mission, and in accordance with the Elohim's precise instructions, Raelian architects have already completed commissioned drawings for the complex of buildings where the most dramatic and extraordinary meeting of world government leaders in history will take place. Not long after we built a small scale model of the embassy based on these drawings, a crop circle appeared in England which bore an astonishing resemblance to it.

I have to say that finance is not the chief obstacle to the completion of this project. The political and diplomatic problems are a thornier issue, and patience and perseverance will be required to overcome them. In this regard, the International Raelian Movement has several times since 1991 made presentations to the Israeli Government and to the Chief Rabbi in Jerusalem, requesting that the necessary extra-territoriality be granted so that the embassy may be built close to Jerusalem where the Elohim created the first human beings. The first temple of the Jewish religion was in fact a previous embassy around which the ancient city was built. The Elohim are now waiting for the State of Israel to grant such extra-territorial status for the new embassy - the third temple - but so far there has been no positive response to the seven requests that have been made.

The first approach was made on November 8th, 1991 on the Jewish New Year, and another official request was made to Israel's Chief Rabbi some months later. The request was acknowledged, and a study of the application began. In the summer of 1993, an Israeli government commission concluded that the Raelian Movement was peaceful in intent and was of no threat to Israel's security. In their report, two rabbis are believed to have concluded that it would be "better not to do anything against Rael in case he really is the awaited Messiah". In November 1993, a further direct request was made to Israel's prime minister, Yitzhak Rabin, when he was in Canada attending the Montreal Jewish Convention. After a month, Mr. Rabin replied through one of his office representatives that he could not comply. If Israel ultimately declines to allow a grant of extra-territoriality, as already indicated, we will most likely establish the embassy on Palestinian or Egyptian territory or in another neighboring state. In fact, the lower slopes of Mount Sinai would make an excellent alternative choice since that is where Yahweh, the leader of the Elohim, first appeared to Moses. Nevertheless, the Elohim would prefer to give Israel the opportunity to agree to this request since that is the true purpose of the State of Israel. Since the message of the Elohim, on December 13th, 1997, we have started negotiations with other countries, and once we have "the go ahead", a final "last chance" request will be made to Israel.

Already, in 1990, as a sign of their special feelings towards the people of Israel, the Elohim agreed to my suggestion to modify their original Symbol of Infinity when used by Raelian Movement branches in the West. The central swastika, which means "well-being" in Sanskrit and also represents infinity in time, was replaced with a galaxy-shaped swirl. This change was made in an effort to help the negotiations for building the embassy of the Elohim in Israel and also out of respect for the sensitivities of the victims who suffered and died under the Nazi swastika during the Second World War. In Asia, where the swastika can be found in most Buddhist temples and where it represents infinity in time, the original symbol is not a problem. This modification of the IRM symbol for the West was, of course, gladly made, and when looking back now and surveying our progress since 1973, I can see that everything is going according to plan.

The International Raelian Movement will one day achieve all the goals set by the Elohim - with or without my participation. I know that it has become self-sustaining and could now function perfectly well without me. Much still remains to be done, and even when at last the great day dawns and the Elohim land openly and officially before the eyes of world government leaders and an international array of television cameras and media representatives, some skeptics, I expect, will still continue to doubt whether these highly advanced human beings could truly have created all life artificially on our planet. The leading members of the IRM and myself are aware that this might be so. But this does not daunt us - quite the reverse.

The Elohim themselves will definitely land here in the not too distant future, around the time of what some call "the singularity"- when everything will be understood thanks to science. It will be no later than thirty years from now and may be much sooner if the truths I have described in this book spread more rapidly around the world.

The Elohim will bring with them all the great prophets of the past, including Moses, Elijah, Buddha, Jesus Christ, and Mohammed.

This long-awaited event will be the most wonderful day in the history of humanity. I hope you will be present when they land at their embassy, and I hope that you are able to share the joy of knowing that you played a part in this wonderful adventure. The area where the embassy is to be built will become the spiritual center of the world for millennia to come. People from all nations will come in pilgrimage to this "holy" place. A replica of the embassy will be built near the real one and opened to the public so that they can see what it is like inside.

But will the Raelian Movement's mission end with the coming of our creators? Not at all! On the contrary, it will be the real beginning of our mission. With the disappearance of all primitive religions, the vacuum will have to be filled with a new spirituality - one that is in tune with the technological revolution still to come.

We are now today's human beings using tomorrow's technology, with yesterday's religions and yesterday's thinking. Thanks to the Elohim, we will be able to reach new spiritual levels by embracing their own religion - an atheist one - that of infinity as represented by their symbol. The Guides of the Raelian Movement will become the priests of this new religion, allowing human beings to feel in harmony with the infinitely small and the infinitely large, allowing them to realize that we are stardust and energies forever.

Laboratories and universities will be built close to the embassy and there, under the guidance of the Elohim, our own scientists will be able to improve their knowledge. In this way, we will gradually approach the Elohim's scientific level. This will enable us to venture out to other planets to create life ourselves, and we will become in our own turn "Elohim" for those we create. On our own planet, Brigitte Boisselier and other scientists of realistic vision have already started out along the path of becoming "intelligent designers" who, as they work for the future, will be fully aware of the true nature of our past and our origins. Through us and through them, spirituality and science will walk peacefully together hand in hand, free at last from the medieval fears that have haunted our past. This will enable us to become "gods" ourselves, as was written long ago in the ancient scriptures - but perhaps rather more accurately or amusingly "atheist gods".

However, let's not forget that our greatest task is to build the embassy for the Elohim so that at long last they can come here and land officially and openly among us! And they will bring to our very troubled yet potentially very beautiful world their profound teachings of love as well as science.

Rael
Quebec, Canada
Autumn 2005

ADDITIONAL INFORMATION

Readers may wish to contact the author or his organization, the International Raelian Movement (IRM), for further information about this book and other related matters. The main global address for the author is:

c/o **The International Raelian Movement**
Case Postale 225, CH 1211
Geneva 8
Switzerland

The official internet addresses of the International Raelian Movement and associated organizations are:

www.rael.org
www.raelianews.org
www.raelradio.net
www.rael-science.org
www.raelafrica.org
www.apostasynow.org
www.subversions.com
www.icacci.org

To subscribe to **rael-science**, which distributes by e-mail a selection of scientific news concerning this book, please send a blank e-mail to:

subscribe@rael-science.org

SEMINARS AND CONTACTS

Each year several seminars are held around the world where Raelians gather to hear the teachings of the Elohim as given by their Prophet Rael. If you would like to participate in one of these seminars or just get in touch with a Raelian near you, please contact one of the local Raelian Movements below. For a complete list of Raelian contacts in over 86 countries, please visit the website: www.rael.org.

AFRICA
05 BP 1444, Abidjan 05
Cote d'Ivoire, Africa
Tel: (+225) 07.82.83.00
Email: africa@intelligentdesignbook.com

EUROPE
7 Leonard Street
London, England, UK
Tel: +33 (0)6 16 45 42 85
Email: europe@intelligentdesignbook.com

AMERICAS
P.O.BOX 570935
Topaz Station
Las Vegas, NV 89108, USA
Tel: (+1) 888 RAELIAN
Tel: (+1) 888 723 5426
Email: usa@intelligentdesignbook.com
Email: canada@intelligentdesignbook.com

OCEANIA
G.P.O. Box 2397
Sydney, NSW 2001
Australia
Tel: +61(0)419 966 196
Tel: +61(0)409 376 544
Email: oceania@intelligentdesignbook.com

ASIA
Tokyo-To, Shibuya-Ku
Shibuya 2-12-12
Miki Biru 401, Japan 150-0002
Tel: (+81) 3 3498 0098
Fax: (+81) 3 3486 9354
Email: asia@intelligentdesignbook.com

U.K
BCM Minstrel
London WC1N 3XX
England, UK
Tel: +44(0)7749618243
Email: uk@intelligentdesignbook.com

ACKNOWLEDGEMENTS

Thank you to The Fitzwilliam Museum, University of Cambridge, UK for granting permission to reproduce *The Baptism of Christ* by Aert de Gelder, 1710. Oil on canvas, 48.3 x 37.1 cm.

Similar thanks go to The National Gallery, London for granting permission to reproduce *The Annunciation, with Saint Emidius* by Carlo Crivelli, 1486. Egg tempera and oil on canvas transferred from wood, 207 x 146.7 cm.

To Colin Andrews (www.CropCircleInfo.com) for permission to use the crop circle aerial photograph taken at Cheesefoot Head in Wiltshire, England in August 1990, thank you.

Thank you to Marcus Wenner for providing the original English translations of *The Message Given by Extra-Terrestrials* and *Let's Welcome the Extra-Terrestrials*, which form the majority of this new translation-reviewed edition.

For the many biblical quotations found within this book, the *Restored Name King James Version*, the *American Standard Version*, the *Darby Translation*, the *Hebrew Names Version*, *The Webster Bible*, and the *New King James Version* have been used as references.

OTHER BOOKS BY RAEL

SENSUAL MEDITATION

An important companion volume to *Intelligent Design: Message from the Designers*.

To open our minds to the future and realize our true potential, we must learn to awaken our bodies more fully to the pleasures of all our senses... that is the vital lesson which Rael has brought back from his journey to another planet.

In this volume, he details the techniques of meditation which the Elohim have designed to help bring us into harmony with the infinite nature of all things.

By helping us to enjoy sounds, colors, tastes, perfumes and caresses more intensely, the teachings enable us to find new creativity within ourselves.

GENIOCRACY

The first English translation of a highly controversial political thesis.

Democracy is an imperfect form of government destined to give way to rule by geniuses - "Geniocracy". Under this system, no candidate for high office may stand for election unless his intelligence level is measurably fifty per cent above the norm. Furthermore, to be eligible to vote, an elector must have an intelligence level ten per cent above the average. Geniocracy is, therefore, selective democracy.

These challenging concepts already apply on the planet of the Elohim. Unless we can come up with something better, they advise us to begin preparing to implement a similar system, since all human progress is ultimately dependent on the work of geniuses.

In this first edition of the book to be published in the English language, Rael describes how such a process might work here - once intelligence testing is sufficiently developed.

YES TO HUMAN CLONING
An amazing glimpse into the future.

In this book, Rael, who inspired Clonaid, the first company offering to clone human beings, explains how today's technology is the first step in the quest for eternal life.

With exceptional vision, he allows us an extraordinary glimpse into an amazing future and explains how our nascent technology will revolutionize our world and transform our lives.

This is a book to prepare us for an unimaginably beautiful world turned paradise, where nanotechnology will make agriculture and heavy industry redundant, where super artificial intelligence will quickly outstrip human intelligence and do all the boring tasks, where eternal life will be just as possible in a computer as in a series of constantly rejuvenated human bodies, and where the world could be a place of leisure and love where no one need work no more!

THE MAITREYA
Extracts from his Teachings.

Rael, the predicted "Maitreya from the West", shares his teachings and insights in this wonderful book of extracts taken from the many Raelian seminars at which he has taught over the past thirty years. A multitude of topics are covered in this book, such as Love, Happiness, Serenity, Spirituality, Contemplation, The Myth of Perfection, Non-Violence, Science, Loving Relationships, and much more. An excellent resource for anyone interested in developing oneself and wishing to live a more fulfilling and joyful life.

NOTES AND REFERENCES

The notes shown below are that of the editor and not of the author.

1. For the biblical references throughout this book, unless stated otherwise, the Restored Name King James Bible (RNKJV) has been used, which utilizes the Hebrew names of *Elohim* and *Yahweh* instead of *God* and *the Lord*.
2. In many French bibles, and in the original French equivalent of this book, the word *science* is used instead of *good and evil*.
3. *in the evening* in the New King James Version (NKJV) of the Bible.
4. *defect* in the New King James Version (NKJV) of the Bible.
5. Written as *Commander of the army* in many bibles.
6. Greek version and Latin Vulgate read *tumors*.
7. Written as *dark cloud* in the New King James Version (NKJV).
8. Passage taken from The Webster Bible (Webster's) due to its use of *on the earth* instead of *in the earth*.
9. In many bibles, the word *armies* is often found in place of the word *host*.
10. The RNKJV uses *EliYah*, but the more popular spelling *Elijah* has been used.
11. Hebrew Names Version (HNV), based off of the World English Bible, an update of the American Standard Version of 1901.
12. New King James Version (NKJV).
13. In this passage, *angels* can be replaced with *Elohim*, as found in the Hebrew version. This is also noted in the footnotes of the New Living Translation (NLT) Bible.
14. New King James Version (NKJV) has been used. The bible quotation of the French bible by Edouard Dhorme would read something like: *Will you spread, with him, clouds that are solid as a mirror of molten metal?*
15. The French bible of Edouard Dhorme, as quoted in the original French Messages, reads like: *Every Man is stupid when he lacks science.*

16. *Yahushua,* as used in the Restored Name King James Version, has been replaced with *Jesus,* as found in other Bibles.
17. American Standard Version (ASV) of the Bible.
18. The French equivalent starts with *Les temps seront venus quand,* ie. *The time will have come when.*
19. The word *fish* has been replaced with the French equivalent *pisces.*
20. This quotation is from The Darby Translation (Darby) of the Bible. It has been chosen due to its use of the word *nations* instead of *Gentiles,* since the Bible quoted in the French Messages also uses the word *nations.* Some other translations of the Bible that use *nations* for this passage are: NLT, NASB, and RSV.
21. The Darby Translation (Darby) of the Bible.
22. *from ancient days I am one and the same* is a quotation from the previous bible extract in the French version. In English bibles, it is usually written: *before the day was I am he.*
23. In 1975, with the authorization of the Elohim, Rael changed the name of the movement to the *International Raelian Movement.*
24. This passage has been modified from the original quotation in the Bible. Most English bibles use the word *life* in this passage, while the French bible by Edouard Dhorme, the one that Rael had with him during his encounter, contains the word *ame,* or *soul* in English.
25. Translated text from *Submission to Authority,* S. Milgram, Paris 1974.
26. Most English bibles use the word *heaven* in this quotation, while the French bible and the French Messages both refer to *cieux - skies* in English. This is confirmed by the Latin Vulgate Bible of 405 AD that says: *coram Patre meo qui est in caelis,* or *my father who is in the skies.*
27. While most modern English bibles use the word *wilderness* in this passage, the French Messages and bible use the equivalent of *desert.* The Latin Vulgate Bible of 405 AD uses the word *desertum.*
28. Often referred to as *spanking* or *smacking.*

BIBLIOGRAPHY

Darby, J.N, *The Darby Translation (Darby)*, 1890.

Fiori, Jean, *Evolution ou Creation*, Published by Editions S.D.T., 77190, Dammarlie-les-Lys, France.

Milgram, S, *Submission to Authority*, Paris, 1974.

Public Domain, *Hebrew Names Version(HNV)* of the *World English Bible*.

Public Domain, *Restored Name King James Version (RNKJV)* - *www.eliyah.com/Scripture/*

Rostand, Jean, *L'Evolution*, Paris, Robert Delpire Editeur, 1960.

Thomas Nelson & Sons, *American Standard Version (ASV)*, 1901.

Thomas Nelson, Inc *New King James Version (NKJV)*, 1982.

Webster, Noah, *The Webster Bible* (Webster's), 1833.

INDEX

A

Abraham   24
Acts of the Apostles   77
Age of Pisces   81-82
Ambassador   94, 172-173, 176, 222-223
Amos   62
ancient writings   151, 155, 207, 216
angel   26, 34-35, 40-41, 53, 65-66, 76, 78, 298-299, 300, 302-303, 308-309
animals   10, 14-17, 21, 39, 61, 93, 126, 160, 164, 193, 197, 215, 262, 265, 272, 330, 331
antennae   36, 139, 323
Apocalypse   176, 206-207, 221, 229, 273, 276, 291-293, 304, 308-310, 312, 324, 332, 337, 344, 348, 357, 365
Apocryhpha   59
Aquarius   81-82, 206
ark   20-22, 32, 37, 240-241, 280, 332
artists   13-14, 92, 110, 186, 201, 258
astronauts   43, 47, 73, 229, 241
atmosphere   9, 11, 21, 30-31, 35, 72, 105, 114, 212, 227-228, 230, 341
atoms   90-91, 154, 211, 239, 252-253, 255-256, 262-263, 329, 332-333, 341

B

beast   14, 21, 61, 247, 263, 303-304
Bible   7, 9-11, 17, 33, 83-85, 88, 92, 97, 99, 106, 108, 229, 247, 249, 263, 310, 324, 335-337, 340, 345, 347, 374, 377-379
bone   49, 166, 191-192, 236-239, 253-255, 284, 298
Book of the Dead   155, 209
Bouvard, Philippe   138, 139
brain   35, 61, 95-96, 108, 110, 112-114, 150, 155, 171, 193, 207, 211, 242-243, 248, 258, 264, 268, 316, 342, 354
Buddha   165, 216, 221, 249, 252, 312, 324, 370
Buddhism   150, 360
Buddhist   89, 369
Buddhists   216, 222, 360, 362

C

candlestick   62

Carbon 14   235
cataclysm   20, 150, 217, 241, 263, 280, 285-286, 291, 298-299, 306, 313, 314
Catholic   8, 123, 128-129, 250, 273, 308, 310-311, 334, 338, 344, 348
cellular plan   175, 192, 236-237, 247, 298, 325, 332, 334, 357
chemical   28, 31, 113, 164, 242-243, 246, 248, 257, 262-263, 265, 327, 333, 339, 342
children   6, 15-16, 19, 30, 33, 38, 50, 58, 91, 97-99, 102, 106-107, 109, 111, 114, 123-125, 127-129, 157, 163, 176, 182-183, 186-187, 189-192, 194, 199, 205, 207, 213, 215, 221, 230, 232, 256, 261, 274, 279, 287, 307, 315, 318-319
chosen people   18, 26, 28, 32-33, 359
Christ   65, 81, 84, 87, 104, 114-115, 117, 124, 249, 343, 345, 370, 374
Christians   177, 215-216, 222, 238, 250, 261, 294, 320, 323, 337, 360
church   80-84, 86-88, 96, 117, 141, 218-221, 250, 261, 308, 310, 337-338, 345, 347-348, 367
Clermont-Ferrand   3-4, 100, 135, 137, 140, 143-145
clouds   12, 38, 40, 44, 298, 340, 377
commandments   28, 54, 95, 175, 358
communication   37, 63, 154, 158, 199, 209, 266, 346, 357
Communism   97-98, 196
computer   156, 169, 175, 192, 237, 264-270, 298, 329, 376
computers   110, 163, 171, 174, 197, 264, 266, 269, 270
consciousness   171, 246, 248, 255, 259, 260, 262, 268-269, 274, 306, 325, 343-344, 348, 351, 353, 359, 361
Copernicus   96, 116
council of the eternals   109, 113, 161, 163, 171, 279, 280, 283, 288, 295
criminals   195, 203-205, 322

D

Daniel   52-55, 336
Darras, Jean-Pierre   131
death   75-76, 98, 109, 112, 150, 153, 155, 174, 184-185, 191-193, 197, 203, 237, 242-243, 247, 262-264, 266, 285, 294-296, 298, 301, 305, 314, 318, 321-323, 336, 344-345, 350, 366
Delilah   36
Deuteronomy   32
devil   67, 80, 116, 249, 276, 281-282, 303, 353
disease   90-91, 213, 215
DNA   336, 342
Druids   124-125

E

Ecclesiastes 61, 337
education 16, 96, 113, 143, 164, 183, 185-186, 189, 190, 194, 261, 267, 268, 339
Egyptians 27-28, 32, 176
Elijah 36, 39-42, 74, 104, 114, 161, 165, 219, 221, 370, 377
Elisha 42
Eloha 84, 136, 161, 227-228, 277, 287, 320
Embassy 94, 102, 117, 173-177, 192, 223, 233-234, 248-249, 251-252, 291, 323, 359-360, 367, 368, 369, 370-371
Enos 19
eternal life 112, 184, 200, 204, 216, 237, 244, 247, 275, 285, 313, 365-376
eternals 109-113, 161-164, 171, 184, 191, 193, 200, 211, 214, 216-217, 220, 222, 227, 237-238, 243, 245, 249, 279-280, 283, 288-289, 295, 306, 320, 324, 356, 361
eternity 50, 108-109, 143, 161, 171, 174, 192, 211, 216, 221, 262, 348
Evolution 92-93, 116, 191, 235, 274, 297, 327-329, 336, 349-352, 355, 366-367, 379
Evolutionists 273-274
Exodus 26-30, 228, 230
Ezekiel 45-52, 105, 166, 221, 336

F

family 3, 98, 135, 157, 173, 175, 192, 199, 215, 268, 315, 323, 344, 347-348, 350
famine 209, 296
fish 14-15, 55-56, 92, 149, 378
flying saucer 5, 47
forehead 167, 191, 236-238, 298, 313, 334
four levels 181, 255
France 3, 8, 126-127, 139-140, 151-152, 158, 310, 319, 330, 334, 356, 365, 379
freedom 8, 110, 114, 140, 157-158, 183, 187, 195-196, 270-271
fruit 13, 16, 18, 35, 70, 124, 188, 262, 278, 328, 330

G

galaxy 39, 81, 210, 211, 369
Gandhi 158, 180, 222
Genesis 10-26, 92, 173, 231, 247, 313, 347
genetic code 236-237, 245, 247, 262-263, 266-267, 269, 297-298, 336
Geniocracy 95, 97, 142, 150, 193-196, 250-251, 336, 364, 375
genius 18, 71, 97, 103, 108, 150, 194, 231, 253, 336

God   11, 29, 34, 36-37, 39, 40, 48, 51-52, 55, 58, 65, 69, 74, 79, 80, 84,
     94, 115-117, 153-154, 182, 184, 216, 220, 239, 240, 245-247, 249, 261,
     273, 276, 281-282, 286, 292-294, 297-298, 300, 303, 309-310, 312,
     336, 344-345, 359, 366-367, 377
gods   26, 153, 155, 208, 278-279, 339, 349, 359, 371
Golden Age   81, 84, 117, 150-151, 194, 197, 206, 246, 256-257, 259, 275,
     291, 303, 306-307, 323, 324, 352
Gospel   68-69, 74-75, 220, 308
Gospels   79, 86-88
government   10, 17, 20, 58, 60, 67, 100, 173, 177, 193, 196, 205, 238,
     277-279, 315, 336, 350, 363, 368-369, 375
Greek   89, 269, 281, 309-312, 339, 377
Guide of Guides   174-177, 192, 195, 215-218, 222-223, 237, 358, 360
Guides   143, 159-161, 172, 174-177, 180, 185, 192, 195, 215-219, 222-
     223, 237, 248, 251, 259, 273, 325, 353, 358, 360, 365, 370

H

heaven   11-13, 24, 26, 29, 33, 41-44, 49, 56-57, 67-69, 71-72, 76-77, 87,
     154, 178, 219-220, 222, 288, 291, 295, 297, 299, 300, 303, 305, 308,
     324, 345, 349
Hebrew   11, 53, 57, 84, 109, 161, 309, 324, 335
hell   151, 190, 215, 296
helmet   169-170, 228-229, 294
Herod   66, 77
Hiroshima   145, 288, 290, 304, 319, 321
homosexual   272-273
humanitarianism   97-99, 142, 193-194, 196, 336
hypnosis   68

I

idols   26, 32, 43, 112, 279
immortality   74
infinitely large   154, 162, 210-211, 216, 244, 370
infinitely small   91, 153-154, 211, 216, 239, 244, 252, 262, 336, 370
infinity   143, 155-156, 171, 178, 181-182, 184-185, 193, 198, 200-202,
     209, 211-212, 220, 231, 234, 236, 239, 245-246, 252-253, 255, 258,
     262, 268, 292, 339, 344-345, 353, 369-370
inheritance   71-72, 75, 93, 97-98, 107, 192, 303, 307
intelligence   15, 18, 61, 67, 71, 83, 96-97, 106, 152, 193-194, 214, 231,
     258, 306, 330, 337, 344, 347-349, 375-376
inventions   95, 164, 194, 206, 233
Isaiah   43, 44, 60, 62, 82-85, 177
Islamic   89

Israel   15, 18, 22, 24, 27-30, 33, 38, 43, 50-51, 55, 63, 64, 66, 69, 78, 81, 84-85, 165, 173, 176-177, 216, 231-232, 289, 338, 359, 360, 368-369

J

Jericho   32-33
Jerusalem   49, 64, 176-177, 305, 314, 359, 368
Jesus   66-69, 73-76, 82, 84, 87, 114, 117, 124, 161, 165, 173-174, 177, 208, 215-216, 218-219, 221, 249-250, 252, 261, 281-282, 289-291, 306, 312, 315, 318, 320, 323-324, 337-338, 345-347, 362, 370, 378
Jewish   8, 33, 62, 84-85, 123, 184, 216, 232, 249, 323, 368
Jews   23, 37, 84, 172, 177, 222, 231, 314, 359, 362
Jonah   55-56
Judges   34-35, 54, 195, 203, 279
Jullian, Marcel   137-138

K

Kabala   88-89, 335, 340
King Solomon   38
Kings   38-43, 54, 297
knowledge   8, 10, 16, 17-18, 20, 23, 39, 44, 54-55, 59, 61, 63, 69, 71-72, 74, 81, 84, 90, 93, 96, 103, 107-109, 113, 117, 122, 137, 174, 180, 229, 234, 293, 324, 336, 340, 351-353, 366, 370
Koran   173-174, 216, 218, 313

L

La Montagne   140
laboratories   233, 276, 278, 304, 331, 342, 370
laboratory   13, 17, 230, 232-233, 277, 279-280, 289, 292, 304, 317, 328, 336, 347, 356, 367
laser   40, 68, 78, 144
Last Judgement   53-54, 71, 109
Latin   246, 309, 311-312, 314, 340, 365, 377
Leviticus   31, 99-100, 247
light   4, 5, 7, 12, 27, 46, 59, 64, 69, 73-74, 78-79, 88-89, 94, 109, 115, 116, 149, 159, 207, 212, 227, 228, 234, 254, 278-279, 316, 324, 332, 337, 340-341, 346, 347, 352, 360-361
Lord   67-68, 199-220, 282, 293, 297, 309-310, 377
love   16, 57, 61, 71, 81, 86-87, 93, 101, 103, 108-111, 116-117, 122, 126, 128, 130, 132, 158, 161, 164, 171-172, 181-182, 184-186, 188, 190, 192-193, 200-204, 211-213, 215-216, 219-221, 223, 232, 242, 246, 261, 271, 274, 278-280, 283-284, 287-288, 290, 306-307, 313, 325, 338, 343, 348, 350, 359-361, 371, 376
Lucifer   276, 278-280, 288

M

machines   45-46, 49, 156-157, 194, 227, 229, 278, 294-295
Madech   122, 124, 140-143, 145
marriage   88, 110, 190, 336
Mary   65
Matthew   65-76, 86-87, 174, 220, 232, 277-278, 281-282, 315
meat   197
meditation   138, 162, 172, 178, 185, 198-199, 201, 207, 212, 248, 257, 344, 364, 375
Messenger   40, 94, 172-173, 177, 200, 208, 288, 290-291, 298, 306, 309, 311-312, 325, 338, 343, 357
Messiah   63, 216, 308-310, 368
metal   25, 43, 45-47, 52, 58, 102, 219, 228, 269, 294, 301, 377
Milgram, Stanley   317
military   18, 33, 95, 100-102, 106, 115, 117, 151-152, 158, 195-196, 206, 233, 315, 320-322, 336, 350
miracles   39, 55, 67, 69, 73-74
money   95, 98-100, 110, 117, 130-135, 196, 205-206, 220, 232-233, 288, 336-337
Morisse, Lucien   132-133
Mormons   89
Moses   26, 28-30, 74, 104, 114, 161, 165, 219, 221, 249, 252, 306, 312, 324, 369, 370
Mount Carmel   39
Mohammed   165, 173, 174, 216, 221, 249, 252, 312, 324, 370
music   92, 111, 130, 149, 160, 162, 164, 170, 186, 201-202, 267, 270, 346
Muslim   184
Muslims   216, 222, 362
mythology   89, 339

N

Noah   20-21, 150, 217, 240-241, 280
nuclear   20, 44, 94, 105-106, 117, 157-158, 196, 286, 291, 298, 300, 302, 303-304, 313, 319, 321-322, 333-334
nuclear weapons   94, 105-106, 157, 196, 286

O

Old Testament   166, 249, 296

P

parable   69, 75, 277
paradise   15, 151, 156-157, 162, 164, 168, 172, 177, 191, 245, 376
patriotism   157
perfumes   15, 264-265, 375

planet of the eternals   184, 193, 211, 214, 216-217, 220, 222, 227, 236, 238, 243, 245, 249, 288-289, 306, 324, 356

planets   30, 61, 70-72, 75, 90-91, 107-109, 153-154, 156, 162, 210-211, 244, 246, 252, 277-278, 292, 340, 367, 370

pleasure   133, 136, 162, 164, 186-188, 190, 199, 202, 206, 211, 214, 217, 242, 256-258, 261-262, 266-267, 325, 337, 343

Pope   87, 124-125, 220, 308, 311

pray   86, 261, 337

prayer   67-68, 198-199, 213, 220, 346

prophet   48, 55, 173-174, 176, 216, 218, 221, 281, 290-291, 298, 306, 308, 311, 314, 347

prophets   36, 39, 41, 65, 161, 173, 176-178, 184, 199, 206-208, 216-218, 221-222, 236, 249, 273-274, 280, 289, 293, 297, 312-313, 324, 337-338, 348, 350

Proverbs   61, 86

Psalms   56-57, 63

punishment   168, 172-174, 186, 188, 215

Puy-de-Lassolas   3, 136, 145

pyramid   269, 284

R

racing   3, 127, 129-131, 133-134, 135-136, 172

RAEL   4, 94, 117, 147, 172, 176, 192, 200, 206, 221-223, 227, 236, 276, 291, 298, 306, 326, 334, 338, 346-349, 352, 356-358, 361, 368, 371, 375

Raelians   222, 237-238, 245, 250-252, 259-260, 270, 272, 275, 312, 327, 330, 344, 356, 359-360, 364-365, 373

recreated   22, 61, 168, 171-172, 174, 192

reincarnation   151, 213-214, 216

religion   88, 108, 173, 176, 182, 184, 206, 221-222, 238, 248, 251, 267, 273, 290, 308, 310-312, 315, 323, 325, 327, 337, 339, 343, 346-348, 360, 367-368, 370

religions   88-89, 115, 143, 152-153, 157, 165, 173, 176, 184, 214, 221-222, 244, 246, 249-250, 280, 293, 314-315, 335, 338, 343, 348-350, 359, 370

resurrection   42, 54, 109, 184

Revelation   64, 81, 115, 172, 176, 207, 229, 293-305, 309-311, 336, 337

robot   163, 166, 168-171, 197

robots   59, 110, 162-163, 165, 166-167, 169-171, 196, 233, 336

S

Samson   35-36

Samuel   36-37

Satan   57-58, 67, 93, 276-284, 288, 303, 320
school   125, 127-130, 152, 205, 233, 261, 327, 367
science   48, 59-61, 65, 72, 74, 107, 112, 137, 151, 153, 156-158, 162, 186, 188, 191, 193, 195, 203, 205-208, 214, 216, 243-244, 254, 275, 309, 313, 317, 327, 332, 337, 342, 345, 351, 370, 371, 372, 377
scientist   8, 115, 292, 316-317, 352, 365
scientists   10-18, 35-36, 44, 67, 74, 92, 100, 109, 113, 115-116, 144, 194, 205-207, 233-235, 244, 253, 255, 263, 266, 274, 276-279, 306, 314-317, 327, 350, 367, 370-371
sensual meditation   199, 201, 212, 248, 257, 364, 375
sensuality   164, 202, 259, 261, 337, 343
serpent   16-17, 31-32, 60, 279
servants   102, 162, 297-298, 303
Seth   19
singularity   370
slavery   157, 362
Smith, Joseph   312
society   10, 143, 151, 153, 161, 180-181, 183-184, 188-191, 193, 195, 198, 203, 205-206, 213, 256, 259, 315, 317, 325, 349-350, 354-355, 361
Sodom and Gomorrah   23-24, 26, 44, 94, 103, 217
Son of man   48, 50, 166, 293-294
soul   82-83, 150, 153-155, 168, 172, 242, 245-247, 249, 336, 346, 378
spirit   11, 19, 41, 45-49, 61, 66-67, 77, 83, 88, 90, 246, 281, 293, 295
sports   110-112, 114, 134-136, 138, 172, 206
Star of David   62, 155
submarine   55-56, 60
supernatural   11, 42, 74, 84, 115, 172, 278-279, 309, 336, 359
swastika   62, 151, 155, 369

T

Telepathic Contact   199, 312
telepathy   6-7, 36-37, 41, 63, 94, 101, 105, 172, 207, 216
television   55, 73, 137-140, 143, 158, 159, 212, 227, 259, 293, 369
theory   114, 327, 329-330, 349-351, 366-367
those who came from the sky   11, 57, 309-311, 335
Tobit   59
Tower of Babel   22
transmission   90, 201, 236, 237, 332, 334
transmitter   35-38
tree of life   17-19, 50, 74, 107
trumpet   28, 33, 293, 295, 299

U

unidentified flying objects   77, 116, 221

V

Vatican   87-88, 220, 232, 249, 273
vessel   25, 27-29, 38, 40, 47-48, 51, 63, 107, 178, 230, 241, 284
violence   129, 150, 156, 158, 162, 168, 195, 203-204, 206, 215, 259, 261, 279, 286-288, 306, 316, 321-322, 351

W

war   34, 94, 114, 142, 151, 158, 195, 231, 241, 298-299, 301, 319, 322, 369
wars   114, 220, 256, 259, 296, 318, 322, 350
weapons   18, 43-44, 94, 105-106, 151, 157, 195-196, 220, 279, 286, 288, 350
witnesses   85, 181, 357
womb   20, 35, 123, 262, 272, 283, 292
world currency   205, 336
world language   152, 205

Y

Yahweh   17-18, 21-22, 24, 26-31, 33-38, 40-43, 49, 51, 55-58, 60, 62-66, 76, 78, 82, 85-86, 161, 164-167, 171, 175, 232, 279-280, 282-291, 295, 302, 305-306, 324, 347, 357, 369, 377

Z

Zechariah   56, 62, 64
Zephaniah   81

Revision: 251207

Made in the USA
Middletown, DE
29 November 2022